Negotiating *So* Everyone Wins

Secrets you can use from Canada's top business, sports, labour and political negotiators

DAVID C. DINGWALL
FOREWORD BY JEAN CHRÉTIEN

James Lorimer & Company Ltd., Publishers
Toronto

James Lorimer & Company Ltd., Publishers acknowledges the support of the Ontario Arts Council. We acknowledge the support of the Canada Council for the Arts which last year invested $24.3 million in writing and publishing throughout Canada. We acknowledge the Government of Ontario through the Ontario Media Development Corporation's Ontario Book Initiative.

Cover design: Tyler Cleroux
Cover image: Shutterstock

Library and Archives Canada Cataloguing in Publication

Dingwall, David C., 1952-, author
    Negotiating so everyone wins : secrets you can use from Canada's top business, sports, labour and political negotiators / David C. Dingwall.

Issued in print and electronic formats.
ISBN 978-1-4594-1110-4 (hardback).--ISBN 978-1-4594-1111-1 (epub)

1. Negotiation in business--Canada. I. Title.

HD58.6.D55 2016   658.4'052   C2016-900038-9
                                            C2016-900039-7

James Lorimer & Company Ltd., Publishers
117 Peter Street, Suite 304
Toronto, ON, Canada
M5V 2G9
www.lorimer.ca

Printed and bound in Canada.

CONTENTS

For Jennifer, Leigh Anne, Jay, Lucas, Shamus and Nancy!

Foreword

When I first met David Dingwall, I liked him right away. He was a twenty-seven-year-old newly-elected Member of Parliament from Cape Breton, and I was the newly-appointed Attorney General. It was 1980 and we were part of a Liberal majority government that would be the final term of office for Pierre Elliot Trudeau. David was an important and productive contributor at an important time in Canadian history that included repatriating the Constitution. Later, when I was Leader of the Liberal Party in 1991, David was a natural choice to be Opposition House Leader. And when I led the Liberals to power in 1993 and became Prime Minister, he was one of the first Cabinet Ministers I appointed. We have been friends since meeting, and to this day we often talk about issues of mutual interest, such as crises in the world, the state of the nation, and the progress of our party and its new leader, whom we both knew long before he followed in his father's footsteps.

From the very beginning, David was a loyal, hard-working and capable public servant, a strong advocate for his region and a passionate supporter of his colleagues. He took his responsibilities seriously and always did his utmost to fulfil his mandate in the face of complex issues. As needed, David was a tough and relentless negotiator, a quality that I admire, and we locked horns many times behind closed doors. But there was always mutual respect and the recognition that each of us was pushing for the outcome we believed was best. Politicians never hold it against other politicians when they are just trying to get their way.

What David learned quickly, and has applied throughout his entire career, is that everything in public life, the private sector and even personal matters happens as a result of a negotiation. During his seventeen years in office and in his career since then, as he has dealt with some very complex negotiations, David has understood and applied the fundamentals of deal making: preparation, consultation, passion, patience and tenacity.

One of his most public successes was the passing of the new tobacco legislation in 1997, which won him an award from the World Health Organization. It was a highly contentious and complex piece of legislation that required David to balance the interests of over a hundred health groups, many different branches of the government and powerful corporate lobbies. He was consultative, organized and focused on building consensus. He was also relentless in influencing leaders in the Party — including me — that the law needed to be tough. In the end, the legislation was enacted by Parliament and became the strongest legislation in the world and a model that was since replicated in many nations.

David has always been a student of negotiation, and it is a great service that he has taken the time to produce this book. There are many qualities about *Negotiating So Everyone Wins* that I admire, but one that stands out most is that it is based in experience. I have never been a big believer in theories or models. I have found that success comes from hard work, relationships and battle-tested skill.

Negotiating So Everyone Wins outlines David's ideas about negotiation, including the importance of being strategic and the need to develop a clear understanding about the interests of the other side. He uses careful and candid examples from his own experiences to illustrate his ideas and shares some of his shortcomings to illustrate where a negotiator can go wrong. The book is also unique because it offers insight from a diverse group of

Canadian leaders in business, sports, labour and politics who sat for interviews to discuss their thinking about negotiations. David has also made the videos of those interviews available online on YouTube and referenced them throughout the book.

Negotiating So Everyone Wins is timely, relevant and practical. Its insights apply to issues as diverse as climate change, Aboriginal land claims and infrastructure development. Through this book, negotiators can become more thoughtful, deliberate and balanced in their approach. They are also more apt to succeed at a time when parties to a negotiation are more than ever before resistant to having the terms of a deal dictated to them. People want to be consulted, considered and involved. And they want a process that is fair, transparent and comprehensive.

In many ways, *Negotiating so Everyone Wins* illustrates a truly Canadian approach to deal making: passionately pursue the outcome you seek while doing what you can to make it work for the other side. And I find it fitting that this book is arriving in print at a time when Prime Minister Justin Trudeau was elected in a majority largely because he emphasized a similar message: work together to achieve the best possible resolution.

The Right Honourable Jean Chrétien, P.C., Q.C.
former Prime Minister of Canada

CHAPTER 1
The Strategic Negotiator

"In business as in life, you don't get what you deserve, you get what you negotiate."

— Chester L. Karrass

On Tuesday, June 3, 1997, I woke up in a very unfamiliar situation: I was out of a job. The night before, as my friend and colleague Jean Chrétien was leading the Liberal Party to another majority government, I had been gathered with my friends, family and supporters as I learned I had fallen 3 per cent short at the polls. The constituents of the Cape Breton region had chosen a representative from the New Democratic Party of Canada and I was not heading back to the House of Commons. It was a devastating blow.

In politics as in life, success is an ongoing negotiation. Throughout 1996 and into the early part of 1997, a major priority for the Chrétien government had been to eliminate the deficit through several cost-cutting measures. Among the most public of these cuts was a significant reduction in Unemployment Insurance support (soon thereafter renamed Employment Insurance or EI). As an MP from a high unemployment area, I had campaigned within my party against cuts that would be detrimental to workers in my riding and elsewhere in Atlantic Canada. But I had been out-voted by my peers who felt this was an important signal to workers and the general public. As a result, labour leaders in my riding went on a campaign against me. And while there were other issues at stake, EI was the lightning rod that led to my defeat. After seventeen and a half years in public office, I was in a position that few people face at mid-career: what will I do for a living?

Three days after the election, I returned to Ottawa to help with the transition to the new government and to begin my own shift into the private sector. I had no idea what I would do next. One afternoon during this period, my longtime assistant Gloria McCarter came into my office looking shaken and grim, telling me, "The manager of your bank in Sydney is on the phone. He is insisting that he speak to you immediately." When I picked up the call, the cool voice on the other end bluntly stated, "Mr. Dingwall, we are calling in all of your loans. You will receive a registered letter at your residence today. Thank you." Then he hung up. Already in shock from the election loss and the uncertainty of my future, I was now in a tenuous financial position as well.

As we all do in times of trouble, I turned to friends and family for support and guidance, which included a conversation with close friend and fellow Acadian Roméo Leblanc, who was Governor General of Canada at that time. Leblanc made a really interesting suggestion: I should follow my lifelong interest in the business of sport and meet with his friend Claude Brochu, the largest shareholder and President of the Montreal Expos. "Maybe there is a role for you with Major League Baseball," said Leblanc.

While meeting at his Montreal office, Brochu let me know that he was a member of the selection committee for the new full-time Commissioner of Major League Baseball. Bud Selig had been interim Commissioner since 1992 and was, by all accounts, the leading candidate to secure the job on a full-time basis. But despite what appeared to be an obvious outcome of the search process, Brochu encouraged me to apply for the job. He explained that there was significant interest in my candidacy. I had been a high-level amateur athlete and was passionate about the business of sport. I was an expert in bargaining and negotiation and had a track record of success in highly complex situations. I had been a Member of Parliament for seventeen years, including time spent as adviser to Prime Minister Chrétien, and Cabinet Minister for a variety of major portfolios. I had worked on both domestic and international policy and was widely connected across North America and the globe. And I had a reputation for finding the right balance between diplomacy and hard-nosed politics. When Brochu had finished explaining why he believed I was being considered, he said, "Even if you don't get it, it will be an experience that might open doors for what you will end up doing next."

After polishing up my résumé, speaking with a few knowledgeable friends and reading up on the business of baseball, I met with a senior representative from Heidrick & Struggles, the global executive search firm handling the process. The interview was a special experience. We talked about the future of Major League Baseball, particularly its growth and acceptance in foreign countries. We discussed immigration and the search firm rep probed into my understanding of the intricacies of that subject. He asked me how my family would handle public life and the extensive travel required of the Commissioner. We talked about the powerful owners and my thoughts on the best strategies for creating alignment and support among a group of very successful and independent people. I asked about Selig, and the search firm rep would only say that the search committee was exploring all options for the position. And we talked about the compensation, which is a moment I'll never forget: he said the pay was between five and seven, and when I realized he meant million and not hundred thousand, I could hardly believe it. Covering my shock was one of my greater accomplishments in the interview.

Elated by the process, energized by the possibilities and feeling pretty good about my chances, I headed back to Ottawa where I telephoned Claude Brochu and then debriefed the Governor General over dinner at his residence. My enthusiasm for the position lasted until I received a letter from Heidrick & Struggles informing me that my candidacy was not successful. I had struck out.

In the weeks that followed, I spent quite a lot of time asking myself what had gone wrong. Did I allow my ego to be overtaken with ideas of fame and fortune? Could I have been better prepared for my discussions with Heidrick & Struggles? Did I fail to manage my relationship with the senior rep? Why didn't I use my Rolodex of contacts who could have spoken up in my favour? Did I understand the criteria for selecting the new Commissioner? Could I have probed deeper regarding the needs and aspirations of Major League Baseball? Could I have reached out to some of the committee members and owners to build relationships and learn more about the state of the game? Did I err in not seeing that Bud Selig was going to be appointed full-time Commissioner and my opportunity lay in another role within Major League Baseball?

In public office, everything we did was carefully planned out and meticulously executed. I was a highly experienced negotiator who rarely made a move without thinking through all of the angles and setting myself up to succeed. But somehow, I had missed a very basic idea: a job interview is actually a negotiation. I failed because I had neither objectively assessed the situation nor been particularly strategic in the process.

As time passed, I learned that Claude Brochu had been right. The experience of that job interview did open my eyes to new possibilities. They were rarely in the realm of professional sports (though I took another shot at it later on), but since that moment, I have been involved in professional work that relies on negotiation: operating a consulting firm that helped businesses deal with government agencies; overhauling the Canadian Mint as its CEO; starting a company that provides Alternative Dispute Resolution (ADR) and negotiation services to public, private and non-profit organizations; dealing with regulators, constituents, governments, clients, board members and senior executives; and acting as legal counsel for law firms in Nova Scotia and Toronto. Through all of those roles, and in my time as a visiting professor at Ryerson University where I am charged with the task of educating students in the ways of negotiation, I have been honing my own skills but, more importantly for the purposes of this book, working to understand and articulate my thinking about one of the essentials of success in life: the craft of negotiation.

MORE THAN EVER, NEGOTIATIONS ARE PART OF OUR LIVES AND WORK

In simplest terms, a negotiation occurs any time at least two parties work to reach an agreement about something. Every day, agreements are made that seem too trivial to think of them that way, but not all negotiations involve large tables, scads of lawyers and thousands of documents. Negotiation is an integral part of our lives because conflict is embedded in the human experience. What you want will not always align with what someone else wants, and you have to find a way to proceed. Common forms of negotiation include complex domestic and international public policy issues; ongoing interactions between businesses, non-profit organizations and government branches; every form of legal proceeding; social arrangements such as marriage, divorce and parenting; sports and entertainment contracts; buying a new car; securing a raise or promotion; and even getting home from work on time. The widespread nature of this activity means that every one of us would benefit from understanding what leads to successfully negotiated agreements, which improve our ability to get what we want. As Chester L. Karrass says, you get what you negotiate in life.

The last twenty years has seen a shift in the mainstream leadership style, which has radically altered the importance of negotiation skills for almost every person in a leadership role. Today's leaders are more collaborative, focused on authenticity and engaged in influence than the old-school command-and-control types. In almost every sector of the economy, there is a heightened need and demand for negotiation skills. And unless they intend to accept other people's terms and fall short of their goals, today's leaders need at least a basic understanding of the stages and processes of formal negotiations. The reality is that negotiation is no longer the sole purview of a specialized group of lawyers, politicians and experts in the art of the deal. It is a skill that every leader needs in this increasingly collaborative and connected world.

When it comes to options for dispute resolution, negotiation allows participants to have a significant degree of control and exercise a fair amount of creativity — two features that lead to mutually beneficial solutions. The same cannot be said of litigation, which is bound by the rigid structures, timelines and constraints of the legal system. The litigation process is a quagmire (see Appendix A). It is time-consuming, expensive and unpredictable. Participants are dragged through Statements of Claim, Statements of Defence, motions, pre-trial sessions, discovery, subpoenas of witnesses and the actual trial, all of which generate significant legal costs and stress. This procedural morass is not true of arbitration, where the outcome of the process is decided by a neutral party. Nor is it true of negotiation's closest cousin, mediation, where participants are still one step removed from guiding the process and interacting directly with the other side. Many lawyers and negotiation professionals often use a

Decision Tree (see Appendix B) to compare the potential outcomes of litigation with the benefits of settling via negotiation, but in my experience, negotiation is the most effective means for resolving disputes and reaching agreements. Yes, those other forms of resolution are sometimes required, but none of them are as flexible, receptive to influence and open to inventive solutions as a negotiation.

In their book *The Practical Negotiator*, William Zartman and Maureen Berman make the same point: "The essence of negotiation is creativity, not legalisms." This line has always resonated with me. While legal precedents are important and relevant for lawyers, most legal activities are actually negotiations. Being creative and accepting control over the process are essential. Negotiations allow parties to understand not only the positions, but the interests of others and to build agreements that attend to those needs in a very precise way.

The creative potential of negotiation means that no two negotiations are the same. This is surely what motivated the late Richard Holbrooke, former United States Ambassador to the United Nations and Special US Envoy who ended the bloody conflict in the former Yugoslavia, to say, "Negotiation is like jazz. It is improvisation on a theme. You know where you are, you know where you want to go, but you don't know how to get there. It's not linear." His insight likely explains why many people are fearful of entering into any kind of negotiation. Unpredictability, pressure and complexity have a tendency to scare people off. I have heard many versions of "let's get to the facts and base all of our decisions on them" or "we don't have time to sit around and talk this all through, let's just get a deal done." That attitude can also be driven by a desire to avoid the extensive effort a negotiation requires. As Michael Wheeler says, "Negotiation is work. It demands concentration, resilience, and creativity in a context where the stakes may be high and the outcomes are uncertain."

Negotiations follow a slightly revised adage used regularly in the fundraising community: people make deals with people. Every settlement or resolution is an agreement between people, and a negotiator's ability to build relationships, use their influence and understand what makes people tick are significant variables in their success. Essentially, the negotiator is the key to the whole process. What you do, who you are, who you have on your team and how you proceed determine the outcome. If the process is like making music, the negotiator is the conductor or composer. This obviously requires a fairly sophisticated skillset.

Because you, as the negotiator, are the defining element in the process, you are on a never-ending journey of learning. Assessing and upgrading your skills is a priority. Increasing your knowledge and developing your talent will improve your record of success and bring enormous value to the people you serve.

BE STRATEGIC

On April 16, 1996 at 1:55 p.m., Mary Clancy, a fellow Liberal MP from Atlantic Canada, rose in the House during the section of the proceedings called Statements from Members, a time when MPs from both sides of the House can make brief remarks on a topic of their choosing. A statement can set the tone for a topic that will be discussed during Question Period, inform the House about something important that has happened in the nation or, as was Clancy's intent, recognize an important Canadian who had died. And so, following statements about the Cape Breton Development Corporation's mining activities and the state of the fisheries across Atlantic Canada, and just after a poem about raw milk cheese regulation from the MP from Blainville–Deux-Montagnes in which he called me "naive" and rhymed "minister" with "sinister," Clancy rose in her place and spoke eloquently about someone I knew:

Mr. Speaker, it is said that no one is indispensable.
Last week, many of us in Canada learned that this
is not so. Gerry Godsoe died in Halifax, leaving a
huge gap that no one can fill. He had advised prime
ministers and backbenchers, premiers and business
leaders on all sides of the political spectrum. He helped
the young and the old, the great and the lowly. He
practised law superbly. He practised politics superbly.
He practised life superbly. To Dale, his wife and other
half, to their three daughters, Suzanne, Stacey and
Laura, I express our sympathy in this, their sudden
and tragic loss. Gerry was taken far too soon and it is
not fair to any of us. Gerry Godsoe, lawyer, thinker,
caregiver, husband, father, son and brother, Canadian
extraordinaire, friend, requiescat in pace.

I had worked with Godsoe on several occasions. A Rhodes Scholar who spent a large portion of his career as a senior partner at Stewart McKelvey in Halifax, he had held various roles during his career, including President and CEO of Nova Scotia Power and a senior adviser to Prime Minister Pierre Elliott Trudeau during the repatriation of the constitution. Godsoe was also Executive Director of the Macdonald Commission, a landmark commission on Canadian economic policy whose recommendations improved the flexibility of the Canadian economy to adapt to international and technological change, reformed the welfare state model to promote social equity and advised the adoption of an elected Senate.

With his scuffed shoes, dishevelled clothes and unkempt hair, it was hard at first sight to see Godsoe as a powerful national figure or talented negotiator. But he was one of the most insightful people I have ever encountered. He was a superb prober who could uncover and distill key information and synthesize it into a coherent understanding of the whole. He was incredibly creative in drafting or presenting a solution to a situation, whether in the charitable, commercial or public policy sector. And he did it all with a pleasant and affable personality that disarmed people and invited them in. Moreover, he did most of it in his mind and in his conversations — long before his actual negotiations began.

An instructive example of how Godsoe thought and worked comes from one of my strongest memories of him. It was 1986 and the Liberal Party of Nova Scotia was in search of a new leader. I was in the middle of my second term as a federal Member of Parliament from Cape Breton and had been re-elected two years earlier by a wide margin. In keeping with a long tradition in our country of federal politicians becoming provincial leaders, many key people in the provincial party were pressing me to "return home" to run for the leadership. I was loving my work in Ottawa, but knew that I needed to give this opportunity serious consideration. I decided to seek the input of the smartest people I knew, and that led me immediately to Godsoe. We sat down over coffee in his Halifax office and I put the question to him: what should I do?

He sat looking out the window for a while and then began asking me questions. Did I like working on national and international issues? What sorts of issues would I be involved in as Premier? How did I feel about being a team member versus being the top dog? Did I prefer complex issues and diverse interests or focused initiatives where I could be directly involved in the course of action? What did my wife, Nancy, think and how would the change affect my family? What would my mentor Allan MacEachen, former Deputy Prime Minister, think and why? What would the party leaders in Ottawa think and why? What were the interests of the provincial leaders who were wooing me and did my own perspective align with those views?

Never once during the conversation did he tell me what he thought. He did not consider it his place to have an opinion on the matter; instead, he helped me sort out what I thought. As a result, I got a firsthand glimpse into the mind of one of the country's leading negotiators.

Godsoe had crafted his approach on the fly to flush out the major issues and point me toward my own thinking. In so doing, he had not only organized and identified all of the issues, he had integrated all considerations into one coherent picture and guided me toward the key questions I needed to answer. And he had done it all in a non-linear fashion, moving across different topics effortlessly so it felt like we were just having a conversation. I had gone there to get advice about what to do and came away with something much more helpful: the essential issues distilled into categories I could work with. On display that day was Godsoe's gift for the single most important quality of a successful negotiator: strategic thinking.

Being strategic is the ability to think through every imaginable angle of a deal or dispute and envision how it will unfold. It's arriving at the bargaining table as if you have been gazing into a crystal ball. It's approaching the discussions with an ability to select your response or course of action based on extensive conversation, accurate information and a wide-ranging understanding of the other side's needs and goals. In essence, a strategic approach is one that gathers knowledge of what can happen long before it actually does, because planning and forethought have constructed all reasonable avenues of possibility. And on the flip side of the same coin, it's not making decisions based on a hunch, gut instinct or intuition. Yes, negotiations are like jazz and we need to improvise on a theme. But great jazz musicians are highly trained and can see, feel or hear the music before it arrives to the world. They're not randomly blowing a horn. That means that you, the negotiator, are not coming up with options in the moment. It means that you are ready to choose from options you understand already, long in advance of arriving at the table. You should never be surprised.

Like Gerry Godsoe, a strategic negotiator has a broad perspective, a stellar imagination and a capacity to envision future possibilities and oblique angles, as if they can watch a movie in their mind of how things could play out. A strategic negotiator is comprehensive in their preparation, relentless in their drive for information and superb at sifting, sorting and synthesizing information so they can put it to use at a moment's notice. They have a capacity to be objective and impartial rather than emotional. They know how to connect to and influence people and are able to predict how others will respond based on an understanding of their interests. And they are highly logical and able to anticipate the sequence of steps that will follow each and every decision, mapping out every contingency. In essence, a strategic negotiator is like a Grandmaster chess champion who can make decisions about their next moves based on their capacity to see future implications of each choice. From opening gambit to endgame, they see the whole board and the whole game in advance. And with every move, they re-calculate and reassess their options in response to what their opponent does or is likely to do.

Everything I have described sounds like a tall order. But it can all be learned. Throughout this book, I offer a detailed outline of a strategic negotiator's qualities, approaches and priorities. Every one of them is connected to the central premise: be strategic and not intuitive. To set the stage, here are five operating principles that should govern your entire approach as a negotiator. Throughout the book, you will see each of these principles illustrated in many ways.

1. Allow enough time to be successful.

The number one error that I see in the law and in negotiations is insufficient time for preparation and process. A negotiator can only achieve a superb outcome if they have done their homework and assessed their options at every step. It is time-consuming to do well, but the time pays off in better outcomes. A strategic negotiator needs to be careful about time commitments to the client (if they are representing one) or to the other side, be aggressive about time for planning and put in the hours to prepare. For example, it's as important to schedule your preparation time into your day planner as it is to schedule the actual negotiation meetings — with the same level of commitment to both. Just ask someone you know about how long it takes a good firm to complete a merger or acquisition.

2. Consider how every part of the process, no matter how small, fits into the overall approach.
Once mandate and goals are established, a strategic negotiator works through how every imaginable element — from relationships to logistics — can be approached to support those goals. This process involves the kind of zooming in and zooming out that Jim Collins and Morten Hansen describe in their book *Great by Choice*. As a negotiator, you develop a plan and analyze even the most minute part of the process (such as the wording of an email) in order to connect each part to the strategic goals and major considerations in play. Many negotiators are capable of focusing on the key issues — like flushing out all relevant information about the market or the performance of a particular product — but so often I find that they fail to act strategically about small things. This capacity for perspective comes with practice and with adopting a disciplined approach to seeking out different angles. The very best negotiators leave nothing to chance, have a plan of action for every contingency and then ensure that the smallest details fit into those plans. As an example, when I started in politics, I was not particularly attentive to my relationship with the media. I focused on being competent and prepared within my portfolio and missed this important factor. It was an oversight that came back to haunt me. So, later in my career, I began the

process of trying to build better relationships with the reporters who covered my beat.

3. Plan backward from your imagined outcome to ensure an efficient and effective process.

Reverse engineering has become a common approach in almost every sector and is essential in negotiations. Often, people can delineate their goals and envision the end they are working toward but fail to work backward from the goals to map all the interim steps along the way. As a negotiator, ask yourself how everything you do from the outset connects to the end vision so that every step supports your efforts. Negotiations are sometimes described as emotional, messy and damaging to the relationships of the parties involved. It does not have to be that way if you are deliberate about how you plan and assess your process. The Japanese are famous for their lean enterprise system whereby they look at the various steps in the process to improve upon each aspect and the overall organization. This is called value stream mapping. I do the same thing in a negotiation. There are too many situational and personal variables to conclude that a single strategy or recipe will work in each and every case. Working backward from your primary goal will allow you to outline the unique steps needed to get there and ensure you have the most efficient and well-run process available, even though you will need to adapt as you go.

4. Make rational informed decisions, not emotional impulsive ones.

Emotion is an important part of a negotiation process, but it needs to inform your thinking, not be your deciding factor. Strategic negotiators map out options, predict alternatives and select a course of action or response based on careful assessments and contingency planning. Making a decision based on your emotional reactions — or on the emotions of your client — will undermine that process. This is not to say that a negotiator should avoid any display of emotion. As with any tactic, an "emotional outburst" can be strategic: righteous anger or a flare of frustration might be the best response at times. The idea here is that a good negotiator is comfortable in their own skin and highly self-aware so that they can assess their reactions and make deliberate decisions — even to erupt with emotion — rather than act on impulse. Yes, a negotiation process involves improvisation and adjustment, but those alterations are informed by information and research, not hunches and gut instinct. You need to know yourself, what pushes your buttons, what you don't know, where you have blind spots, which people complement your skills and what you are and are not good at. Self-awareness is a lifelong pursuit and can be gained from experience and reflection. And from brutal honesty and input from others. Surround yourself with people who are supportively candid. And constantly ask yourself, "Am I getting this right?"

5. Remember that no deal is sometimes the best deal.
You don't just want to reach an agreement. You want to reach an agreement that is right for you. Not every negotiation can be concluded successfully. Policy positions, price, timing or quality issues may be so different for each of the parties that agreement is impossible. Don't be alarmed if, after entering a negotiation, you find that it cannot be concluded successfully. Sometimes the best strategy is to walk away.

In exploring what it means for a negotiator to be strategic, it can be helpful to look at models provided by experts in the field. The approach I am advocating can often take into account or make use of a variety of positional possibilities for a negotiator.

THE QUALITIES OF A GREAT NEGOTIATOR

"The number one thing is to be willing and able to walk, which means that you have done your preparatory work so you know exactly what this company is worth to you, how you are going to add value, what other terms and conditions matter to you and where the risk is. You have to have a clear bottom line. And not be bothered by the fact that they are going to try to get more or they perceive that it's worth more. If they say it's worth more, then you say, "Then you shouldn't sell it to me, you should sell it to someone who is willing to pay that price.' It's important, psychologically, not to say, 'Success is me getting this deal.' We say, 'Success is getting the deal on the terms that we want.' The second thing is being mature and not being emotional. Being very calm. And staying relaxed. And recognizing that deals generally take a lot longer than people expect them to."

Watch the interview at tinyurl.com/negotiating-clark-qualities

ED CLARK, former President and CEO of TD Bank, 2002–2014.

One of the leading practitioners in Alternative Dispute Resolution is Alan Stitt. A lawyer by profession, Stitt operates the largest dispute resolution company in Canada and has conducted mediation and dispute resolution workshops in Canada, the United States, the Caribbean, Europe, Africa, Asia and Australia. Stitt is also an Adjunct Professor at the University of Toronto Law School and lectures at the University of Windsor Law School, teaching courses in negotiation and in ADR. In his book

Mediating Commercial Disputes, Stitt makes an argument that a negotiator is best served by taking a principled approach rather than either of the other major options he has observed, which are competitive and co-operative bargaining.

Stitt outlines that a competitive bargainer is strictly focused on the outcome of the negotiation and does not consider anything other than "winning." Negotiators like this often get good substantive results, yet they are prone to downsides like deadlocks, damaged relationships and the potential to miss out on some very creative solutions because of a single-minded focus on a particular result. The competitive negotiator also develops a reputation for being a "hard-ass," which can limit their effectiveness and hiring potential. At the other end of the spectrum is the co-operative negotiator, who is largely focused on the relationship and will do whatever is necessary to preserve it, even if that involves making substantive concessions. The advantage of the co-operative negotiator is that relationships remain intact, even enhanced, and creative solutions are much more likely to arise. However, this approach typically means a lesser chance of getting a good deal because of the concessions made to preserve relationships. These negotiators can develop a reputation as a "softie" and some clients will be unlikely to retain them.

A principled negotiator, according to Stitt, can take advantage of the merits of both the competitor and the co-operator by approaching a negotiation with a focus on the underlying issues and interests involved on both sides. Stitt's thinking is grounded in the seminal work *Getting to Yes: Negotiating Agreement Without Giving In* by Roger Fisher, William Ury and Bruce Patton of the Harvard Law School, from which arise the phrases "focus on interests not positions" and "hard on issues, soft on people." Stitt's description of the principled negotiator is built on the following seven elements of *Getting to Yes* that maximize the likelihood of reaching a good deal while maintaining positive connections with the other side: alternatives, interests, options, legitimacy, communication, relationship and commitment.

The principled negotiator has been a kind of movie star on the negotiation scene for the last twenty years, and there are significant merits to this approach. But my position is that there are times when it is not the right attitude. It is entirely possible that a strategic negotiator might, after methodically and accurately assessing all of the options available in a given negotiation, conclude that the best approach is any one of Stitt's three — competitive, co-operative or principled. Point being, there is no one guaranteed approach to negotiations that makes the most sense all the time. The strategic negotiator works to see the entire process unfolding in advance and then chooses the options and approaches needed based on a rational assessment. So while Stitt's model is helpful, I have summarized it mainly to illustrate that the strategic negotiator can operate in many modes, depending on the requirements of an individual negotiation stage or entire process.

PURPOSE OF THIS BOOK

This book is meant to provide you — the strategic negotiator — with a wide array of options that will aid you. The negotiator's skills, knowledge and style matter more than anything else, including the scope of the subjects or artifacts under discussion. This is why this book is about you and your skills rather than just focused on a dissection of the negotiation stages and phases. My purpose is to offer valuable suggestions and ideas about your craft to help develop your capacity to lead your side to a positive outcome in every bargaining process. We can all improve our approach, and I envision this book as part of your professional growth.

Throughout, I have offered a variety of stories from my own career in politics, the private sector and education. I have also included instructive content from the leading negotiators I interviewed for the Ryerson Negotiation Project. Their expertise encompasses public policy, commercial ventures, sport and charitable organizations, and their insights offer diverse perspectives on how to approach negotiations in a strategic manner. In most cases, their comments have been transcribed as they were delivered in the interviews, but in some places I have combined a few comments spread over time into one quotation because the way the remarks were delivered made them difficult to understand on paper. Either way, the words are always theirs, not mine, with occasional edits for focus and clarity. (If you want to watch the complete interviews, follow the links included in the Ryerson Negotiation Project Video Interviews section.) Throughout, I have also outlined my own ideas about negotiation along with references to leaders in the negotiation field whose work has informed my own. In this way, I hope for this book to be an ongoing reference for you and to lead you to other resources of interest and value.

The book is built upon an age-old premise: a thing can be understood by breaking down its parts and looking at how each relates to the other. In all of the sections that follow, I have attempted to separate out the key elements so you can examine the parts in detail. Any process has steps that can be learned. Some are sequential and some not. Either way, examining parts and steps provides the framework you need to accurately and carefully predict and prepare as you proceed through any negotiation.

I begin with an outline of the fundamental competencies that a negotiator must possess and then look at a handful of game-changing approaches that can set you apart and demons (habits or situations) that can sewer you. I then explore issues related to your mandate as a negotiator and the ways that you should approach communication, both on your team and with the other side. Last, I take you through everything you need to consider at each stage of the process: the set-up, designing and forming the deal, working live at the table and closing.

THREE KEY LESSONS

"There are some lessons that are generic in negotiations. One is always be respectful. Don't vilify the other side. Two, always leave a way out for compromise so that when compromise happens, there hasn't been winners and losers, in a classic sense. The third is, make timing your friend. You have to be deliberate about what you put on the table when, in terms of the timing of what you are doing. Is what you are doing going to give leverage to what you want to achieve?"

Watch the interview at tinyurl.com/negotiating-harder-lessons

PETER HARDER, former Deputy Minister of Foreign Affairs and current Senior Policy Adviser at Dentons and President of the Canada China Business Council

ESSENTIAL QUALITIES OF CHARACTER

I have one final note about becoming the best possible negotiator, beginning with a reminder that a negotiation is about reaching an agreement. Throughout this book, I (and others) will emphasize that a negotiation is not a war in which you are out to conquer and destroy the other side. The best approach is one that seeks mutually beneficial agreements that consider the long-term health of the relationships and the overall system. It is about genuinely viewing the process as shared and the outcomes as achieved by working together.

As a result of this emphasis, two essential qualities of character are civility and respect. I have found that when you are civil with others and respectful of their views, even if you don't agree with them, there is a much greater chance of achieving what you are hoping for, both now and in the future. People who are rude or who shout, swear, intimidate, bully, threaten or humiliate are not strategic negotiators. There is no place for this kind of behaviour in a process whose goal is a viable and beneficial outcome for all involved. Incivility poisons the atmosphere and relationships and will sink the negotiation.

As a leader and negotiator working to raise your game, hold in mind that you will be at this for a long time. Who you are and how you proceed are fundamental aspects of how your career will unfold. And they are the central drivers of your ability to reach an agreement. As a result, civility and respect are lifelong qualities to emulate. In over forty years of professional life, I have met people on both the domestic and international scene from public office, not-for-profits and industry. The best of the best are invariably civil and considerate, regardless of their position.

This book is about learning how to succeed in negotiations by focusing on the skills and qualities of the negotiator. It is also about learning how to do it the right way so that you achieve the effective deals and impressive reputation that lead to sustainable success. If you hold in mind that the art of negotiation is fundamental to every kind of leadership, this book will extend and enhance your skills as a leader by improving your approach to every kind of strategic interaction.

TAKEAWAYS

YOU GET WHAT YOU NEGOTIATE IN LIFE

1. Seek agreement — look for mutually beneficial solutions, not win-lose dynamics.
2. Core competency — leaders have to be capable negotiators in this day and age.
3. Creativity and control — you have more influence in a negotiation than in litigation or arbitration.
4. Relationships matter — people make deals with people.
5. Learn and grow — you need to constantly assess and upgrade your skills.

BE STRATEGIC

6. Plan your time — ensure you are able to carefully and completely plan, prepare and respond.
7. Sweat the small stuff — assess and anticipate every aspect of the process no matter how minute.
8. Reverse engineer — imagine the outcome you intend and plan the process you need to get there.
9. Be rational — making decisions based on emotion and impulse is a dead end.
10. Be ready to walk — remember that sometimes no deal is the best deal.

ESSENTIAL QUALITIES OF CHARACTER

Approach negotiations with civility and respect to optimize the potential of reaching the current agreement and to build a long-term reputation as a superb negotiator.

CHAPTER 2
Fundamentals

"The quality of a person's life is in direct proportion to their commitment to excellence, regardless of their chosen field of endeavor."

— Vince Lombardi

In Cape Breton, three topics regularly come up in conversation: the weather, the fishing and what the heck the government is up to now — not necessarily in that order. As an MP from a Cape Breton constituency, that habit of talk meant that my name came up on a regular basis and a steady stream of citizens came to see me. The meetings were invigorating, challenging and a constant reminder that government exists to serve. This was particularly evident when I met with local fishermen. They were passionate about their calling and craft, deeply embedded in the traditions of the sea and engaged in a constant struggle for their livelihood, especially during my time in office when fish stocks were in rapid decline and the government was regulating the fisheries. From fishing quotas to the rules for employment insurance, there was no shortage of issues for us to discuss.

When the fishermen came to see me, with or without an appointment, sometimes during regular business hours and sometimes not, the meetings were intense and focused. And it was through these meetings that I met one of the best negotiators I have ever come across, Herb Nash, who was (and still is) the President of the Glace Bay Harbour Authority. A lifelong fisherman who is, to this day, representing the interests of his trade, Nash didn't look like your typical negotiator. He was average height, well over 200 pounds, usually had a cigarette hanging from his mouth and often had three or four days of stubble on his face. He spoke with the distinctive Cape Breton accent and emphasized his point with thick hands that had been pulling in traps and setting lines for years.

Nash didn't have a high school diploma, but he was a walking encyclopedia of information about the fisheries. He knew all of the facts and would research the scientific studies used to justify claims about fish stocks and compare those findings to every other available piece of information. He knew all of the quotas and regulations for everything from lobster to redfish to groundfish, and he knew the exact history of the fishing registry. Nash studied every fisheries report, reading every line and following up on every claim. And if he didn't understand something in a report, he would take it to the home of a schoolteacher he knew, sit down at the kitchen table, fling it open, poke the page in question and ask, "What does this mean?"

Nash followed every conversation about fishing in the House of Commons and at the federal Senate Fisheries Committee by getting a copy of the minutes. He did the same with the European Parliament. And he had a huge network all over the world. He knew everyone from fishermen and their families to representatives in the Ministry of Fisheries and Oceans to consultants who worked for the Ministry to representatives from all of the political parties who were on the fisheries file.

Nash was informed, careful, knowledgeable and plugged in.

When I knew he was coming to see me, I had to be on my game. He'd remember exactly what I said last time and if I strayed from that, he would not hesitate to interrupt me: "No, no, no, Dave, that's not what you said." And he had done his homework to find out if I followed through on my promises. He expected answers to all of his questions and if my facts weren't exactly right — if I offered a statistic at 3.2 per cent when it was actually 3.4 per cent — Nash would correct me. If I had been quoted in the media, he would look into what I said and call me on it: "No, no, no, boy, that's not what you said. You were in the paper. Which is it, Dave?" Or he would read what other politicians or officials were saying and point out that it was inconsistent with a printed report: "Brian Tobin over in Newfoundland said this, but that's not what the Ministry is saying." His knowledge of the fisheries was so extensive that I learned something new every time I met with him. In fact, I assigned a staffer named Sandra McLeod to follow-up with him after every meeting, partly so that we could learn from him. He would advise us to read this report or that report and his interest and assertions pushed us to know everything we could.

To this day, I can still hear his voice as he hammered away at me about the issues. He was never abrupt and it was never intimidating to meet with him, but did I ever have to know my stuff. He was an ardent and seasoned advocate for the interests of fishermen. And there was never any grey area about where he stood on quotas, international regulations, issues related to the operation of small crafts — anything that affected the rights and livelihood of fishermen.

Nash is a beauty. One of the best negotiators I have ever seen, he is a shining example of a subject matter expert, an ardent representative of the interests of fishermen and the value of mastering the fundamentals. Our interactions might best be described as constructive adversarialism, a kind of productive disagreement underpinned by a fair representation of the interests of both sides. Whatever you call it, Nash reminds us all to be informed, be prepared and be strategic.

A strategic negotiator masters the basic skills, sub-processes and subjects that form the basis of the craft. No two negotiations are exactly the same because the issues, people and magnitude of the subject matter vary. But there are recognizable patterns in every quest for resolution that make it possible to delineate and analyze component parts of the approach that can be refined — especially if a negotiator is going to be strategic and proactive about the actions and responses in all stages of the process. As I have said, avoid making decisions in the moment based on gut instinct or emotion. Great negotiators think through how they will respond in any given situation and arrive to each interaction with the other side prepared to execute a strategy rather than react. And they focus on developing skills and understanding the complex parts of the negotiation process.

PLANNING

"You don't work until you are tired. You work until you get it perfect." That's how David Peterson summed up the process of planning what would be Toronto's successful bid for the 2015 Pan American / Parapan American Games. Peterson is former Premier of Ontario, former Chancellor of the University of Toronto and founding Chairman of the Toronto Raptors. He is an expert who is often called on to manage highly complex negotiations. So when the province wanted to take a stab at hosting the games, then-Premier Dalton McGuinty called Peterson personally and asked him to lead the team.

"We worked for a year and a half preparing our presentation and laying the groundwork for our bid," explained Peterson during his Ryerson Negotiation Project interview. "We had to have a complete bid book with plans that covered every element of hosting the Games, including every detail about venues for sixty different sports. We had to go through details such as where the badminton will be played, where the athletes' village will be located and how the transportation, food, entertainment and medical support will work." Peterson and his team also had to visit forty-two countries to meet with the Pan Am officials who would be voting on the proposals. These meetings involved hearing the concerns and interests of the parties and then taking them into account with the planning process. Often, Peterson would fly to a place such as Mexico overnight, attend a two-hour meeting and then get back on the plane to Canada.

Peterson also explained that he and his team had to be incredibly precise about planning for the visit from the evaluation committee — a part of the process that can make or break a bid. "There were six members of the committee and we had to move them all over Ontario to show them the various venues we intended to use. We had five hundred people involved in planning the committee's transportation by car, boat, train and helicopter. We could not afford for one thing to go wrong in the timing. It was like a political campaign, and we had people who had planned campaigns for all three parties involved — experts in this kind of coordinated planning. People who knew how to plan and how to adapt as they went along. There were no compromises. We had to get it perfect. More was expected of us because we are Toronto. It's not a developing nation. There was a higher standard expected from us."

The end result was a presentation that many involved described as "Olympic calibre." More importantly, Peterson and his team succeeded in landing the Games for the City of Toronto, largely because of their commitment to a comprehensive, detailed and precise planning process. "Good planning conserves your resources, prevents wasted effort and, in the end, will save you enormous amounts of time and money," concludes Peterson.

PREPARING FOR A DEAL IN ANOTHER COUNTRY

"You have to do your homework and try to understand as much as you can about the culture and society you are dealing in, because they can be very different from each other and from the way that we deal with things here in Canada.

"I would always go to the Canadian Consul General at the Canadian Embassy or to the local office of Ernst & Young or Deloitte, one of the big accounting firms, and, if I could, a local office of a North American law firm. The people there will either be from that country but be very familiar with North American approaches, or they will be from North America and be very familiar with the particular country. They give you the lay of the land — don't say this, make sure you do that, et cetera. I would also seek out the Canadian Trade Offices — in every country, there is a trade commissioner whose job is to facilitate Canadian business in that country. You can also just Google Canadian businesses that work in the country.

"I remember when we were going into Turkey where it is difficult to figure out exactly how to do business. I found that there were some Canadian mining companies, who are very different than media companies, but they were able to help us understand how things worked in Turkey. There are also usually business councils — like the Turkish-Canadian or Chinese-Canadian council — so you can get the lay of the land. As much as you can, you need to get a PhD in that country."

Watch the interview at
tinyurl.com/negotiating-asper-location

LEONARD ASPER, former CEO of Canwest Global Communications Corporation and current President and CEO of Anthem Sports & Entertainment

Watch the interview
with David Peterson at
tinyurl.com/negotiating-
peterson-planning

In most major endeavours, the leadership will require a detailed roadmap. In the business world, corporate directors and financial lenders always want to see your business plan. They give enormous weight to it and will be very focused on what it fails to address. The same is true for non-profit organizations, government agencies and institutions that operate in the international field. In a negotiation, your plan is an essential first step and needs to have a clearly stated objective supported by numerous options that might unfold along the way. A seasoned negotiator recognizes the importance of planning and openly works with the team to anticipate the various twists and turns that will inevitably occur.

There are a variety of elements to take into account, most of which link to one another: the mandate and how to develop it; the makeup of your team and the individual roles within that group; the time frame; various alternatives; the quality of the information you need and where to get it; how you will resolve deadlocks and impasses that you can foresee; financial interests and their potential effect on the negotiations; your best guess about the information that the other side has; and a strong sense of the issues the other side is likely to raise and how you will respond to them. And, as I will outline in chapter 3, a substantial amount of time is needed to talk about how to develop critical relationships that will positively influence the process.

Obviously, the amount of planning required is in direct correlation to the complexity and scope of the issue. If you want a pair of socks when you enter Hudson's Bay in Toronto, you don't need a comprehensive plan. You will either find some socks or end up down the street at Holt Renfrew. But when the stakes are high and there are multiple moving parts, you need a plan. As Michael Wheeler writes in *The Art of Negotiation: How to Improvise Agreement in a Chaotic World*, "In any context, a well-conceived planning process sharpens objectives, exposes possible obstacles, illuminates potential paths, even though the exact route may not be determined until the interaction is well underway."

As I said at the outset, one of the classic errors that negotiators make is not allowing sufficient time for a proper process. I have been amazed at how often lead negotiators fail to commit enough time to the planning process under the assumption that they can figure it out as they go along. It's the wrong way to think about planning. Take the time needed to map everything out — especially when the planning process requires an extended group. Finding a time when all members of your side are available to meet or ensuring that you have access to the experts and individuals you need is complicated. The more you can plan ahead, the more likely you are to get what you need.

The advantages of proper planning are numerous. First of all, you can consider the long-term implications of what you are proposing and what you might end up accepting. The mere act of physically sitting down and planning out alternatives allows you to understand how satisfactory each possibility will be in terms of the mandate and goals. This process is critical to determining when to accept or reject an offer and if or when to continue negotiations with the other party. Discussing alternatives will also put you and your team in a position to explore the various options for how the negotiation will proceed and help with collecting the information needed both to substantiate claims you will be making and to rebut assertions put forward by your counterpart — a process that can save an enormous amount of time and money later on. There are significant synergies that flow from getting your team together to discuss alternatives, options and information, and teams often find that some of their best ideas come up during those planning sessions.

It is also important to remember that some of the options chosen during the planning process will come out of discussions with your counterpart on the other side. This is one of the reasons that throughout my day as legal counsel, I try to convince clients that it is very important that they build relationships with the other side before they go to a negotiating session. Whether you have known the other party for some time or they are completely new to you, devise a strategy for how to build rapport and come to a better understanding of each other's needs in the process. Negotiations are about reaching agreement. The more you know what they need and want, the better able you are to fulfill your own mandate.

EXPERTISE

There is no substitute for experience and expertise. You can develop yourself into a world-class negotiator, but if you are involved with unfamiliar subjects or contexts, all the skill in the world isn't going to help. More and more, we are seeing negotiators specialize in certain industries and areas. Some of us are still considered to be experienced generalists who can manage cases in different fields, but there is so much technical expertise in many agreements and disputes that, at a minimum, it is important to acquire team members who are well versed in the area, whether it is non-profit, public or private. Negotiators who think that they can operate in any sector and do so exceedingly well are not being totally candid with themselves or their clients, because it is a significant strategic advantage to know an industry well.

Subject expertise is a main reason why we are seeing more and more in-house experts and consultants who can advise about specific governmental Request for Proposals. The requirements for those applications are so complex that it is a huge advantage to have someone present with experience on the governmental side of the equation who can guide you through all of the various stages. Clients of mine who have been able to see that hiring someone with detailed knowledge is an investment rather than a cost have reaped the rewards of that expertise, because they are ready to respond to whatever comes up in the process.

This need extends to all sectors. When dealing with a major merger acquisition proposal, engage team members with specific expertise and experience, such as tax law, asset valuation, financial statement analysis, and relevant legislative regulations and case law parameters. If dealing with a commercial arrangement that involves a major procurement of technology services, construct a team that includes specialized technical people, financial experts and operations or sales personnel who understand the fine details of the industry. In the public sector, acquire experts in negotiating a collective agreement, introducing new policies or revamping existing programs.

In addition to the presence of subject experts, the strategic negotiator also studies the industry in question and does everything possible to develop a rich understanding of what is involved. The more you can integrate your expertise and knowledge of the negotiation process with an understanding of key relevancies to this particular kind of negotiation, the more effective you will be. It is the duty, if not the fiduciary duty, of the negotiator and the team to fully understand all of the elements of the negotiating process.

PREPARATION

Legendary basketball coach John Wooden said, "A failure to prepare is preparing to fail." He might as well have been describing a negotiation. With plans and expertise in place, it is important to go through a meticulous process of preparing for every possible contingency that may arise. Trial lawyers spend hundreds of hours, days and weeks preparing for opening statements, direct examinations, cross-examinations, motions for disclosure and closing arguments. They develop a theory of the case and then work exhaustively to understand and organize the facts. More than anything else, especially in cross-examination, the facts will be the determining factor before a trier of fact. That is where the motto "one fact per question" comes from. And this level of detail is why trial preparations are so time consuming.

Negotiators have to approach their cases with the same zealous attention to detail, and there are several key areas that I advise paying close attention to.

Establish Goals

It seems obvious, but you and your team need to have a clearly defined set of goals as the process begins. You can only succeed in achieving your mandate if you know what you want to accomplish. In addition, take time to map out the goals of the other side. Consider all of the issues at hand and look at all of the parties involved and the interests behind their stated positions. Assessing these factors will help to anticipate what they are likely to suggest for the agenda sequence and how those suggestions affect your ability to meet your goals. If you aren't very clear about what you are trying to accomplish, it is difficult to get to those targets.

SWOT Analysis

SWOT stands for strengths, weaknesses, opportunities and threats. Some time should go into preparing a SWOT analysis of your proposal as well as that of your counterpart. This valuable analysis provides perspective on the situation that will guide your ability to assess alternatives. It is surprising how often items that you would label as a strength will be perceived as a weakness by another party. The mere fact of holding a discussion about the various exposures, weak links and strongholds of your side can help you prepare more effectively.

As an example, consider how a company negotiating with a government ministry could analyze its adversary using the SWOT framework. A *strength* of the government is its deep pockets; a large amount of money can be made available for the negotiation. A *weakness* is that the government is subject to political pressure. If an agency, special interest group or corporation makes demands, the negotiators will have to respond. An *opportunity* for the government

ASSESSING A DEAL AND ACQUIRING RELATIONSHIPS

"In some sense our acquisitions model is asymmetrical. The business leader must endorse the deal. You would never do a deal when the corporate development team thinks it is a good deal but the business leader says no. The deal has to be linked into the strategy. If you don't think you are going to add value, operationally, to what you acquire, you shouldn't be doing the deal in the first place.

"But, if the business leader says, 'I want to do this deal,' and the acquisition team says, 'We shouldn't do this deal,' we won't do the deal. Obviously, it comes out of a discussion with me where I call that, but it just wouldn't happen inside our organization that if the corporate development team says 'I don't like this deal' that I would overrule that. It's the same way that we run our risk department. In theory, I can overrule my Chief Risk Officer, but I have never overruled my Chief Risk Officer.

"In our case, relationships are quite important because it would be very rare that we would try to acquire something when we were not trying to acquire the management. We would rather pay more and get something that is working well in which we are actually acquiring talent as part of the deal. But if that is what you are trying to do, there is a side process that has to go on, which is to recruit the management team that you are acquiring.

is its significant capacity to delay if desired — it can initiate both valid and invalid mechanisms that slow the process down, such as sending an issue "to committee." Finally, a *threat* the government faces is negative public opinion resulting from media scrutiny, such as often happens when complex environmental clean-up processes are delayed and the public perceives the government to be stalling.

"The clearest example would be when we bought the Commerce Bank in the United States, which has a business model that is very similar to the Canada Trust model. They are open seven days a week. They are open at night. They do these wow things. They give cookies to the dogs, they have dog bowls. They have fun. They make banking a fun experience for the employees and for the customers. There was no point acquiring the Commerce and then losing the management team. So it was quite critical that we recruit the management.

"What I always say to people is 'Would you hire the people who are coming with the company? If you wouldn't hire them, why would we buy the company?' So when you look at the relationship between business development and the business leaders, in general, the business leader's job is to recruit the management team."

Watch the interview at tinyurl.com/negotiating-clark-relationship

ED CLARK, former President and CEO of TD Bank, 2002–2014

Team

In 1995, the Supreme Court of Canada struck down tobacco legislation on the grounds that it was unconstitutional. Once again, the tobacco companies were victorious in the courts, and tobacco products with all their deadly ingredients were free from regulation. In January 1996, Prime Minister Jean Chrétien assigned me to take over as Minister of Health, which meant navigating though the legislative and political quagmire around the writing and passing of a new bill was now my responsibility. Stakeholders from across the country were anxious to meet with me to explore legislation that would protect Canadians, and especially young people, from the lure of tobacco products and the subsequent addiction and health concerns that follow. Most of all, health groups wanted to meet to express their outrage at the Minister of Health for not moving quickly enough, and the issue became their rallying cry from coast to coast to coast. Of course, the tobacco companies held that everything was fine and consumers should be allowed to decide for themselves.

When I arrived in the Ministry, I discovered that the department had no backup plan. We had to start from scratch to build legislation that would pass the constitutional test while still having enough weight to be effective in the marketplace. We had to first develop new legislation, analyze its constitutionality, assess the political landscape at all levels of government and then develop and execute a plan. Right away, I knew I needed talented people on the team who could complement my skills and share the load of what needed to be done. Fortunately, there was a young woman named Athana Mentzelopoulos on the staff. She was exceptionally bright, hardworking and strategic and, as I would learn over the course of the year and a half that we worked together to enact the legislation, she was not timid about engaging with people who didn't share her view. Unfailingly polite and often smiling, she would confront officials at all levels head-on about their concerns, positions and role in the process.

When Mentzelopoulos and I first met to discuss the project, she expressed concern that she did not know a great deal about the political process. I told her not to worry about that aspect of her job — that was up to me as Minister of Health. Her role was to engage with all members of the parliamentary committee, the various interest groups, the Prime Minister's office, the House Leader's office, members of the media and senior members in the Upper Chamber — the Senate. She took on the task with zeal and was an indispensable force. She and I met almost every morning to coordinate and then she would go off to various meetings all over Parliament Hill to put our plans into action. Her wise counsel and strategic contributions were an important part of our success and a testament to the value of an effective team.

On December 2, 1996, Bill C-71 was introduced and read for the first time in the House of Commons. Over the next few months, ending with a vote on March 6, 1997, of 139 yeas and 37 nays — 35 of which were from the Bloc Québécois — the legislation was enacted with relatively little opposition and was passed by the Senate on April 16, 1997, with 75 yea votes and only 1 nay. At the time, the legislation was considered the most comprehensive in the world for the regulation of the manufacture, sale, labelling and promotion of tobacco products.

My experience at the Ministry of Health underscores the need to assess your team and put together a collection of people who can, working together, cover off all of the skills and knowledge required by this particular negotiation. When designing the core team and identifying various stakeholders who will operate in an advisory capacity, consider all legal, financial, technical and industry-specific elements of the deal. Are there particular subject experts that you require? Also, think through the exact number of people you will have on the team and how many will actually be at the table. I generally don't counsel organizations to have the exact same number of people on their side as the other team, but I do always advise that there be at least two of your own people in the room at all times. With the team established, ensure that every member is prepared for their specific role and that everyone understands each other's job. Will there be a good cop and a bad cop? Will someone be assigned to take notes? Who will be assigned to observe body language and other non-verbal communications and bring notes back to each caucus? What information do you need to collect and who will collect it? Who is the lead negotiator? Who is the logical person to make thoughtful and timely interventions? Effective coordination of skills, interests and responsibilities goes a long way toward ensuring team success. Most of all, make sure that you have people who want to put in the time and effort required to participate in the preparation of documents and strategy. On the flip side, if some people around you dislike the negotiating process or believe it is beneath them, it is obvious not to have them on your team.

Resources

It goes without saying that you need to collect as much relevant and compelling information as possible about the subject at hand, because there may be instances where internal information is absolutely crucial to your preparations. You may even want to retain a third party to help acquire specific or technical information. It is also important to ascertain from your counterpart a variety of information as you move along in the negotiation, perhaps by forwarding a series of questions to them in advance of sitting down at the table.

If at all possible, try to get the other side's organizational chart. Also, complete due diligence to establish who the decision-makers are likely to be in the negotiation process, because it might not be the lead negotiator or anyone sitting at the table. Consider studying annual reports, industry reports, books, media analysis, business journals and promotional literature. Your analysis might also include academic studies, interviews with suppliers, magazine articles and government reports.

But having the information isn't the whole story. Piles and piles of studies, reports and books are of very little use unless they are understood, integrated into the overall presentation and organized in a manner that makes them easy to access as needed. Information-rich presentations are highly compelling. Difficulty accessing the information you need when it is needed looks sloppy, as does presenting ideas and arguments that are disjointed and potentially inconsistent. I have seen this time and time again: people presenting to senior regulators with a mountain of paper but no capacity to have the necessary information on hand when a particular question is asked. Or lawyers who are so haphazard in their preparations that the information might as well be back at the office, because they cannot access it at will or have a crucial document readily available.

Edward Greenspan, the famous Canadian trial lawyer who died in 2014, was brilliant at this. If there were five elements of a case — like *mens rea* or motive — he would have a file folder for each element. As those issues came up during the trial, he would calmly open the file and refer to that information or follow the questions he had scripted in advance on that subject. Flawless preparation.

Time Frame and Schedule

Time is an incredibly valuable and important resource, and it is essential to be clear about the scope of the work. What are the time boundaries for this particular negotiation? Do you have a month? Two months? Six? What is the expected date of conclusion and who expects that timing? Be sure to obtain these details from your superiors, but more importantly, know the time frame for the other side, because not knowing can lead to significant problems. For instance, there are many businesses that try to conclude labour agreements with their respective unions without enough consideration of time frame. They begin the process very early and are anxious to have the matter wrapped up quickly. Most unions, however, are cognizant of this tendency and act accordingly, controlling the process by controlling the timeline. In order to successfully commence and conclude a negotiation, understand what the other party deems to be an appropriate time frame.

In addition, determine the time restraints on your team members. They may have other commitments in their work or have personal conflicts such as holidays, doctors' appointments or family obligations.

Scheduling requires careful attention once the overall timeline is in place. Begin by sorting out the hard deadlines that each side needs to work toward. In commercial arrangements, the parties typically give themselves a certain period of time in which to conclude the deal. But in many instances, there may initially not be a deadline or it may be vague. It is wise to get some consensus on this issue, and it could be an item for the agenda when you sit down with the other side to discuss the time frame. Of course, it is also, like every element of a negotiation, a process that will help build your relationship with the other side and could yield potential advantages if you are strategic about how to proceed.

After establishing basic deadlines, I advise mapping out your team's milestones in terms of deliverables and accomplishments. This might even involve preparing a critical path that comprises timing, must-do's and an overview of all parallel activities in the sequence that are to be completed at certain points.

Anticipating Questions and Arguments

When I was CEO of the Royal Canadian Mint, one approach to substantially raising our operating revenue was striking international deals wherein we would provide services to other nations. One such instance occurred when my senior team and I travelled to Thailand to meet with currency officials about a potential $50 million contract. In preparation for the trip, we went through every question we could foresee being asked. Will you or your representatives be available to us at all times? Will representatives travel to Thailand as needed? Who will be assigned to manage this project? What are their credentials? Can you give us examples of instances where you have provided similar services? Can you provide us with a list of references? These are questions that anyone considering a significant investment would think to ask, and so we spent considerable time preparing our answers in advance.

The best way to answer a question effectively is to know it is coming. A strategic negotiator prepares for everything that the other side will ask in the process and, in some cases, this involves having clearly defined responses to deliver in as comprehensive but genuine a fashion as possible — canned responses are deadly and need to be avoided. Be informed but not stale or stiff. I always advise my clients to prepare for questions about their experience, knowledge, integrity, professionalism, accessibility, creativity, reliability, availability and flexibility, especially when the negotiation in question is a seller-buyer situation. It is also important to prepare for what you are going to ask the other side, including sketching out possible responses to your inquires. It is all part of a careful and detailed preparation that leads to success.

On the subject of questions, I'd like to mention one particular aspect that is critical in your effort to demonstrate that authenticity is in your DNA: what to do if you don't know the answer to a question. It is fundamental to be honest and ethical throughout the process so that the other side can never mount a legitimate argument that you are bargaining in bad faith. To that end, you can always respond, "I am sorry, I don't know the answer to that question. I will look into it and get back to you as soon as I can." It's a small thing, but it goes a long way to building relationships, strengthening your case and advancing your interests.

Incentives for the Negotiators

In 2008 when the American banking system was in meltdown mode and the financial crisis was in full swing, Canadian banks were admired around the world for their wise approach and careful planning. Ed Clark, President and CEO of TD Bank from December 2002 until his retirement in November 2014, is widely regarded as one of the most strategic and insightful leaders in the industry. During his tenure at TD, Clark led the bank through an extended expansion in the United States, fuelled by a specialized team of business development experts that he created for the sole purpose of making principled, informed and careful decisions about potential deals. Among the various elements of TD's approach, Clark was very careful about how he arranged compensation for his acquisition experts: "Every time we had a complicated contract or acquisition, we handed it over to that group. They get paid for doing a good job, not necessarily for making the acquisition. If we walk away because it was too pricey or we don't like the risks, we have a celebration for that team and it's the same celebration as if they had completed a deal. We try to create opposite incentives so that you don't get deal fever spreading. You want your business leaders to be looking for opportunities to grow, but you can resist deal fever spreading if you put a counterweight on it by having a group that gets equally rewarded for saying 'I don't think we should do this deal.'"

Watch the interview with Ed Clark at tinyurl.com/negotiating-clark-incentives

In your preparation time, give serious consideration to the incentives of the negotiators on the other side. Are they agents acting on behalf of a principal, the person whose interests are being pursued in the negotiation? Will there be a bonus paid if a deal is reached? Is there a direct correlation between the size of the deal and the monies that will be paid to the negotiator, as happens with sport and entertainment agents? Also, look closely at your incentives and those of your team members to objectively assess the role that incentives might play in influencing thinking and behaviour. Will the end result be a pat on the back? Or is something more substantial in the mix?

Administrative Details

I once organized a meeting where there was significant tension between the participants that I felt was a distraction from the discussions, and I needed to do everything possible to keep the focus on the issues at hand. I arranged for the furniture for the meeting to be set up in a semi-circle facing a whiteboard where the issues of the discussions would be presented. By physically arranging the room to orient the participants' sightlines, I was able to influence the extent to which the group stayed focused on the topic at hand.

My advice about administrative details and logistics is that no detail is too small to consider. However achieved, whether by assigning a particular team member to make ongoing suggestions for an approach that might bolster the cause, or just making it a regular part of your own thinking, be sure to consider little things.

There is a long list of administrative details, so I'll point to one as an example: meeting logistics. Where will the meetings actually take place? How will the designated meeting place impact the negotiations? And if there is no choice about where to meet, be aware of the situational factors that may colour your judgement and thinking. Do the meeting rooms have easy and quick access to fresh air? Are the individual caucus rooms well-equipped with communication capabilities? Are the rooms in a noisy location (e.g., near construction)? If the media are involved, is there a separate area where they can be located?

Another meeting consideration is choosing between playing host or being a guest. Conventional wisdom touts the advantages of meeting on your home turf on the basis that a familiar setting will put you and your team at ease. But when you travel to your counterpart's office, you convey a very strong message: you want to make a deal. Also, it can be very revealing to visit the other side at their place so as to collect valuable information about them. As a negotiator, my general preference is to hold meetings at my or the other side's home location. Brian Burke, President of Hockey Operations for the Calgary Flames and former General Manager of the Toronto Maple Leafs, primarily enters into single-party contract negotiations with players and their agents. This is his view: "Most GMs or assist GMs won't go to the enemy's office. They make the agent come to them. I always thought it was a sign of respect that I would go to their office to present and explain the offer. You have a way better chance of making a deal if the agent feels they have been treated with respect."

Watch the interview with Brian Burke at tinyurl.com/negotiating-burke-location

But there are many highly successful negotiators who don't feel the same way, often related to the nature of the negotiations that they are engaged in. Buzz Hargrove, former National President of the Canadian Auto Workers union who represented the interests of 256,000 members in extended collective bargaining with the major auto manufacturing companies, has a different perspective: "I learned from experience that it's better to have the bargaining at a hotel. When you take people away from the communities where they live and work, they are away from the pressures they face and the interruptions that can get in the way, like people running home to dinner with their family or being called on to deal with an issue in the plant. Those issues are important, but when you are bargaining, you need to make sure that there is total focus on the process."

Watch the interview with Buzz Hargrove at tinyurl.com/negotiating-hargrove-location

ALTERNATIVES

In the very early stages of any negotiation, it is imperative to give careful consideration to an alternative to a negotiated agreement — what to do if the negotiations do not go well and you need to pursue another course of action. This can happen when the other party has a fairly strong case which will preclude you from achieving your objectives. In that situation, pay attention to the other options. Every negotiator needs to deal with the hand they have been dealt, and it is extremely important to know whether what is on the table meets your mandate better than the alternatives. The only way to do that is to know what the alternatives are.

In *Getting to Yes*, authors Fisher, Ury and Patten introduce the idea of a BATNA, a Best Alternative to a Negotiated Agreement. Based on this work, the program on negotiation at the Harvard Law School suggests following four steps when assessing the BATNA.

First, list alternatives to settling for the offer on the table, such as mediation, beginning a litigation process and getting into discovery before trying to reach an agreement or starting an arbitration hearing. Second, evaluate the strengths and weaknesses of each alternative to determine if one of them is better than what is being offered at the present time. Third, decide on which course of action to pursue if the negotiations fail. Finally, calculate what Roger Fisher calls your "reservation value." This is the value of the best alternative and is, by definition, the value of the lowest deal you are willing to accept. In this way, establishing your BATNA is also a way of assessing the relative value of the options that are on the table.

Assessing your BATNA can be time consuming, particularly if you are in a multi-party negotiation, but a careful calculation of alternatives will enhance your confidence and give focus to the negotiations. That calculation can also prevent you from giving up a good deal in the present in favour of a BATNA in the future. And remember to explore the BATNA of the other side to have a sense of their view of the negotiations. You might be surprised when you list their options, because their alternatives may well be limited, which will influence your thinking and approach. And when looking at the alternatives for the other side, be careful to remember Fisher's advice that while most meaningful negotiations occur between organizations, a deal is reached by the individuals involved. Considering the incentives of the negotiators when assessing their BATNA is as important as assessing the offers on the table. Ask yourself how the negotiators are compensated, how long have they worked with the company and what their reputation considerations are.

When in a multi-party negotiation, assessing the BATNA of the other parties can be a daunting exercise. In fact, it may be nearly impossible. Nevertheless, put pen to paper and sketch out your best estimate of the alternatives for each party. At a minimum, this will ensure you are well prepared and can be more creative in the next round, or next set, of negotiations.

PATIENCE

"Minister, you sleep in. And then we will spend the day chilling out so we are rested for the meetings." That's what Marc Rochon said to me at the tail end of a flight to China in spring 1994. Rochon was the President of the Canadian Mortgage and Housing Corporation, and I was travelling with him to work out a deal for a twenty-six-acre site in Beijing to showcase Canadian housing products. He was a seasoned veteran who knew all about travelling back and forth across the planet and the importance of being well rested before heading into significant meetings.

When I arrived in Toronto to join Rochon for the overnight flight, I had been going since 5 a.m. I had started the day by reading cabinet documents and then attended caucus, prepared for and attended Question Period, and met with the senior team before getting on a flight from Ottawa to Toronto. When I got there, I was bagged. And after the long intercontinental flight, I was feeling the effects and needed a chance to rest. So Rochon's advice to "chill out" was perfect. I slept in the next morning and then we spent time seeing the city and getting acclimatized. We even went for a haircut, which was pretty funny given how little hair I have. But we took our time, got ourselves ready and were in the right state of body, mind and self when we arrived at these very important meetings, moving patiently and carefully to see them through.

Our approach was consistent with the emphasis on patience that Chinese leaders and their counterparts in Japan are quick to embrace, unlike their North American peers who tend to rush in an effort to get the deal done. Our sense of urgency can often work against our focus on strategic decision making, and in many instances, it can do irrefutable harm to the reputation of the negotiator and the success of the negotiation. Good negotiators have both the ability to persist and the mindset that they will do whatever it takes to achieve their strategic goals. Be impatient at your own peril.

THE QUALITIES OF A GREAT NEGOTIATOR

"Preparedness — someone that really knows the facts of the situation. Knows the business of the client, understands the client, understands the client on the other side and how far they are willing to go, understands how badly the deal is needed by both sides, understands the lawyer on the other side and what it takes to get them to move. It all goes back to being really well prepared."

Watch the interview at tinyurl.com/negotiating-lean-qualities

RALPH LEAN, Distinguished Counsel in Residence at Ryerson University's Ted Rogers School of Management

Here are five important aspects of patient behaviour, which are, in turn, expressions of my key emphasis on being strategic, careful and prepared.

1. A rested body.

If you are tired, rundown, and multitasking, the likelihood of being patient at the negotiating table is low. Just as Rochon advised, make sure you and your team are well rested. I have often heard people say, "If only I had a good night's sleep, I would have been more effective." Good judgement and effective listening skills, not to mention appearance and ability to be civil, come from being well rested.

2. Manage and plan your time.

I counsel executives and participants to be very conservative about their time. If there is a week planned for the negotiations, assume it will take three or four weeks to complete. This advice rarely goes over well with the client, but I try to help them see the benefits of being aware. Furthermore, I share with clients that negotiations are a marathon, not a sprint. There are hills and valleys before reaching an agreement. Just consider a negotiation over a high-end asset like an exclusive piece of real estate or a commercial property, and you can get a sense of the time involved. From the due diligence to track down the appropriate paper to interviewing people associated with the transaction, copious amounts of time and energy are required. Then, considering that the other side might not be readily available to exchange information or meet at a moment's notice, time slows down quite a bit. Likewise, members of your own team may not be readily available for in-depth discussions.

3. Relationships are not developed overnight.
As I have said, be very deliberate about building relationships — a topic that I will explore in depth in the next chapter. But developing a relationship with the client or your opponent takes a considerable amount of time. Plan to put in the time, and that diligent effort will enhance the entire negotiation, especially when you approach those relationships with a specific goal in mind.

4. Pay attention to what they are saying.
When at the table, it takes a great deal of stamina to listen carefully to everything that the other side is saying. But failing to do so may lead to missing an essential point of the argument and leaving your opponent irked by your behaviour. People know when you have stopped listening. Often, negotiators, me included, try to listen and write at the same time. The reality is that you are likely to miss something. The best approach is to stay focused on what is being presented and have another member of the team take meticulous notes of the dialogue.

5. Be strategic.

This is a theme throughout this book that is particularly relevant to the topic of patience. Rushing to a decision too quickly based on an intuitive sense that it is the time to strike, likely means losing sight of your strategy and overall goals. In my experience, this is a side effect of poor time budgeting, unreasonable expectations from clients or partners and the need to comply with demands from other agencies like external regulators. More often than not, negotiators don't organize themselves so that they can conduct negotiations strategically. And while some argue that taking more time at all stages of the process will lead to an increased cost to the client, I am not convinced that is the case. I think that slowing down to get it right the first time is more likely to lead to an agreement that meets your interests and saves money for your client.

ATTENTION TO DETAIL

I was once involved in acquiring a significant publicly traded company when all of the necessary parties gathered for a marathon weekend session to advance the process. It was the middle of summer, and by Friday afternoon it was 32 degrees Celsius outside, a temperature that would continue all weekend. We discovered that the building we were housed in for the purposes of these significant discussions had the air conditioning turned off Friday afternoon at five for the whole weekend. Unluckily, the maintenance man responsible for the air conditioning had gone away for the weekend. There was no one else who could turn on the AC. Needless to say, the tone of the meetings shifted considerably as the weekend progressed.

Throughout this chapter, I have been emphasizing the fundamentals of a strategic approach to negotiations. A recurring theme is that little things can make a big difference. As we wrap up the chapter, I want to expand on what seems obvious but is, in my experience, not the common practice. Being very careful about every action and response from you and your team is essential. It is a time-consuming and trying way to live and work, especially in complex, long-term and intricate negotiations with multiple parties. Paying attention to all of the details is challenging even for the most experienced negotiator.

Remember the quote from David Peterson on planning? "You don't work until you are tired. You work until you get it perfect." When he and I sat down for the interview, he also talked about the process used for final approval on the Pam Am presentation. "We had brilliant and creative people on the team, but it was up to me to ensure that we had the most coherent and complete presentation possible. At the end of the day, I approved every single comma and went through the agony of writing and rewriting the document. Only I could judge if the final product was there, and I was not prepared to delegate that — the tone of the presentation. There had to be one mind pulling it all together, and in that case it was up to me."

Watch the interview with David Peterson at tinyurl.com/negotiating-peterson-detail

To illustrate the point, let's look at some examples of where careful attention to detail can be a make-or-break proposition:

1.   Being unintentionally rude in the early stages of the negotiation process can sour working relationships.

2.   An email whose tone appears to be accusatory can result

in the other party reciprocating both in tone and in substance.

3.   Forgetting to copy an email to a member of your team or indeed to the regulator about a particular issue can create gaps or generate frustration.

4.   Failure to have a much-referenced document readily available to share with the other party can put your authenticity into question and diminish needed trust.

5.   Being social and friendly with only a few members of the other team can come back to haunt you when other members resent that behaviour.

6.   Making assumptions about the other party's authority without having it verified can impact the negotiating process.

7.   Failure to fully agree on what both parties will communicate to the media after a negotiation session can cause confusion and potential embarrassment for everyone.

8.   Holding a meeting with ten or twelve different parties and finding out at the last minute that the washrooms are on another floor impedes efficiency.

9.   The young man who was supposed to deliver coffee to a meeting ending up at the wrong building and participants going without creates obvious vexation.

10.   Confusion over timelines or lack of coordination about when the negotiations will start, when there will be a break and when discussions will conclude can lead to tension, disappointment or ill will.

11. Failure to take time for the lead negotiator to actually practise their opening statement in front of the team can lead to getting the meetings off on the wrong foot and inadvertently undermining your goals right from the start.

Attention to detail can be even more important in situations where you are acting as an agent for a group of individuals who, for example, need to have something negotiated for the purposes of a commercial arrangement. Ensure that you are clear not only about your authority in the process, but also about the dos and don'ts of your principal. If you are familiar with the principal and have a good working relationship backed up by shared experiences, you may not have to discuss those issues, but it is always wise to be very careful and detailed about the principal-agent relationship. And even when you do have a good rapport and it seems redundant to raise questions about how the relationship is going to work in a particular case, I think it is better to be safe than sorry. I have been in many different situations where the principal has indicated a course of action that has not been an obvious extension of past practices and it has created some level of muddle with the agent negotiating on their behalf. Equally, if ever an agent yourself, you may be in a situation where you are uncomfortable with what the principal is requesting. It is a good idea to sort through the details in advance to avoid an emotional situation at some stage in the process that will not be advantageous to the negotiations.

You also need to ensure that everyone on your team is clear about the nature of any strategy, option, concession or alternative you are pursuing. To do so, be very detailed in the conversations so that everyone is on the same page as the negotiations proceed, especially when the price, the cost or the fee are not the central issues at stake. I have always invited my colleagues to ask questions and press me for clarity if they are not feeling confident about the direction we are going.

THE QUALITIES OF A GREAT NEGOTIATOR

"Ted Rogers was one of the best negotiators I have seen. He was a unique individual and the hardest working person I knew. At times, I would be driving home to North York at two in the morning and I would pass his house and the light would be on and he would be in there working. When he went on vacation, he often took six or seven briefcases with him because he was always working. He was always ahead of the game and he always knew what you were thinking and could answer a question on any topic at any time."

Watch the interview at tinyurl.com/negotiating-godfrey-qualities

Paul Godfrey, former CEO of the Sun Media Group and former President of the Toronto Blue Jays

Needless to say, the quantity of details involved in the negotiating process can be quite cumbersome. And as much as you will hear me beat the drum of time throughout this entire book, I know that a realistic feature is our lack of time. We all lead very busy lives that pull us between high pressure jobs, families and friends. We have events that we must attend, meetings that cannot be delayed and other files and issues to attend to. As a result, do what you can to use time effectively. One key technique is to circulate agendas in advance that highlight "outstanding details to be addressed." No matter how large your team is, efficient and focused discussions about all of the issues in play are critical. And when engaged in a team process, be sure to assess people's workload to divide up the work realistically and have it completed well within the time frame.

And remember that checklists are a simple but highly effective way to build up systems for careful consideration of the little details that matter. From logistics before meetings to various details about the opposition to discover, a checklist is a valuable way of making sure nothing is missing.

TAKEAWAYS

PLANNING

1. Allow sufficient time — foresight and anticipation are time-intensive activities.
2. Hold planning sessions — group meetings create clarity, new ideas and alignment.
3. Be exhaustive — discuss every issue, process and element that comes up.

EXPERTISE

4. Acquire experts — enlist team members with extensive knowledge of the sector.
5. Educate yourself — understand the industry in question as much as you can.

PREPARATION

6. Set goals — establish clear objectives your whole team understands and supports.
7. Do a SWOT — assess your position and potential exposures in advance.
8. Complete the team — ensure you have all of the necessary skills, capacities and experience.
9. Acquire resources — collect all relevant and compelling information.
10. Organize files — develop an efficient system for accessing materials as needed.
11. Determine time frame — solidify the total timeline for the negotiation.
12. Schedule the work — establish deadlines, milestones and workflow to guide your team.
13. Anticipate questions — make a detailed list of enquiries and responses for both sides.

14. Assess incentives — consider how compensation for negotiators might play a role.
15. Administrative details — attend to every logistical and procedural detail with care.

ALTERNATIVES

16. Assess alternatives — estimate your/their Best Alternative to a Negotiated Agreement (BATNA).
17. Know your reservation value — identify the lowest offer you are willing to accept.

PATIENCE

18. Be rested — take care of yourself so you can stay focused and attentive at all times.
19. Plan your time — ensure you budget ample time for each stage so you have options.
20. Invest in relationships — put in the time needed to nurture rapport on both sides.
21. Pay attention — listen closely to everything the other side is saying.
22. Be strategic — make decisions based on plans and goals not gut and instinct.

ATTENTION TO DETAIL

23. Nothing is too small — ensure every little detail is taken care of.
24. Be meticulous — ensure that every action, no matter how small, is exact.

CHAPTER 3
Game Changers

"A good hockey player plays where the puck is. A great hockey player plays where the puck is going to be."

— Wayne Gretzky

"Why don't you ride with us?" It was an invitation I'll never forget. I was standing with my daughter Leigh Anne on the tarmac of Canadian Forces Base Shearwater outside of Halifax in June 1995. It was the beginning of the G7 summit, which was being held in Atlantic Canada for the first time — a historic event that had been long anticipated by all involved. As a Member of Parliament from Nova Scotia and a minister in the Chrétien government, I had been heavily involved in bringing the summit to Halifax and had been assigned the task of greeting several key foreign dignitaries as they arrived. The visitors I was waiting for in that moment were of particular importance for Canada: United States President Bill Clinton and his wife, Hillary, two of the most prominent and powerful political figures of our time. It was up to me to initiate the personal interactions made possible by an event like this. As I waited for Air Force One to land, I was focused on making a positive first impression and reviewed various topics of conversation to set the tone for the

Clintons' visit. In politics, everything counts and you have to do the little things well.

The complicating factor in this particular case was their daughter. We had received word that fifteen-year-old Chelsea would be arriving with them. In accordance with proper protocol, I had arranged for my daughter to join me in meeting the plane. We were to speak with the Clintons briefly and then travel in separate vehicles to a boat that was to sail into Halifax Harbour. At least, that was the plan. Just prior to the Clintons' arrival, we learned that Chelsea was not able to make the trip. My daughter decided that she would still take the trip to CFB Shearwater, since we had made arrangements for her to miss school and travel with me.

The ground crew pulled the deplaning stairs up to the door on the side of Air Force One and Leigh Anne and I took the proper position at the base to greet our guests. The Clintons descended the stairs, we welcomed them warmly to Canada and Halifax, and I introduced my daughter. The President explained, in his famous Arkansas accent, that Chelsea was very sorry that she could not attend. He then "suggested" (a presidential suggestion, however polite, is essentially an order) that we ride with them in the presidential limousine that had been flown in the day before.

The Secret Service led us to the motorcade and the Clintons invited us into the car. While experiencing the thrill of being inside the presidential limousine, I was also mentally sorting what the conversation could be. I had not anticipated the four of us being alone together for the fifteen minutes it would take to get to the boat. But as we settled in, trying not to look too awestruck by the whole experience, I quickly realized that it wasn't going to have much to do with me. In fact, I didn't say a word the entire time.

The Clintons were focused on my daughter — and they were incredibly well briefed. They asked her questions about her role on Student Council, how she was doing with her saxophone (an instrument the President plays), the nature of the curriculum in the local schools and what kind of dance she preferred. She answered their questions thoughtfully and carefully, with an ease and poise that made me both proud and envious. I am hardly that relaxed at the best of times! And because the three of them were talking, I had an opportunity to observe these two political figures in action.

The President's probing skills were masterful. He spoke smoothly, made eye contact, was sincere in his questions and had a warm and welcoming tone. Hillary Clinton was precise and detailed in her questions with a different but equally inviting quality. They were able to elicit a great amount of information from my daughter in a short period of time while also making her feel like she was talking to a family friend. The Clintons' interest in and attention to what mattered in her life had a profound effect on her. It also had an effect on me, leaving me equally impressed and feeling a personal connection that shaped my view of them immediately and ever since. The Clintons were exceptional at establishing a strong bond in a very short time and created an event so significant in my daughter's life that I told the story at her wedding — over two decades later.

What I saw on display that day was pure personal and political power. The Clintons are the kind of people who shape every interaction into an act of influence that transforms political processes. Their capacity to build relationships, listen actively, ask probing questions, convey authenticity and express interest puts a spell on people. These skills drive their ability to raise funds, influence decisions and lead people. To me, they are examples of strategic negotiators who can alter the outcome of a process just by participating in it. And they represent a model that every negotiator should keep in mind as they develop their skills and hone their craft.

In my years of experience with negotiations — both in public and private enterprise — I have learned that there are certain elements of a negotiator's approach that change the game. The Clintons had just about all of them. These are qualities and emphases that have a significant impact on the outcome of negotiations and set certain negotiators apart from even the best of the good ones.

BEHAVIOUR AND ATTITUDE

"We judge ourselves by our intent, but we judge others by their behaviour."

— Stephen Covey

This is one of the most powerful — and most simple — ideas for a negotiator to hold in mind. Covey's idea is that people respond to what they see because they do not have access to what is happening inside. If you appear angry, condescending, impatient, loose with the facts or careless with the truth, you will be judged accordingly. The strategic negotiator is aware of how they are being perceived and is deliberate about their actions.

In my executive coaching and negotiation seminars, participants are often amazed when they watch themselves on video and witness the significant gap between their intentions and their behaviour. In a negotiation, once the introductions are over people often shift into a very different mode, behaving in an adversarial or abrasive manner that may or may not be deliberate. Most people don't think that managing or altering their behaviour is important. Or they argue that their approach is "just the way I am," illustrating a failure to recognize the powerful impact of behaviour. Ultimately, how we act — from eye contact to tone of voice to decisions about which information to share or not share — says more about our interest in making a deal and willingness to be reasonable along the way than anything we say.

You are always on display, and the actions you demonstrate (good or bad) are likely to invite the other side to reciprocate in kind. Did you mean to be so impolite? Was it your intention to appear uninterested in what the other party was saying? Why did you refuse to share the independent, third-party report with the other side? Everything you do sends a signal, and you are best served if those actions are deliberate and support your goals. For example, when attempting to foster relationships, tone of voice has a significant effect. If it comes across as harsh, discourteous and disruptive — whatever your intention — you are likely to offend the other party. And your body language is even more important. From social graces to an attentive posture to polite gestures, adopt a physical manner that is inviting and engaging.

ADAPTING TO CHINESE CULTURE

"The cultural challenges in China are really significant. Even for somebody who understands China like I do, you realize all the time that you will never be able to be 100 per cent immersed in the culture.

"One of the biggest differences is what they call the context of your communication. Canada is considered a low context culture. Much of what we mean is in what we say. It's very straightforward. You don't like me, you tell me you don't like me and you tell me why. In China, as in many Asian countries, it's high context communication. Most of the meaning is not in the words but is in the body language or in what is not said. To be able to operate in that environment, you need very good radar. Because if you don't have it, you just barrel your way through and you might be making mistakes that you don't understand."

Watch the interview at tinyurl.com/negotiating-kutulakos-culture

SARAH KUTULAKOS, *Executive Director of the Canada China Business Council*

Attitude is an equally crucial element that is entirely ours to shape. John Maxwell says it best: "We have only limited control over what we experience. However, we have complete control over our attitudes. Whether our outlook is up or down, expectant or reluctant, open or closed, is completely our choice."

To begin with, the strategic negotiator has a mindset that values people and sees negotiation as a shared process of achieving a mutually beneficial result. Taking a kill-or-be-killed attitude, or looking down on the other side, is neither co-operative nor productive. The best negotiators I have met are unfailingly positive, eager to work together and warm and welcoming. During a negotiation process, ask yourself what kind of attitude you want to portray. No matter how you feel, how busy you are, what personal stress you are experiencing or what your feelings are toward the other party, arriving with the right attitude can change the outcomes. Perhaps you are tentative about the upcoming negotiations or your BATNA is not very good or the other party is a subject-matter expert or you really need this deal to sustain your economic interests. I have been in those situations. Avoid negative thoughts or talk about defeat, and remind yourself of the need for a positive approach. I achieve this by carrying a five-by-seven-inch card with this inscription: be positive, smile, and use humour. You would be amazed at how effective this reminder has been over the years. Yes, if the other side is angry, condescending, difficult, or worse, acting like a bully, I always stop and firmly address the problem. But I quickly return to a positive and open approach that indicates my desire to achieve an agreement. Hostility is a dead end.

Behaviour and attitude are interrelated: they influence and shape each other. And while human resource gurus and psychologists might disagree with me, I feel that behaviour, rather than thinking, has the most important influence on attitude. In other words, behaviour influences attitude more than attitude influences behaviour, which can create a positive spiral. As Keith D. Harrell says, "Attitudes determine your feelings, your feelings determine your actions, and your actions determine your results."

AUTHENTICITY, INTEGRITY AND TRUST

Listen to Carol Hansell, a former Director of the Bank of Canada and a leading corporate governance expert, describe her approach to negotiating: "Courtesy and integrity are so important. Not just in how you speak to people, but in the manner that you treat them. If someone calls you, you phone them back. If someone asks you for an appointment and you aren't going to be able to take the meeting, tell them that. I can't function as a professional unless the person to whom I'm speaking believes everything I say. So if someone asks me if something happened and I say that it did, they know they can bank on it because I always proceed with honesty and integrity. And if I can't answer a question, I will tell them that I cannot answer and I will tell them why. I would never want to be a position where someone could say that they can't trust what I say — that would be the end of my ability to function as a professional."

Watch the interview with Carol Hansell at tinyurl.com/negotiating-hansell-trust

Authenticity and trust are crucial game changers for the strategic negotiator. You need to be who you are — but the best possible version of yourself. Do not adopt a false position in a negotiation. People can spot inauthenticity very quickly. This means being truthful and giving answers when you know them and not when you don't. Never be reluctant to say you aren't sure about something. There is no shame in having to go back and check a fact — it happens quite often. Be up front about what you know and don't know. And don't make promises you have no intention or authority to fulfill. Nobody respects that shady sales rep who offers a preferred discount in exchange for an agreement and then is unreachable after the deal is signed.

Former Premier of Ontario David Peterson says that trust is the "single most important commodity. If you lose that, everything is lost."

Watch the interview with David Peterson at tinyurl.com/negotiating-peterson-trust

I have found that the key to building trust is an authentic and integrity-driven approach, an idea at the heart of Stephen Covey's bestselling book *The Speed of Trust*. He writes, "trust is not some soft elusive quality that you either have or you don't; rather, trust is a pragmatic, tangible, actionable asset that you create much faster than you probably think possible." As already mentioned, Covey also emphasizes that our behaviour — not our intention — builds trust in relationships, and so we need to focus on the impression we leave. This is one more reason to monitor and track the messages your behaviour is sending, especially in relation to the proposals you are making. As Janice Payne, a highly decorated and recognized pioneer in labour law, says, "It's very important not to misrepresent or overstate things. It's very important that when you say something, it is correct and the party on the other side can have some comfort that it is correct. I deal with the same lawyers over and over again, and I learned very early that these are relationships that matter and they mustn't be spoiled."

Watch the interview with Janice Payne at tinyurl.com/negotiating-payne-trust

A person who makes outlandish propositions, offers and counteroffers will be viewed as either playing a game or untrustworthy. Individuals who make reasonable, thoughtful and comprehensive submissions during a negotiation are easy to deal with. This doesn't mean they give you everything you want. It means they are level-headed, willing to listen and be flexible, and building a foundation for a resolution.

Trust is also essential because in negotiations, as in life, we tend to come across the same people over and over again. Brian Burke explains how trust works in the NHL: "We all have a high stake in acting properly all the time, because it's a merry-go-round. The agent has a lot to lose by not being honest and ethical. I have a lot to lose. So I think most of the behaviours are in fact professional, educated and civil. I need to be trustworthy, prepared and as transparent as possible with players and agents. I try as much as possible to tell players everything that is said in a meeting if they are not in the room."

Watch the interview with Brian Burke at tinyurl.com/negotiating-burke-trust

In summer 2010, I had a personal experience in the hockey world that exposed me to an expert negotiator with a reputation for being direct and upfront and a capacity to be both honest and strategic. My long-standing interest in the business of sport led me to look into becoming the next Executive Director of the National Hockey League Players' Association — my second attempt to enter the business of sport. Early in the process, I had interactions with Donald Fehr, who had been hired by the NHLPA to help with the search for a new Executive Director. Fehr had worked for the Major League Baseball Players Association from 1977 to 2009 and was widely considered one of the world's leading experts in professional sport bargaining and legal issues. I emailed Fehr about the position and he responded quickly, indicating that I should send along my résumé. Soon after, Fehr called to invite me to meet with the search committee in Chicago and deliver a presentation outlining my ideas about the future of the union and the state of the collective bargaining between the players and the league. During that call, I asked Fehr a question that had been on my mind for some time. Rumours were circulating that Fehr himself was considering taking the job, so I asked if that was true. He didn't miss a beat: "I am considering it, but I haven't made up my mind."

Fehr opened the meeting in Chicago by telling the group what he had told me about his own candidacy — that he was undecided. I was then interviewed by Fehr and a panel of players, gave my presentation and headed back home. The next day, Fehr called to say that the players were not interested in pursuing my candidacy. Throughout that summer, rumours continued to swirl in the media that Fehr was going to take the job, but both Fehr and the NHL Players' Association leadership denied it. Then in December, news broke that Fehr had indeed taken the job.

I am not privy to the details of how Fehr became Executive Director of the NHLPA, and I did not ask him about it when

RELATIONSHIPS AND CREDIBILITY

"I can think of two examples, one from each side, that are about relationships and credibility.

"We always had a committee that dealt with provisions for substance abuse in the workplace. One time, we were settled on a collective agreement; we'd withdrawn the strike deadline; we had voted on it. And then one of our key guys on the substance abuse committee came to me — he's a reformed alcoholic — and he said, 'I thought we had something, but we don't have it and the company says they are not going to do it. And we have to have it.' I could have said to him 'it's over' — but I didn't.

"I went to the company representative and said, 'Look, this guy has been around the union and the company a lot of years and he somehow had the impression that he had something and the language doesn't support it — you gotta give it to him.' It was about having credibility. So when I looked that company guy in the eye and said I have to have it, he knew that I had to have it. It was something he could do on his own and he did it for me out of respect for the relationship."

Watch the interview at tinyurl.com/negotiating-hargrove-trust

"In our 2005 bargaining — things were good — they were selling a lot of half-ton trucks and SUVs at that time. During the process, the company negotiators in Canada had agreed to a certain amount of paid time off — and it was quite significant over and above the other things that we had — and we had already taken it to the bargaining committee when Rita came in to me and said that Gary Cowger was trying to reach me. He was the Vice President for labour relations for General Motors around the world. I knew him and respected him.

"When I took the call, he said, 'Buzz, I'm in trouble.' I said, 'What do you mean?' He said 'I can't do the work time. If you tell me I have to do it, I'll do it, but it's going to cost us dearly and it's going to cost you investment. Somehow our guys screwed this thing up and I can't do it.' Again, credibility. I knew Gary and I knew he wouldn't say that unless it was a real serious problem for him. So I called my key guys together and told them, 'We can't do this. This is about our relationship with GM. This is about the next investment in engines in St. Catharines or Oshawa.' And then I went to the bargaining committee and I laid it out to them. I said to them the relationship is too important. We are going to be around a long while. And I was able to call Gary back and say that we would give up those days. Those are important things for the relationship."

Watch the interview at tinyurl.com/negotiating-hargrove-trust-2

I interviewed him for the Ryerson Negotiation Project. But I know two things: first, he did not hide from me that he was considering the position and, second, he has been enormously successful in that role, partly because of his integrity. People know that if he tells you something, he means it and will follow through.

RELATIONSHIP BUILDING

Recently, I was involved in a divorce proceeding that was particularly contentious. I was representing the husband, with whom I happened to have a long-standing relationship, and the wife was represented by a lawyer I knew well. This is a common situation in the world of legal proceedings. In this case, these established relationships were a critical component of our ability to reach an agreement in a matter of days. For example, the opposing counsel and I were able to have several frank conversations about the situation — all without breaching the confidence of our clients — that moved the proceedings along by acknowledging the acrimony between the participants and working together to construct an agreeable deal to both sides. In a sense, we worked together to achieve our separate mandates to best represent the interests of our clients.

My relationship with my client was even more important. During meetings in my office, he offered extended tirades about his wife (in language not appropriate for public consumption) and lengthy advice about how to manage the proceedings with her. Eventually, in the middle of yet another onslaught when he was again was deaf to my responses, I put my hand up with the palm facing him. When he eventually stopped talking, I suggested that he and I change seats. He looked confused, so I invited him again to come to my side of the table. Once seated where he had been just a few moments before, I began a mock tirade of my own, opening with "since you are obviously the lawyer here . . ." and continuing on with my own colourful language. This seemed to be the only way to illustrate to him that he was being unreasonable, unresponsive to my guidance and offering bad legal advice to a seasoned professional. In other words, he was trying to teach multiplication to a calculus class. The ploy worked and he began to listen to me more as we proceeded, though not without bitterness and complaining.

The story is not meant to emphasize that theatrics are helpful in a negotiation — though they can be at times — but to point out the importance of relationships. I could never have gotten away with that with someone I didn't know, and he would never have listened to me if he did not trust that I wanted what was best for him. The relationships on all sides made progress possible and, in this particular case, were really the hinge of the deal. Positive relationships can set the great negotiator apart from the rest. Building a bond is generally accepted as critical in international diplomatic work but often overlooked in domestic issues, whether they are personal, commercial, corporate or legal.

THE QUALITIES OF A GREAT NEGOTIATOR

"Trust is an essential quality. Trust of your team. Trust of your adversary with whom you are seeking a resolution. They have to trust that you can deliver and they have to trust that you will hold confidences that are, by the very nature of the negotiations, brought to you by the other side."

Watch the interview at tinyurl.com/negotiating-harder-qualities

PETER HARDER, former Deputy Minister of Foreign Affairs and current Senior Policy Adviser at Dentons and President of the Canada China Business Council

As the saying goes, success is often about who you know, and while this mindset is regularly emphasized in business circles, it is rarely applied with consistency in negotiations. Time and again, I have seen negotiators fail to realize the impact of relationship-building on both sides of the table. Of course, a negotiator needs to be strategic about relationships and cultivate them with goals in mind. Tim Sanders emphasizes this in his book *Love Is the Killer App: How to Win Business and Influence Friends.* He notes that relationships in business are assets to be organized, managed, cultivated and leveraged. From the beginning of your career and through every negotiation process, be on the lookout for important connections and be conscious of nurturing them in formal and informal settings. And avoid the common trap of paying attention to the relationship only when the negotiations are in trouble. At that point, it is simply too late. Your effort to connect will be obviously inauthentic and may lead the other side to conclude that they can't deal with you.

Why are relationships so important? Here's how Leonard Asper, President and CEO of Anthem Sports & Entertainment, answers that question: "I think relationships are almost the most important thing you can have. Everybody is smart. Information is a commodity you can get — everyone has access to it. But I think the big delta — the X factor in success — is the quality and scope of your relationships. Deals get done based on people trusting each other, being comfortable with each other and just liking each other. You want to hang out with people that you like — especially when you are talking about a partnership."

Watch the interview with Leonard Asper at tinyurl.com/negotiating-asper-relationship

Shared experiences build relationships. Working together — whether across the table or on the same side — is one of the best ways to build a connection. That's why so many of us have deep bonds with our colleagues. But relationships also develop through time spent in other contexts. Who should you be taking to lunch this week? Is there a way to spend some time chatting with an opposition lawyer before a meeting? What kind of conversation takes place when the meeting breaks? Can you go for a drink with someone to discuss the case offline? How do you spend your personal time? Are you building long-term relationships that help? Think about these questions and proceed with a plan. And make sure that you are always genuine so that how you come across in a social setting confirms how you appear in meetings. A personality disconnect will put people off.

Cameo appearances get cameo results. If you don't put in the effort, you won't build a rapport. Little things like phone calls and emails help but aren't the whole story. Don't be an unannounced stranger: for example, neglecting to keep a regulator up-to-date with your issue and then contacting them only when difficulties arise. Keep in touch and build the relationship. Out of sight is out of mind. Find meaningful and genuine reasons to be in front of the other party. Attend social or industry events or just drop by to find out what is taking place on the other side. Buzz Hargrove invests time in people: "If you are going to be the leader of the bargaining committee, you have to make sure you understand the people you are working with. You have to find out what makes them tick and what drives them. You have to spend time getting to know people. You can't do it over the phone. You have dinner, you go for coffee, you spend time at the bar at the end of the night when the honest conversations happen. And you have to do the same with management. Spend time with them and get to know them so there is a relationship."

Watch the interview with Buzz Hargrove at tinyurl.com/negotiating-hargrove-rapport

On top of what you do offline, your approach to the actual bargaining process ought to consider relationships. One of the most respected experts on negotiations and conflict resolution is the late Roger Fisher, the Harvard Law Professor and director of the Harvard Negotiation Project who co-wrote the book *Getting Together: Building Relationships as We Negotiate* with his colleague Scott Brown. This influential work in the negotiation field informs many of the ideas that I outline in this book. Six messages in particular speak directly to the issue of relationship development:

1.   Try to be unconditionally constructive by always looking for ways to advance the process for both sides.

2.   Process and substance are distinct but related — an open and transparent approach can affect the outcome.

3.   Do not be afraid to discuss differences and avoid having an elephant in the room.

4.   Balance emotion with reason and take a break if things get too hot for real progress or healthy interactions.

5.   Be hard on issues and soft on people so that you can achieve outcomes while taking care of relationships.

6.   The devil we know is easier to handle than the devil we don't.

I want to close this section on relationships with a story about the United States residents who bookended Bill Clinton's time in office.

George Herbert Walker Bush, the forty-first President of the United States, was Vice-President for eight years prior to taking on the top job. Before that, he had been US Ambassador to the United Nations, US Ambassador to China and Director of the CIA. He had a long history of relationship-building and, more importantly, had simply been around forever and seemed to know everyone. In fact, during his presidency he was on a first-name basis with many of the key world leaders.

When Iraq invaded Kuwait on August 2, 1990, Bush Sr. began to form an international coalition and eventually obtained a resolution from the United Nations to invade Iraq and drive Saddam Hussein out of Kuwait. Prior to the United States–led bombings of Iraq, the President called many of the world leaders on several different occasions and asked some of them to help bring others into the coalition, such as when he contacted Canada's Prime Minister Brian Mulroney to ask his assistance in encouraging France's President François Mitterrand to support the UN resolution. Bush also sent his Secretary of State, the renowned James Baker, to visit well over forty countries to secure their support for the initiative.

Bush Sr. was a skilled and experienced diplomat, and his effort to build the coalition meant that when the bombs finally fell on Iraq, it was a unified international force for peace. I know from experience that passing resolutions in the United Nations is an extremely difficult process, one that Bush Sr. mastered. The Gulf War was a relatively short and unanimously successful military campaign that left the world with a positive impression of the United States and sustained its reputation as a superpower.

By contrast, when George Walker Bush became the forty-third President in 2003, he seemed to think that, because the United States was the world's only superpower, certain things would flow automatically. This mindset was evident as Bush Jr. led the United States into what would eventually be the "shock and awe" attacks on Iraq and the ensuing war, which the United States entered into with the support of only a few Western nations, most notably the United Kingdom. Bush Jr. publicly declared that this was just fine with the United States.

When Bush Jr. was attempting to rally world support, he invited Canadian Prime Minister Jean Chrétien to the Oval Office. I was not present for the meeting and don't know what transpired, but I know that the day after Chrétien arrived back in Ottawa, he did something many of us thought would never happen: he publicly announced that Canada would not be supporting the United States if it took armed action against Iraq. Like Bush Sr., Chrétien was a seasoned politician in regular contact with world leaders. Canada's lack of support for the United States intention was a strong signal to the world.

From what I know of the process, Bush Jr. made very few personal calls to world leaders and was, at times, derisive toward other nations that did not support his efforts, including some snide remarks toward the French that soured relations with that nation. (The United States also pursued a nation-wide attempt to rename french fries as freedom fries.) Rather than speaking personally with foreign leaders, Bush Jr. often chose to convey his message through the media or by delegating communication to members of his administration or to British Prime Minister Tony Blair. In addition, Secretary of State Colin Powell hardly travelled in the months prior to the Iraq War. Powell would later claim that modern technology such as email rendered personal diplomacy less important and that he saw his European counterparts frequently at the United Nations meetings in New

York. Overall, the approach by the second Bush administration fostered and reinforced the impression that the United States had little interest in or respect for the views of others and that matters of war and peace were for Washington alone to decide. It was an approach that led to the invasion of Iraq, record debt levels in the United States, a prolonged war that was not supported by the majority of the leaders in the Western world and significant damage to the reputation of the United States in foreign capitals.

TIME, ENERGY AND MONEY

Years ago, I was hired by a firm that provided services to the Government of Canada. The firm of over one thousand employees felt that it had an exclusive deal with the government to provide the service. After a smooth initial period in the working relationship, the government started to hire other suppliers to provide a similar service, which was contrary to the exclusivity provision. The issue percolated for months and months until my client, before engaging my services, issued a multi-million-dollar action in the Supreme Court of Ontario. Soon after I came on the file, I advised my client to drop the lawsuit and focus on negotiation, mediation or arbitration. My argument was that the deep pockets on the other side would drag out the proceedings and make the entire process not worthwhile in terms of time, energy and dollars. I felt that if my client pursued mediation, a deal could be reached. But they were bent on suing, so we proceeded with the suit.

As I had worried, the government used its financial resources and muscle to prolong the case. It challenged us at every opportunity, on every issue and sought motions to defeat and strike our claim before the Ontario courts. When the suit had dragged on for close to five years, my client decided to pursue arbitration. The Government of Canada quickly suggested the use of a mediator and the case was resolved in four hours — an amazing result compared to the extended court battle. In the end, my client received tens of millions of dollars in compensation, the contract was terminated and the two organizations have not worked together since. To this day, the senior administrators of the company say they wish they had listened to my advice. Their failure is a common one — not of ego or ignorance, but of a miscalculation about the time, energy and resources that pursuing a particular course of action will involve. Smart negotiators are aware of the implications of their decisions.

It is a red flag if you find yourself in the midst of a negotiation saying, "I have too much time invested into this matter, therefore I can't turn away." Always be willing to walk away. Have a clear and accurate grasp of the implications of every available course of action. The goal of any negotiation is to get a deal that makes sense for you, not to get a deal done at all costs. Continually assess your options as objectively as possible at every stage in the process. And if a deal begins to go sour, arrange for an extended caucus with your team to discuss progress made, challenges that remain and next steps. Check in with your mandate to see if you are on track. Walk away if you conclude that you can no longer achieve your goals, no matter how much time has been invested in the process. Sure, it is important to talk, talk, talk in a negotiation, but if it is not heading toward an outcome that serves your needs, don't continue.

Monitor your attitude toward time and energy closely, as well as that of your team. Everyone should be eager to participate, clear about the role they play in the process, and patiently willing to do whatever is needed to achieve a deal beneficial to both sides. As you assess the relationship between the current state of a negotiation and your mandate, be frank about the time and energy being spent. Don't allow team members to hide their frustrations and deny that time is of the essence. And never undersell or undervalue your time and energy or convey to the other party that you have a limited amount of either. If you do, it is easy for them to slow down the process and force your hand.

PUTTING IN THE TIME TO BUILD RELATIONSHIPS

"You might have some meetings across a boardroom table, but that is not the end of the process. That will not get you where you need to go in the transaction. This is a difference between a relational culture like China and a relatively transactional culture like North America.

"If you have something to do with an American company, you go in, you negotiate, you shake hands and you are done. In China, there will always be a dinner after the meeting and multiple stages to a negotiation that will not all happen at the table. Many of those things will happen at or after the trust has been established through the building of a personal relationship. I know a lot of Canadians that have said 'Geez, all these dinners' or 'It takes an awful lot of time.' It does. But if you don't do it, then you cannot build up the necessary trust."

Watch the interview at
tinyurl.com/negotiating-
kutulakos-relation

SARAH KUTULAKOS, Executive Director of the Canada China Business Council

Beyond time and energy, it is important to assess and measure financial costs in two particular ways: the actual negotiations and the outcomes that are being proposed. I believe it is critical to have a budget for the negotiation process and to stick to it. People who vaguely assert that negotiation processes are just the cost of doing business miss an opportunity to creatively and effectively ensure positive outcomes. Having a clear budget will guarantee support from the principals and your superiors and will shape your thinking about the length and nature of the talks, the number of people on the team, the need for outside consultants or experts, travel, and administrative expenses. These are all considerations that a budget will force you to address. Make them part and parcel of your approach. But even more important are the financial implications of the deal you are working toward. You need to be careful, detailed and resourceful in assessing value at every stage. For example, if negotiating a technology procurement, know everything about the costs of the acquisition and potential revenue generation. If you are the buyer, know where the equipment is being made, the labour costs, the transportation costs, supply costs, assembly costs and marketing costs. In addition, understand how you are likely to sell the newly acquired product and, if you are a reseller, how you are going to cover the incurred costs. This is where assessing margins is critical: what is the industry norm, what is the norm for the company and what is the spread that you believe you are working with? The market has ample information on costs, margins and profitability. Take advantage of it to assess the impact of the purchase and establish the parameters of the deal you are willing to accept. And make sure that you run the same analysis on the impact that this purchase will have on your own company.

Assessing financial implications is time consuming and complicated. But this is one of the key areas that can transform your ability to get the right deal to meet your needs. The more you know about various options, the better. Work well ahead of time and surround yourself with financial people who can fully model the projections. Leaving these calculations to the last minute simply means you will not have the answers needed to make good decisions. And if you find that your superior is resistant to spending time delving into budget analysis, that's a red flag as well. Never proceed into a negotiation with vague information or vague goalposts. Have a budgetary strategy.

Part of that strategy should include time spent assessing the cost and/or investment that you and your team have put into the negotiation, as well as the difficulty involved in entering into a new negotiation. For example, keeping a diary of total hours spent in meetings, preparations, discussions, strategizing, caucusing and so on is helpful in assessing the current situation as well as subsequent situations.

ACTIVE LISTENING

"Courage is what it takes to stand up and speak; courage is also what it takes to sit down and listen."

— Winston Churchill

One night in 1982, early in my political career, I drove into the Nova Scotia countryside with Dr. Carl Buchanan, who would become President of the 1987 Canada Winter Games, and a friend of mine named Ray Paruch, who is now a Municipal Councillor in Cape Breton. Our destination was scenic Lake Ainslie on the west side of Cape Breton Island to visit Allan MacEachen, Deputy Prime Minister of Canada under Pierre Trudeau. One of Canada's elder statesmen, MacEachen had been a cabinet member under three Prime Ministers and would become Leader of the Opposition in the Senate in 1984. As such a dominant force in Canadian politics, our intention was to speak with MacEachen about my electoral district applying for and hosting the 1987 Canada Winter Games. The cottage was quiet and remote, the perfect location for an extended discussion about the merits and implications of hosting an event like the Games in Cape Breton.

Five hours passed before the three of us poured back into the car and headed for home. During the long conversation, we offered substantive explanations about the need for the Games, the benefits of hosting them and the immediate and long-term impact on the local economy, especially the tourism industry.

We went through every element of the proposal with MacEachen and did all we could to influence this senior official and seasoned politician of the merits of our proposal. In the end, we were successful in securing the Games for the county and the province, because of that evening as well as other significant efforts by a host of people involved. But I will always remember that moment not for the role it played in securing the event, but for MacEachen's listening skills.

He was completely focused throughout the conversation, looking directly at whomever was speaking. He occasionally interrupted but only with clarifying questions about each detail so as to connect all the pieces together. And he pressed us on our logic: What is the proposed capital cost? What are the proposed operating costs? Does the municipality have the economic wherewithal to be the sponsoring community to host these games? What political support do you have from the Premier of Nova Scotia? We answered his questions as best as we could — some better than others — and when the topic was exhausted, he thanked us for coming and said he needed time to reflect on the issue. We drove away feeling heard, energized by the possibility that we might succeed and valued by one of the country's leading politicians. Active listening is a masterful skill for demonstrating attentiveness, extracting intelligence and showing appreciation for everyone involved. MacEachen illustrated all of these positive effects, and we felt good about his genuine interest in our position.

People love to talk and they love it even more if someone is sincerely listening to what they have to say. Use active listening skills to promote this dynamic. Combine your undivided attention with specific probing questions, and reflect back to the speaker what message you are hearing to get confirmation that you have understood correctly before moving on. Include body language cues, such as sustained eye contact, an upright posture, sitting on the edge of your seat, an open expression and nodding your head. The speaker will feel valued and heard and you will acquire relevant information. This kind of listening cannot be faked. You either do it or you don't, and if you don't, it will limit your ability to build trust. Anne Golden, former Head of the United Way and CEO of the Conference Board of Canada, puts it this way: "Above all, people have to be respected. I learned early on that if I was talking to someone while I was doing something else — like today when people are talking to you while they are on their BlackBerry — they don't feel respected. Even if you can multitask, it doesn't convey that you are listening. You have to engage with people in a way that lets them know they have your undivided attention."

Watch the interview with Anne Golden at tinyurl.com/negotiating-golden-listening

Golden's comments point to another key element of active listening: stop talking and avoid interrupting unless asking a clarifying question. This approach requires patience and an ability to avoid distractions. The greatest listening sin of our times? Attending to your smartphone during a conversation. That might be fine in the informal interactions of your workplace, but it is a damaging approach at the negotiation table. Serious conversations require more of you. Allow people the time and space to speak fully. As Leonard Asper says, "I have learned to really make sure that I don't interrupt people and listen very carefully. And I often check in with people to see if they have had a chance to say everything they wanted to say. I find it creates very positive energy in the room if people feel listened to. And it creates difficulties if people don't feel listened to. You can see them boiling up from the frustration. I also make a point of following up with people after a meeting — via email or live — if I have the sense that they had something else to say."

Watch the interview with Leonard Asper at tinyurl.com/negotiating-asper-listening

One way to become a top-notch active listener is to develop into a great note-taker. The simple protocol of asking if you can take a few notes sets an encouraging tone and conveys thoughtfulness. Because you are recording key details, your prompts for elaboration, repetition or an example are legitimate and indicate your engagement. Note-taking is a formidable method for building rapport, especially since a person who is writing is less likely to be talking, distracted by gadgets or interrupting. Not all negotiators have to be liked, but if you can get the other side into the mood of sharing information and believing that they are being heard, you have a much better chance of advancing towards an agreement. And keep in mind that if you opt to give your undivided attention directly to the speaker, you can always have someone else on the team taking notes.

If you are engaged in international negotiations, be aware of the various interpretations of active listening body language in others cultures. For instance, in North America, nodding your head conveys agreement. In Japan, however, nodding your head means that the message has been received but not necessarily agreed to. And in Bulgaria, nodding means disagreement. Developing cultural awareness helps with every strategic advantage of the negotiator, and especially with the game changers outlined in this chapter.

PROBING

One of the greatest questioners is a character none of us have met: the great Los Angeles detective, Lieutenant Columbo. Portrayed by Peter Falk, Columbo came across as dishevelled, disorganized and odd. He asked a series of conversational, open-ended questions to put people at ease and get them talking. Then, from the nuggets he collected, he began to track down the truth about the case, with each episode moving toward his famous and deceptively offhand line: "There's just one more thing." His skill was a potent combination of allowing his adversaries to feel good about themselves and then asking exceptional questions that got to the truth of the matter.

Probing for information is an essential skill that a strategic negotiator should hone and use widely. Active and effective probing is a game changer because you are guaranteed to acquire more information than otherwise, which makes you more capable of fulfilling your mandate and getting the deal you desire. From day-to-day activities to intense interactions at the bargaining table, ask questions to collect information that might be critical later in the process. Like Columbo, a good questioner can control a process through simply inviting the other side to give fuller details and explanations. And of course, asking questions is always preferable to arguing with the other side over differences of interpretation.

In general, negotiators are wise to use interrogative questions that begin with who, what, when, where, why and how. In particular, the more open-ended questions — why and how — collect broad information about processes and uncover what the opposition thinks about them. Open-ended questions are the heart of a negotiator's probing techniques to expand your understanding of the various issues on the table. By asking open questions, you learn what the respondent thinks is important. You may access a perspective you've not considered about facts and positions you know quite well. Of course, when a situation requires a narrower focus and closed answers, the skilled negotiator can opt for the simpler who, what, when and where questions or even shift to a cross-examination style by asking questions that can only be answered with yes or no.

In the early 1990s, I was the Opposition House Leader for the Liberal Party of Canada, and we were faced with a formidable opponent in the House — Prime Minister Brian Mulroney. He was a great debater, had a superb capacity for recalling facts and was always extremely well-briefed by his impressive staff. As a result, we quickly learned that if we approached Question Period with open-ended, multi-part questions, we were doomed. It was no effort for Mulroney to avoid answering that kind of a question and to use the time to promote whatever was on his own agenda for the day. In response, we made a change in protocol for the party. Any member of the Liberal opposition who wanted to ask a question in the House was to report to Room 601 of the Parliament buildings in advance of the sessions. There, with all of us sitting together, I led every MP through the process of refining their questions so that they would yield the kind of responses we were looking for. Ask a general question and Mulroney would speechify eloquently. Ask a pointed question with the purpose of eliciting specific information and the "ums" and "ahs" came out!

Another tool in the probing arsenal of a skilled negotiator is the reverse question. This is when you answer a question with another question in an effort to hear what the other side is thinking. For example, you might say, "I'm not certain — what do you think the situation should be?" I find this technique yields a great amount of information. My colleague Dr. Maurice Mazerolle, Director of the Centre for Labour Management Relations at the Ted Rogers School of Management at Ryerson University, calls answering a question with a question "returning the porcupine."

As with all other aspects of negotiations, it is best to adopt the right tone and attitude when probing for information. If sarcastic and flippant, you will most likely get a similar response. The same is true if you are positive, thoughtful and genuine. For the most part, the best attitude is a curious approach to life. Develop a curious mind and interact with people on the premise that you are trying to understand their world. A genuine interest in your counterpart will go a long way toward building rapport and creating trust — and eliciting a lot of information. You may be surprised by how often people will disclose volumes of information if you ask good questions in a curious and interested manner. And it doesn't hurt that showing a genuine interest makes you more likeable. People are more open, even in a negotiation, with others they like and enjoy being with. Social occasions are a superb setting for effective questioning techniques — especially open-ended questions — to collect information from the other party. This may happen during a break in the negotiations, over a coffee, or at lunch or dinner. Showing interest by asking questions clarifies the information you already have and builds the relationship.

As with every other negotiation strategy, always practise and prepare: practise good probing techniques and prepare questions well in advance. Start by making a list of the information you need and imagine the answers the other side would give. Then, flip the exercise around and map out your responses to similar questions that might be asked of you. As you prepare mentally or through making notes, keep in mind that good questions are short questions. If you are long-winded and offer multiple elements, it is likely that the other side — just like Brian Mulroney — will use the opportunity to talk and not address the crux. Like all of life's important skills, practise probing with effective questions until it is second nature for you.

Brian Tracy, an entrepreneur who produced an audio program called *The Psychology of Selling*, stresses the importance of good quality questions. Let me share with you some of his findings:

1. Situational Questions:
You need to collect information about the other party at various stages in the process, especially the early interactions, that will help you to confirm your research and assumptions. This might involve questions about a current situation, holidays they have taken or the role they play in their organization. With this kind of questioning, it is critical that you are friendly and warm and prolong the dialogue — otherwise people will read through your questions and be concerned about your motivation.

2. Problem Questions:
It is essential to try to collect information about both the implicit and explicit needs of the other party. I tend to spend most of my time focused on understanding the explicit needs of the other side because I can typically arrive at an understanding of their implicit needs as well through this focus. It is important that you verify your assumptions about the other party's needs, so don't be in a hurry to move away from this type of dialogue.

3. Impact Questions:
Once you have a sense of the needs of the other party, you can move on to having them describe the impact of that need. This will give you valuable information about their rationale for various proposals. It will also allow you to collect information and begin to assess the negative effects that will occur if they are not able to fulfill those needs in whole or part.

4. Solution Questions:

With a shared understanding of the other side's needs and the impact of those needs in place, probe for an understanding of what they believe to be the best solution. This may initially lead to superficial or quick answers, but you need to probe to understand, in detail, how they foresee addressing their needs. Ensure that they outline for you why their solutions are appropriate, fair and necessary; pay close attention to their body language and what is not being said; and be sure to take detailed notes while pressing them to elaborate. In general, I find that people exaggerate the solutions they perceive, especially early in the deliberations, so you should keep that in mind when listening to the solutions that are being proposed.

5. Reaffirmation Questions:

A seasoned negotiator applies the very best active listening skills possible, which often involves questions that clarify what the other side is expressing in terms of needs, impact and solutions. In essence, these questions play back for the other side what they have said while probing for additional or related information that will expand on your understanding of the topic. Throughout, focus on providing them with ample opportunity to explain their thinking so that you can fully understand their needs.

TAKEAWAYS

BEHAVIOUR AND ATTITUDE

1. Focus on what can be seen — we are judged by our behaviour, not our intent.
2. Be deliberate — make thoughtful choices and practise inviting behaviours.
3. Expect to be mirrored — positive and negative actions tend to be reflected back at you.
4. Start with attitude — attitude leads to feeling, then to action, then to results.
5. Be constructive — be positive, smile and use humour.

AUTHENTICITY, INTEGRITY AND TRUST

6. Be real — people can sense when you're inauthentic and will distance themselves from you.
7. Actively build trust — trust is an asset to be carefully developed.
8. Develop credibility — acting with integrity means that your words and actions will be believed.
9. Be honest — if you don't know something, say so and then go find out and report back.

RELATIONSHIP BUILDING

10. Never underestimate connections — cultivate and leverage good relationships.
11. Set yourself apart — everyone has information; not everyone has positive relationships.
12. Invest time — get to know people both during the work and in social settings.
13. Get personal — email and phone calls are not enough; live conversations build rapport.

TIME, ENERGY AND MONEY

14. Assess in advance — plan for the amount of time required for the negotiation.
15. Monitor your attitude — you and your team need to be patient and stay energized.
16. Allocate resources — have a budget for the negotiation process itself.
17. Understand outcomes — assessing financial implications is time consuming and necessary.

ACTIVE LISTENING

18. Use your body — make eye contact, sit upright, lean toward the speaker and nod your head.
19. Stop talking — keep your ideas and your thoughts to yourself.
20. Interrupt as needed — if you are going to talk, ask only clarifying questions.
21. Avoid distractions — you can't fake focus and attention; put your devices away.
22. Take notes — writing things down conveys genuine interest in the content.
23. Validate the speaker — make sure they feel heard, valued and respected.

PROBING

24. Be like Columbo — ask open questions and attend carefully to the responses.
25. Control the process — the more you probe, the more you know about the other side.
26. Narrow when necessary — use cross-examination-style questions for yes or no answers.
27. Keep it short — long-winded questions elicit rambling, off-topic answers.

28. Reverse the flow — answer a question with another question if you need more information.
29. Choose questions wisely — apply the Art of the Questioner to get the information you need.

CHAPTER 4
Demons for Negotiators

"When you are offended at any man's fault, turn to yourself and study your own failings. Then you will forget your anger."

— Epictetus, Greek Philosopher

In the late 1990s, I worked as an adviser to several established corporations, one of which was Sun Microsystems Canada Inc., a division of the multinational parent company of the same name. Sun provided computer software, hardware and services that included developing workstations for the UNIX operation system and creating the well-known programming language Java. Sun was a major player in the industry and in 2010 was purchased by Oracle Corporation for $7.4 billion. My contact at Sun was Regional Director Jacques Chartrand, a former executive from Canadian Airlines and a consummate professional: careful, positive, accurate and exceptional with people. He worked tirelessly to achieve success and was consistently focused on meeting the needs of his customers and establishing first-class relationships.

I came to work with Chartrand and his executive team at Sun because they were interested in becoming a major provider of products and services to various Canadian municipal, provincial and federal government agencies. On my suggestion, Chartrand arranged for his team to meet with the government representatives by hosting a half-day working session. The goal was for the Sun executives to develop a better appreciation of government needs and concerns, showcase their products and solutions, answer questions and, most of all, for us to get to know each other and begin to build relationships that could benefit both sides on a long-term basis.

The session went extremely well because Chartrand and his team prepared carefully and executed effectively. They were thorough and thoughtful, and it was evident that the various government officials were impressed. They also allowed ample time for discussion about durability concerns and impact on existing operations and costs. Our feeling at Sun was that the session was a great success and that both sides benefitted from the exchange of information and professional dialogue. But in several post-session interviews with government representatives in attendance that day, we discovered that an event had occurred after lunch that had had a significant negative impact.

Chartrand had arranged for a special speaker at lunch, an American tech expert who added energy to the sessions by exposing the group to some cutting-edge insights about the industry. The presentation was engaging, but the speaker went off script at one point and spent some time making extremely negative comments about one of Sun's major competitors — Microsoft. Negative selling is a fairly common technique in the United States, and if the audience had been filled with American government officials, the comments may have been better accepted. We Canadians are sometimes perceived to have politeness in our DNA, with "sorry!" being one of our favourite words (especially when other people bump into us). Whether the cultural stereotype is true or not, in this audience of Canadian government officials — many of whom had spent millions of dollars purchasing products and services from Microsoft — the negative comments did not go over well and took some of the momentum out of the session. The remarks may have felt appropriate to the guest speaker, but the message the audience received was that they were idiots for having bought from Microsoft.

Needless to say, Chartrand and his team were not keen to imply either that these potential customers had been fools or that Microsoft was a bastion of charlatans. In time, after many more efforts to build relationships with a renewed emphasis on the benefits of Sun's products rather than the negatives of the competition's, Chartrand and his team were able to regain the momentum and move forward with several departments and divisions of the different levels of government. But they would have been far better off if the sessions had occurred without the negative selling. This was an important learning experience for Chartrand, his team and me about the downside of bad-mouthing your competition. It also illustrated the importance of knowing your audience and making strategic decisions to support your goals rather than assuming you know what works.

Evolving into a skilled and effective negotiator requires a strong understanding of the fundamentals and of game-changing techniques, but it also requires knowledge of the major pitfalls that can derail your success, such as running on assumptions as the American presenter did. In my experience, the majority of difficulties that occur in a bargaining process arise out of errors made by the negotiators themselves. This is why I call the errors Demons.

EGO-CREEP

In 1980, I was a twenty-seven-year-old first-time MP from Cape Breton. My party, the Liberals, had a majority government led by legendary Prime Minister Pierre Elliot Trudeau, who would serve until 1984 when he retired from politics. Like any ambitious, young and determined professional, I was bent on being competent, successful and respected. Also, like young people can sometimes be, I had yet to learn all of the nuances and graces required to be those things. I lacked the kind of lessons you can only get from experience. But I was about to get a hard one during a meeting in 1981 about the coal mining industry in the Cape Breton.

Since the nineteenth century, coal mining had been a major force in what became known as Industrial Cape Breton, but it was in decline by the late 1970s and the government was often involved in negotiations with the United Mine Workers of America. In particular, there were frequent meetings with one of the most legendary figures in the history of Cape Breton: William "Bull" Marsh. Bull Marsh was born in 1922 and had been a coal miner since the day his father came home and handed a pair of pit boots and a helmet to his sixteen-year-old son. At the time, coal was still shovelled by hand into buckets deep inside the seams. In 1958, Marsh became the youngest ever President of District 26 of the United Mine Workers of America, a post that he held for an unprecedented twenty-two years. His tenure led many to conclude that the mining industry had been extended thirty years longer than would have been possible without his efforts. With the industry in Cape Breton in decline for some time because most of the remaining coal was out under the sea and not cost effective to extract, the federal government had been operating DEVCO — the Cape Breton Development Corporation — since the late 1960s. DEVCO was mandated to slow the pace of the industry's decline and delay the substantial effect of the layoffs on the local economy. In 1965, there were 6,500 miners working in Cape Breton whose livelihoods were in part a credit to Marsh's influence on the government.

So when I arrived to a meeting about funding for the coal mining industry to create jobs in 1981, I was well aware of Marsh and his reputation. Marsh and his team were presenting on why the government should increase funding for the mining in the area.

I was focused and determined to make an impression, so I asked a lot of questions and demonstrated my knowledge of the facts whenever possible. The meeting proceeded fairly well and when it was over, I felt I had done a decent job. As it was wrapping up, Marsh approached me and asked to have a word. I was keen to extend the conversation and build the relationship, so I was pleased he had more to share. He leaned close, looked in my eyes and said in a low, slow voice, "When you speak, I fucking listen. So next time, when I talk, you better fucking listen." And then he walked away. It was like getting blasted by a sandstorm. He left me standing there in shock with a memory I still carry into every meeting. I am indebted to Bull Marsh for reining in an emerging ego that had been a barrier to our proceedings and relationship.

NOT TAKING CREDIT FOR A CONSENSUS

"Never give the odour of knowing it all. They call it diplomacy for a reason, and if you want to have influence, you do it quietly because you want people to come back to you. If you take ownership for the consensus that you were a part of achieving, you will lose the credibility of both parties you have brought together for the next time. And conversely, you will enhance it if it has worked and you have allowed them to take credit for it."

Watch the interview at tinyurl.com/negotiating-harder-credit

PETER HARDER, former Deputy Minister of Foreign Affairs and current Senior Policy Adviser at Dentons and President of the Canada China Business Council

If you enter negotiations and find that the other party looks strong, speaks well, has a great grasp of the issues, is likeable and behaves passionately, you may find yourself a little intimidated. Different people handle those situations differently, especially if they are genuinely in awe of the other person, but it is normal for the emotion to affect how you proceed. The trouble is that it can lead to overcompensating for what you may feel are your shortcomings by trying hard to impress: speaking more often or more loudly, sharpening your tone or sending out signals that you are the better player. With Marsh, I was guilty of talking and interrupting too much, even though I thought I was being productive. And it can happen the other way around as well. If you come across a negotiator who seems to lack experience, has trouble communicating effectively or appears dishevelled and disorganized, there is a risk you will conclude that your superiority will carry you through. In both these situations and indeed many more, what happens is what I call ego-creep. It's a rather natural behaviour, but one that a skilled negotiator will crush immediately on appearance.

So how does a strategic negotiator avoid ego-creep? First, they recognize it for what it is — behaviour that is driven by a twinge in the ego or a sense of insecurity that leads to overcompensation or altering the planned approach. Second, the negotiator focuses on the mandate and the goals contained within it and makes strategic decisions about how to act rather than reacting based on a sense of insufficiency. Third, their focus is not on being the best known negotiator in the history of humankind but on achieving the best possible agreement in this particular situation. If you find yourself feeling the need to beat the other negotiator, it is a sure-fire sign of ego-creep, which in my view does not arise out of competence and a genuine sense of command but rather out of insecurity and self-doubt. Confidence in your preparation and skillset may be appropriate and well earned, but that is not the same as ego. Step back and return to deliberate and strategic actions. A successful agreement is often the side effect of the negotiators' actions, but it ought not be driven by a desire to win and prove something. It has to be about what makes the most sense.

Egos are also an issue for the principals in negotiations, not just the negotiators acting on their behalf. One of the best examples comes from major league sports where owners can meddle in the day-to-day operation of their teams to serve their own interests and get their name in the papers. Sometimes, a big ego can lead to success, but it can just as likely lead a team to run a deficit and decrease the owner's net worth. And, as Carol Hansell explains, this kind of ego-creep can negatively affect normal business negotiations for the same reasons: "I have been in situations where my client is really just looking for the best solution being met by somebody who has got ambitions to be seen in a particular way in a public light by creating a name for themselves. That kind of self-aggrandizement leads to the other side demanding things that don't really belong in the deal, which can lead to confusion and can drag out the negotiation in an unproductive way."

Watch the interview with Carol Hansell at tinyurl.com/negotiating-hansell-ego

In essence, everyone at the table — from principals to agents — has to put the needs of the deal ahead of their own personal interest in making an impression. The most successful negotiators I have seen always set aside their own egos to carefully and strategically pursue their goals, while also looking for ways to get the other side what they are seeking. The focus always needs to be on the mandate, not personal gain.

BIAS

In his book *The Psychology of Judgment and Decision Making*, Scott Plous explains a concept that he calls confirmation bias, which "is the tendency to search for, interpret or prioritize information in a way that confirms one's belief or hypothesis." Almost anyone can fall into this form of bias, and it is particularly risky for a negotiator because adopting a skewed perspective on the facts of a case to confirm your own view can lead to missing critical elements in the process. Thinking strategically requires assessing your own thinking to see if you are missing anything or looking to have your own biases confirmed.

Anchoring bias is another pitfall for any negotiator. This is a tendency to reach conclusions early on based on the first wave of information and process. Sometimes called a first impression bias, this rush to judgement might happen if you're in a hurry and feel pressured to reach an outcome. An anchoring bias may also emerge when you have little relevant experience or knowledge or when you are personally invested in the situation. Any conclusion based on early impressions or personal interests can lead you and your team far astray. I once hired a young man into a position of responsibility on the recommendation of an acquaintance who had worked with him in a community setting. The young man had been through an interview process, but it was the glowing recommendation that secured him the job. The reference described the young man as dedicated, prompt, detail-oriented and a superb communicator. Within three weeks, it was clear that those were not actually his traits. He was seldom on time for work, had a confrontational tone and rarely returned phone calls. In this case, the reference's anchoring bias was based on a positive personal relationship and little knowledge of the new context the young man would shift into. His skewed view led me into a hiring I had to permanently undo within three months.

THE QUALITIES OF A GREAT NEGOTIATOR

"Keep your humanity and keep your values. People of values are respected more than people with no values. People get a sense of what would you die for . . . the things you really care about. You don't have to wear them on your sleeve and you don't have to trumpet them all the time, but people of values and depth are taken much more seriously than people who aren't. Keep your humanity — always think of it from the other person's point of view and try to be sensitive to their needs and try to be as kind and humane as you can be. At the end of the day, this is an art not a science. It's about finding things that we have in common with people who are far more similar than different than us."

Watch the interview at tinyurl.com/negotiating-peterson-qualities

DAVID PETERSON, former Premier of Ontario, former Chancellor of the University of Toronto and founding Chairman of the Toronto Raptors

It probably goes without saying that having a bias in favour of yourself can interfere with a successful process. Sometimes called overconfidence bias or the overconfidence effect, this is basically a prejudice in your own favour based on an overestimation of your clout or skill. This is a difficult one, because if you generally believe that you are better than you are, you are the least likely person to see it. This is the kind of bias on display when a person habitually overestimates how they did on a test ("I nailed it!") and then blames a lower than expected result on the teacher, an unfair assignment, a fellow student who led them astray in the studying or any other external factor. Essentially, an overconfidence bias does not take into account real, objective data about performance. Instead, a person overestimates their performance and believes their contributions are more valuable than they are. Needless to say, this bias seriously interferes with a strategic approach to negotiations. If at the end of each day, you reach inaccurate conclusions about the power you hold and the effectiveness of your approach, you will lose touch with the reality of the negotiation in a hurry. The best antidote to this bias is to appoint a person of trusted experience and perspective to your team to provide daily feedback about your performance. And then you really need to accept their comments and advice. You are not asking something as basic as "how'd I do?" but rather checking your conclusions about the specifics of the meeting against your teammate's. Debriefs like this are an important part of any negotiation process. The trick here is that an overconfident negotiator doesn't check in enough with others and can trivialize contrary conclusions. The only way out of town with this bias is to actively recalibrate your perspective with objective feedback and data, which means admitting and addressing areas of weakness.

Of these three biases, negotiators are most often guilty of a confirmation bias. Once having established a position or perspective, they then only seek information which will buttress that position. Since this risky approach is fairly common, it's one to especially look for. Avoid it by having a complete understanding of the issues at hand, both those that support your interests and those that work at cross-purposes to your goals. And maintain flexibility in your thinking so you can respond and adapt as the negotiations unfold. It is also wise to avoid the use of heuristics to confirm your view. These are rules of thumb based on past experience or educated guesses. They are mental shortcuts that can be very misleading during a negotiation because they assume that something will unfold in the present as it did in a past experience, such as making a concession when it appears that the situation is similar. This is generally not a successful way to meet the interests of your team or client today. Develop a plan, stick to your mandate and be very careful not to let a confirmation bias cloud your thinking or the thinking of anyone on your side.

One way to ensure that these various biases are not a factor is to approach negotiations with the same discipline required of lawyers and professors. At law school, students are taught that they must always ascertain precedent in order to substantiate a point of view, and the courts expect this level of preparation from all lawyers. Judges adopt multiple perspectives when looking at the information presented. And academics are required to understand and assess the contrary point of view whenever they make an argument. It requires discipline and structure to obtain a balanced and informed view of a negotiation. And keeping an open mind until the right time to narrow is a hard-earned skill.

NEEDINESS

"Why don't you take it home for the weekend?" It sounded like a great offer. My late friend Alan Joseph, a car salesman who worked near my home, suggested that I take a new silver 1985 Ford Taurus station wagon home with me to "try it out." Alan was a warm and gracious man of great humour and kindness whom I had known through thick and thin. But in this moment, he was using an ingenious negotiating technique.

My wife and I had three young children, and I was balancing the demands of a young family with my life as an MP, which included long hours and extensive travel back and forth from

Ottawa. We had needed a new car for some time, and I woke up one Saturday morning determined to get the issue settled quickly so I could move on to other things. I headed over to see Alan at the dealership and as I arrived, I committed error number one for a potential buyer: "I really need to get this wrapped up quickly." What salesman wouldn't want to deal with someone whose number one priority is speed rather than negotiating a lower price? Alan gave me a quick tour of the wagon before offering it to me for a few days. I thought it was a great suggestion, so I drove it home to show the family. Soon after I had it in the driveway, the kids were dancing around the front yard excited about their new car and we were all doing loops around the neighbourhood. So when I went back to the dealership later on to talk to Alan about the deal, I wasn't considering alternatives at all. This was the vehicle we wanted.

Alan was a great guy, but in that moment he must have seen dollar signs floating over my head. He knew full well that I would be walking out with that car, and he didn't have to go out of his way to lower the price to make it happen. And that's exactly how it went. My neediness to get the deal done left me with less money in my pocket than if I had made it clear that I had all the time in the world to look at options.

Needing to get a deal done quickly is a huge problem for negotiators. If you enter into a negotiation pressed for time, your attitude and behaviour will betray your desires to the other side. Negotiators seized with this mentality tend to make large concessions early on, talk too much or exhibit an over-eagerness to close well in advance of the end of the game. These are all signs of neediness, and I would counsel you to monitor your mindset about getting a deal done and avoid being in a rush situation. It will not lead to the best deal for you and your side. Of the signals negotiators send that indicate they are needy, the one I have seen most often is non-stop talking. If you find yourself talking at length, recognize it and stop. Of course, if the other party is keen to go on and on, let them. And watch for a high-pitched tone of voice, rushed delivery or indications of a dry mouth. These signs of stress indicate an anxiousness to reach an agreement.

In *Start with No*, author Jim Camp refers to neediness as the "greatest weakness" in the negotiating process. He writes, "You do not need this deal, because to be needy is to lose control and make bad decisions." I agree. The likelihood of making a bad decision or settling for a deal that doesn't fit your mandate is much higher if you "need" to get something done. What Camp suggests as an alternative is to focus on "wanting" a deal, a different emphasis that creates focus, planning and passion in the place of a narrow-minded emphasis on a resolution. We all want to accomplish things in life, but desires do not have to be compulsions. I need food but I want a new car. I need water but I want a cottage on the lake. I need to be safe but I want a new arrangement with my employer. Neediness gives your opposition leverage. It makes you vulnerable. A much stronger position is to be clear about your mandate and patiently work toward the best deal possible.

NAIVE REALISM

Lee D. Ross, Professor of Humanities and Sciences at Stanford University, defines naive realism as "the belief that we see reality as it really is; that the facts are plain for all to see; that rational people will agree with us; and that those that don't are either uninformed, lazy, irrational or biased." His description is a powerful way to understand one of the substantial risks that all negotiators face: assuming that the way they see the situation is accurate without taking the time to test and assess if that is actually the case. This is like mixing a confirmation bias with overconfidence, with a credulous view of the "obvious" nature of things before us and a disregard for any person who sees differently. It is an approach that can have significant negative consequences for a negotiator or, even worse, for a person caught in a legal web. Such was the case of Donald Marshall, a famous wrongful conviction case in the history of the Canadian justice system and one that blazed a trail for other high profile wrongful conviction cases such as David Milgaard's and Guy Paul Morin's.

In one of the twists of my life, I knew Donald Marshall in early 1971, just before the incident that changed his life and made him a household name. He and his close friend Sandy Seale were buddies with my best friend Alan Joseph, and we were all in our late teens. Alan had a job sweeping up dressing rooms and the lobby at the old Sydney Forum, and it was there that I met the two young men and got to know them a bit. They were good guys. Seale was friendly, outgoing and funny. Marshall was more reserved but warm-hearted. When news broke on the night of May 28, 1971 that Marshall had inflicted what would be fatal stab wounds on Seale, it was difficult to understand how that could happen. Donald went to prison for life, a sentence he would serve for eleven years before being acquitted by the Nova Scotia Court of Appeal in 1983. I had attended law school while Marshall was imprisoned and had become a Member of Parliament in 1982, so I had followed the case for both personal and professional reasons. Marshall continued to battle with the justice system after his release until he was fully exonerated in 1990. That exoneration was made possible by a Royal Commission conducted from 1986 to 1989 by Chief Justice Alex Hickman, which found that the criminal justice system had failed Donald Marshall from the moment of his arrest in 1971 up to and even beyond his acquittal in 1983 and which made recommendations regarding the role of police and Crown prosecutors.

What actually happened that night is now known. Seale was walking back from a dance when he met Marshall in Sydney's Wentworth Park. As the two young men chatted, Roy Ebsary, who was later described as having a "fetish" for knives, hailed the pair from a side street and asked for a light. An altercation ensued and Seale died from his wounds the next day. Five days after the incident, Marshall was arrested and charged with murder and the case hurried through the justice system. When Marshall was acquitted in 1983, the Crown Attorney was obligated to make all of the evidence in the case available without any determination of its usefulness. The case was then studied in law schools and university classes for years in an effort to determine why Marshall had been convicted. At a minimum, it is clear that the police spent very little time attempting to establish an alternative theory about the murder and focused on the fact that Marshall had had some run-ins with the law as a young man, though none that were particularly violent. The facts seemed plain to the police and other possibilities were discounted as unrealistic. It is also clear that the Crown Attorney approached the case with a narrow view of the facts and rejected alternative conclusions about what may have happened.

I am not an expert in this case, but like most lawyers and politicians who have a rough sense of the history, I know that one of the main issues was that the Crown and law enforcement officials ignored evidence that could have led them to doubt their conclusions. They were operating from the mix of a confirmation bias and overconfidence that I am calling naive realism: "this is the only possible view of the situation." Many believe, as do I, that racism informed that bias, as Marshall was a young aboriginal. When anyone looks at a body of evidence and picks out the pieces that support a pre-existing view, it generally leads to negative and even damaging results. And while the impact of an inaccurate view of the facts during a negotiation process is not as severe as the destruction of a young man's life, we can all learn a lesson from that situation.

THE QUALITIES OF A GREAT NEGOTIATOR

"You have to make sure you always operate in good faith. Otherwise, the trust relationship that you are trying to build with the other party will not get established. If the trust is not there, it doesn't matter how patient you are or which facts are laid out on the table. You really can't move forward. That is your base."

Watch the interview at tinyurl.com/negotiating-singh-qualities-1

MARTIN SINGH, Partner at Precise Pharmacy and federal leadership candidate for the New Democratic Party, 2011–2012

I have been in many situations where the other party sees one certain view of the case that ignores several reasonable interpretations of the facts. Disagreeing with their lens has sometimes led to name calling or the suggestion that I am being intentionally difficult and objectionable. When that happens, two things come to mind. First, that the other party desperately needs its interpretation of the facts to be accepted as true, to the point where it is likely a deal-breaker for them in the negotiation. Second, if their objections are over the top, that they have fallen into naive realism and can only see one interpretation of the facts. This is a dramatic mistake that a strategic negotiator avoids because they know that there are many interpretations in complex situations. They also know that even when facts are relatively easy to interpret, there can be different conclusions reached as to what they mean. In any disagreement about the facts or how they ought to be interpreted, I am always careful to respect the other side's conclusions. But I also suggest a valid second, third or fourth interpretation. If you do not clarify other possibilities, you may be faced with ripple effects that come back to haunt you during the process.

ASSUMPTIONS

In 1984, at the height of the Cold War, American scholar and Russian history expert Suzanne Massie was called to the White House to meet with President Ronald Reagan. Reagan called on Massie because he had read her book *Land of the Firebird: The Beauty of Old Russia* and wanted to better understand Russian views. That day began an ongoing relationship in which Reagan and his wife, Nancy, interacted regularly with Massie about the Russian way of life. During that first conversation, Massie taught the President that Russians were in fact highly religious, despite the state's opposition to religious doctrine, and the President used that insight as a starting point for conversations with Russian General Secretary Mikhail Gorbachev. But the most famous outcome of the relationship between Massie and the Reagans came at a luncheon in 1986 at the Reykjavík Summit. "You know, the Russians often like to talk in proverbs and there's one that might be useful," Massie told the President. "You're an actor, you can learn it in a minute." And then she explained the phrase Доверяй, но проверяй, which in English would be pronounced "doveryai, no proveryai." Translated, it was a phrase that became famous: "Trust, but verify." Reagan explained at the signing of the INF Treaty in 1987 that the phrase described "the extensive verification procedures that would enable both sides to monitor compliance with the treaty." Gorbachev would later indicate that Reagan's use of the phrase was a turning point: he felt he could work with this President who had gone to the trouble to understand Russian culture. This is an example of a world leader in the depths of negotiations making sure he strategically covers all the bases in his preparations. It is also a wonderful phrase to help us avoid a significant trap for negotiators: relying on assumptions.

Entering into any negotiation process with an assumption about what matters to the other side or, for that matter, what matters to your side, is an error to be avoided. Assumptions about the appropriate price without confirmation of market value, the quality of the product without objective reports and testing or the timing of shipments without the track record of the delivery company can lead to difficulty. As the President said: trust, but verify.

I have an example from everyday life to illustrate how a series of assumptions can botch a process. The story has to do with a set of cottage doors that needed to be painted and, while I would love to frame it as being about a "friend" of mine, that would be dishonest. This is actually a story of a complete mess I made by making a series of assumptions.

Our family cottage is situated in rural Cape Breton on the Bras d'Or Lakes. It is a lovely structure built up over time and a place dear to the hearts of the extended Dingwall clan. The doors in question lead onto the porch, and when they needed to be repainted, I acted with a military general's certainty of success and proceeded without input from anyone in my family or circle of friends. I just figured that my concept was so solid that it was foolproof, and especially the decision to use an exterior automotive finish that would provide longevity, exceptional colour and a distinctive look. As I planned out the work, I assumed all that was required was to ship the doors to an automotive shop where a close friend of mine, an expert in automotive finishing, could take care of the painting. I approached a local building supply centre and asked them to remove the doors, replace them with a temporary option and transport them to the automotive shop. Based on the conversation with the building supply outfit, I concluded that this could all be done in five to seven business days. Sixteen weeks later, I had my snazzy doors at an absurd cost of over $12,000 and more than a few difficult moments with my spouse.

What assumptions led to this mess?

1.   That the doors could easily be shipped from the cottage to the automotive shop, fifty-five kilometres away. Given their size, a special flatbed truck had to be ordered.

2.   That the doors were in good shape. Not true, so I had to purchase new doors.

3.   That purchasing new doors would take a day or two. It took three weeks because they had to be shipped in from another location.

4.   That the new doors would be delivered to the automotive shop for the finishing. In a mix-up, the old ones of inadequate quality were sent to the shop.

5.   That the finished doors could be transported back to the cottage using the same flatbed truck. Not so. To avoid scratching, a specialized truck had to be engaged for the blanket-wrapped doors. My friend Tommy Young provided and drove the truck, lifted the doors and, despite much chuckling along the way, was a complete gentleman throughout the process.

6.   That the building supply centre would send the promised installers when needed. There were none available who could do the job for several weeks.

7.   That the installation would be the end of it. However, we discovered that the doors were rattling in the wind and didn't fit very snuggly. Two more visits from the installers were needed to tweak the doors.

8.   That as a result of all this, things would be fine. However, high winds were lifting the doors from the side of the building to the point that they were beginning to rip away. We needed specialized hinges and the installers back all over again.

9.   Clearly, my motto had been "trust, but don't bother to verify." The moral of this story is that with any new endeavour, do your homework and really understand what you are getting into. Every strategic negotiator needs to accurately assess costs and time. Yes, the doors looked fabulous in the end, but when friends and family refer delightedly to "Dave's doors," they aren't celebrating my impressive ability to make an entrance.

TAKEAWAYS

EGO-CREEP

1. Watch for the creep — it usually comes from feeling intimidated or insecure.
2. Don't overcompensate — you will speak louder and more often than required.
3. Avoid feeling superior — even if the other side seems to be inexperienced or disorganized.
4. Squash a desire to prove something — return your focus to the mandate.
5. Put the deal first — you serve it, it doesn't serve you.

BIAS

6. Seek alternative views — confirming only your perspective will skew details and conclusions.
7. Be patient — relying on first impressions may anchor your outlook too early in the process.
8. Assess your talent honestly — overestimation and overconfidence distances you from reality.
9. Develop discipline — test your position using precedent and contrary arguments.

NEEDINESS

10. Don't rush — you will make early concessions and pursue a close before it's wise.
11. Exercise restraint — non-stop talking is a clear signal of neediness.
12. Swap need for want — this gains control and avoids a narrow-minded emphasis on resolution.

NAIVE REALISM

13. Accept complexity — there is no such thing as a single, obvious reality.

14. Respect the flexibility of facts — they mean different things from different perspectives.
15. Grant the rationality of others— you're not the only one who can think and reason.
16. Test and assess — find the gaps in your position to know how to address them.

ASSUMPTIONS

17. Doubt assumptions — both yours and theirs.
18. Trust — expect the other side to be truthful, conscientious and upright.
19. But verify — seek the information you need to ensure your trust is well placed.

CHAPTER 5
The Mandate

"Industrial capitalism brought representative democracy, but with a weak public mandate and an inert citizenry."

— Don Tapscott

If you worked for Jean Chrétien, you could always count on knowing where he stood. If you had a proposal to submit or a perspective to share, he would listen, ask questions and expect you to know what you were talking about. And then he would tell you what he thought — clearly and directly — while connecting your ideas to the larger issues of the government. When you went to see him, you needed to be on your game and ready to be precise, detailed and passionate about your case. So when I attended the first ever cabinet meeting of a Chrétien government in November 1993, it was no surprise to hear his expectations of the thirty-one ministers in the room laid out in clear, specific and comprehensive terms. It was just his way.

The twentieth Prime Minister of Canada, Chrétien was a seasoned veteran of the Canadian political scene. He had been an MP continuously since 1963 and in the Liberal cabinet from 1965 to 1984. His values of tolerance, respect, caring for those in need and financial prudence were among the many attractions of his candidacy for the Liberal leadership. And his political savvy and confidence helped him win the election in a landslide, leaving the outgoing Tories with only two seats. Left of centre on social issues and right of centre on fiscal issues, Chrétien arrived at that first meeting with a clear directive from the Canadian people that included addressing the deficit and streamlining the government. Chrétien knew exactly how he wanted the government to run and his process for selecting and empowering his ministers was an expression of his experience and insight. Prior to that first cabinet meeting, we had all been through a rigorous selection process that included being vetted by the RCMP for security clearance and being questioned about potential conflict of interest and ethical issues by the Honourable Mitchell Sharp, personal adviser to the Prime Minister. We had also had personal conversations with the Prime Minister about our interests with respect to cabinet positions and our ideas about the emphasis of the government.

Once Chrétien had decided where he wanted us to serve — in my case, that meant taking on a half dozen economic portfolios — he began the process of establishing our mandate. First, he gave us a letter, copied to our Deputy Minister, that outlined the responsibilities of the minister and the priorities that would guide us. Then, he followed up with several live conversations to provide additional detail, revisions or updated priorities. This meant that prior to arriving at that first meeting, all thirty-one of us had a sense of our individual responsibilities and shared emphasis in government. Then, in the meeting, he focused on how he wanted the government to operate. After thirty years in office, most of them spent as a member of a cabinet or shadow cabinet, Chrétien knew exactly how he wanted the cabinet to function and how important it was to be crystal clear with his team, especially about the relationship between the Prime Minister's office and the ministries. In particular, he spoke to his five key structural ideas for overseeing the government during his tenure as Prime Minister.

1.   He wanted each minister to work closely with their senior public servants. Since they have the responsibility of running the operations of the government, Chrétien believed the public servants ought to be involved in offering suggestions to their ministers and providing sound policy options. He also eliminated the role of Chief of Staff in each ministry as a cost saving measure and as a means of obliging the ministers to deal regularly and directly with their non-partisan staffers.

2.   He wanted ministers to conduct themselves with respect and thoughtfulness not only to public servants, but to MPs and the many stakeholders connected to each of the respective ministries.

3.   He knew that ministers could not be experts on every subject that came to the cabinet table, but he expected them to be extremely knowledgeable of their departments. In return for the pressure to really know their stuff, Chrétien left us mostly alone to run our affairs, but that confidence was quickly withdrawn if he learned that someone was not on top of their file.

4.   He made himself available for easy and regular access, but it was clear that he did not want to be engaged in minor or time-wasting proposals. Everyone knew that if you wanted to speak to the boss, it had to be important — quick meetings, clear information, description of the problem and then seasoned advice and direction from the top.

5.   He intended to establish and support a powerhouse senior staff and made it very clear to us about how ministers

should interact with them. He placed three powerful, thoughtful and highly competent individuals in place who contributed significantly to the success of our government. Peter Donolo was to be Director of Communications and all key messages and engagements with the media would go through him, with ministers having limited contact with the media. Eddie Goldenberg was to be the Prime Minister's principal secretary, charged with reviewing each minister's focus on both the government's overall mandate and on their individual mandate letter. And Jean Pelletier was to be Chrétien's Chief of Staff — his voice and representative. The former Mayor of Quebec City and close friend of both French President Jacques Chirac and Chrétien, Pelletier had a shrewd political mind, ran a very tight ship and was tight-lipped, which led to few if any of the anonymous leaks that had plagued previous Prime Minister's offices. This triumvirate became one of the most effective PMO staffs in history, and their ongoing interactions with ministers ensured that their vision and influence held sway in every government matter.

"No matter what happens in this room," said Chrétien in the meeting, "when we leave here, we speak with one voice." It was a message that set the tone for the four years that followed when I worked closely with him as a senior cabinet minister. And it was an emphasis that he maintained through his entire tenure as Prime Minister. By being proactive, consistent and clear about the mandate in terms of goals, process and emphasis, Chrétien created the conditions for a highly successful government and established himself as one of the most effective Prime Ministers to take up residence at 24 Sussex Drive.

As it did under Chrétien's leadership, the concept of a mandate plays a significant role in politics and legal proceedings, but it is equally important in any kind of negotiation. In simplest terms, a mandate describes the arrangement or agreement between a negotiator and whomever they are representing to achieve a particular outcome. It includes a clear outline of all goals, details about how those goals will or will not be achieved, identification of long-term considerations and a description of the negotiator's authority regarding which decisions they can make on their own and which require approval from the client. In essence, the mandate outlines what a negotiator has the power to do and what they are supposed to accomplish.

As a negotiator, your clients can range from yourself to another individual to a large organization to a group of different parties with shared interests. Your ability to succeed in each context begins with the degree to which your mandate is clear, detailed and, most of all, agreed to by all parties on behalf of whom you are negotiating. Failing to develop the mandate creates the risk of making decisions counter to your client's desires and increases the likelihood of the other party being able to exercise some clout in having you follow their mandate. A poorly developed mandate also creates the possibility that your process may misrepresent the desires of your client or that you engage in approaches or behaviours that the client does not support. It's not strategic to operate on a wing and a prayer, with a vague sense of what you are trying to accomplish. Keep in mind that the best negotiators don't want just any deal; they work for the one that best fits the needs and interests of the client. Closing the deal is important, but your forethought and preparation make the best outcome possible. And the mandate is the tangible sign of that preparation. As Carol Hansell explains, "Understanding your client's objective is critical. As lawyers or governance council, we are negotiating on behalf of the clients. It is important that the client's tone, demeanour, posture and priorities are being reflected. You need to spend a lot of time talking to your client about what they are trying to accomplish and what their endgame is, rather than just looking at specific parts of the negotiation. Unless I spend a lot of time talking to the client and unless they are open with me, I won't know what their instruction means."

Watch the interview with Carol Hansell at tinyurl.com/negotiating-hansell-mandate

ORAL VERSUS WRITTEN MANDATES

Over the years, I have received mandates through an oral briefing and in writing, the latter of which is usually crafted after extended conversations with the principals involved. Discussion and dialogue are of utmost importance at all stages of a negotiation and in long-term relationships, but there is no substitute for a written mandate. Spoken communication is never perfect; there is always a degree to which the parties walk away with a different understanding of what happened. In particular, people often make assumptions during conversations that create confusion about the instructions relayed to the negotiator. Whether it comes to you in writing and you follow up with detailed conversations to ensure you are clear or whether you receive it orally and then transcribe it for the client or superior to confirm, ensure that the mandate is written down for all to see and agree to.

A common approach these days is to follow up on a client meeting with an email that outlines your understanding of the mandate. This allows all involved to go through the items slowly and agree with the negotiator's characterization of the goals and powers outlined, with time to have further discussion wherever there is a lack of alignment. I advise clients and others to be very specific in summarizing their mandate in writing so there is limited confusion. It is far better to be clear at the beginning of the process than to get well down the road toward an agreement and come across a difference of view.

One temptation to accept an oral mandate occurs when a negotiator receives direction from a superior and doesn't want to appear stupid or unnecessarily inquisitive. Sometimes these oral instructions are vague, uncertain or confusing, especially if the superior has not carefully thought through the situation. This creates a significant risk that the negotiator will get burned later on when the superior says, "that's not what we agreed to." Though you might be right about how the situation unfolded, why put yourself in a situation where you have to correct the boss? Plus, getting into a mess on a significant deal because the mandate wasn't clear isn't good for anyone. In those cases, it is your job to raise all questions with your superior so that you are set up to succeed. For the most part, you will find that your email after the meeting is welcomed for being a specific, direct, efficient and detailed clarification of what was discussed, which will help you succeed in the negotiation and build your reputation as a professional.

This approach is useful beyond situations in which you receive your mandate from a superior. After almost any interaction about the what and the how of a given negotiation, I tend to follow up with an email summarizing the details. And it is often the case that I draft the written mandate myself following a conversation. The process begins with a live meeting with the individual or group I am representing, guided by a checklist to ensure that all aspects of the mandate are discussed. I then prepare a short summary of the conversation outlining specific goals, time frame, authority and other relevant material. The result is a detailed, clear and accurate mandate that helps all of us. In fact, I would go so far as to say that while many negotiators will tell you that they love to close a deal on a handshake and a verbal agreement, almost all of them see the value of having a written mandate before they begin.

Written mandates are especially important for the broad range of negotiations with a principal-agent arrangement. This is a common set-up for lawyers, with the mandate typically ascertained under the auspices of a retainer agreement. However, these agreements do not always address the parameters of the agent's authority or the contingencies for various predictable circumstances. Beyond the lawyer-client relationship, principal-agent situations are unique in that they create a wide range of opportunities for what I will call "mischievous" behaviour — situations where either the agent or the principal can act in ways that undermine or ignore the other. In general, people proceed in good faith and work together to the best of their ability, but when you are negotiating on behalf of a principal, especially if your relationship is reasonably new, be sure to spell out the parameters of the mandate very carefully, including specific goals, time frame and authority. And, as always, I believe that the onus is on you — not your client or superior — to ensure the mandate is clear.

Written mandates come in a wide variety of forms and can sometimes be embedded in an organization's core functions. As seasoned franchise agreement negotiator Michael Cleaner explains, "The mandate would be developed from the annual strategic plan of the organization which would decide how many new locations we are going to open or how much land we are going to acquire to bank for future development. And those goals would have a budget attached to them. As a lead negotiator, I would have been part of producing the strategic plan. We took the strategic planning process very seriously and we reviewed the strategic plan at the end of every quarter. It wasn't something that we stuck in a desk and then dusted off a year later to look at and see how we had done. We would pull it out each quarter and ask ourselves if we needed to make any revisions based on current conditions."

Watch the interview
with Michael Cleaner at
tinyurl.com/negotiating-
cleaner-mandate

EXPECTATIONS AND STRATEGIC GOALS

"I always think — what does the ribbon cutting look like? What does that ceremony look like? What I say to my own team is, at the end of the day, what's the discount that we want — what's the profit that we need — what is the endgame that we want to achieve? I do that at every negotiation at the very front end rather than having it morph along. We say, 'What does success look like?' so that before the meetings start, we know what we are trying to accomplish and have a clear estimate of how things will turn out."

Watch the interview
with Paul Zed at
tinyurl.com/negotiating-
zed-mandate

That's Paul Zed, Chairman of the President's Advisory Board for Rogers Communications Canada and former Member of Parliament, talking about proceeding into negotiations with a clear vision of the endgame. Establishing a mandate with clearly stated goals is a crucial part of success.

When it comes to envisioning success, I think it is really important to dream big. In their book *Built to Last: Successful Habits of Visionary Companies*, James Collins and Jerry Porras call this a Big Hairy Audacious Goal. Their emphasis is on a company's strategic business statement, which should be both bold and possible, but you can use the same idea to picture your success. Many of the leading experts in negotiation believe that you need to have inspiring goals or you will fall short in accomplishing your objective. This is also the approach that I have taken since leaving public life when I mentor young people. One of the most important things I can do is to help them set high expectations for themselves. I then help them to develop a comprehensive plan of how they will strategically achieve those goals, because if you build from your current position, you are more likely to be successful. The same is true in negotiations. Everyone involved needs to develop a shared stretch goal or BHAG — an ambitious vision of what is possible, an objective that would be a great success to achieve. People rise to meet high expectations.

With that stretch goal established, be both strategic about how you proceed and realistic about what is possible. You can assume that the other party will be prepared, have a clear set of goals, understand the situation and know the impact of concluding a successful arrangement. Therefore, an inspiring goal cannot be over the top. If excessively unrealistic, unbelievable, or unattainable, it will eat away at your credibility and the credibility of your propositions. Be aspirational within the elastic possibilities of reality.

Ed Clark ambitiously expanded TD Bank's interest into the United States through an ongoing series of acquisitions led by a team of business development specialists. Though he had a stretch goal, he was always realistic and accurate in his expectations and in how he and his people represented their success. "Transparency is the whole foundation of your relationship with your own employees, the Board, shareholders and regulators. We believe firmly, just tell it like it is. It is enormously comforting for people to know what is actually happening. If you asked the members what they like about being on the Board, most of them will say that they like that I start every Board meeting by saying, 'Here are all the bad things happening right now at TD, here are all the things that are going wrong, here are all the problems that I am stewing about. It's not upward delegation. I own all of this. But you should know about it. I would not want you ever to be blindsided.' An expression I use is Round Down, not up. The good news will go up easy enough. People want to know about the things that are going wrong, and if you are going to present views, make sure that you are not exaggerating."

Watch the interview with Ed Clark at tinyurl.com/negotiating-clark-goals

RATIONALE

When David Andrews, President and CEO of the American Hockey League, was applying for the job he has now held for over ten years — a period in which he has overseen a massive expansion of the league — the needs of the league and the rationale behind what he would be doing in the job were embedded in the interview process. "One of my strengths is strategic planning," Andrews explains. "From the very beginning, even before I took over as President of the league, in my interview for the position I basically crafted a strategic plan for the league and said that if I was selected, I would present this to the Board for support."

Watch the interview with David Andrews at tinyurl.com/negotiating-andrews-planning

Andrews's approach allowed for a simultaneous conversation about his candidacy and the goals of the organization, so that from the very beginning he and the AHL Board were in alignment about what they were hoping to accomplish and why it was a priority.

Understanding the rationale of the mandate is essential if you are going to execute it effectively. Negotiations are not simple and a mandate on its own is not comprehensive enough to set you up for success. To cope effectively with the twists and turns that will inevitably occur, a negotiator needs a deep understanding of what the negotiation means to both parties in order to be clear about where it might go and what to do if the goals need to be adjusted along the way. Specific goals are a significant motivator and are used widely in areas such as sports, sales and education to spur people by focusing their attention. But goals not rooted in a clear understanding of rationale are less than ideally lucrative and generative. A broad understanding of why you and/or your client is proceeding into a negotiation is essential.

With this understanding in place, you can then set about creating specific goals based on the rationale in such areas as the bottom line value of the products or services you are negotiating over. Entering a negotiation with a "I'll do the best I can" or "let's see how it goes" mindset is very dangerous. You do not want to take a chance in the negotiating process, and clear, identifiable goals within the context of the rationale will help with that. I often ask clients, whether in law or business, to spell out in detail the rationale behind the mandate so that I am abundantly clear about "the why" of what they are trying to accomplish. Pursue that angle with the principal you are representing, and put your probing skills to work to help them flush out what they mean and discover what has not yet been expressed.

As Paul Zed indicated when he envisions the ribbon cutting, be clear with the client about what success will look like — a question that many of the great negotiators I know ask at the beginning of any process. Answering requires real clarity about why the negotiation is happening and what the specific goals ought to be. For example, success could simply be a particular price for a product or service or a certain length of agreement. But it might be more complex, such as the quality of the long-term relationship between parties and the ways that relationship is represented and supported in the contract. Parties to a negotiation — even if just two members of your team — ought to take the time to envision in specific detail that will be considered success. For me, success is always more than just the monetary figure contained in an agreement. It can include the term, issues of quality, dispute resolution, renewable options, testimonials, contingent liabilities and a host of other items, all of which will be reflected in the agreement. The more you can be clear about what you are trying to accomplish and what success looks like based on the rationale, the better.

GETTING AGREEMENT

This is how Buzz Hargrove describes the process that he and his union leadership used to secure support from their members: "As we were heading toward the end of a collective agreement, we would hold membership meetings and conduct surveys, asking people to identify what they thought the priorities of the union should be and then, prior to submitting our final proposals to the companies, we always had a final membership meeting and went through them all again and they were voted on. And then when bargaining is over, you have to go back to the membership for ratification."

Watch the interview with Buzz Hargrove at tinyurl.com/negotiating-hargrove-agreement

Hargrove's approach represents an important consideration: establishing agreement about the mandate, especially when there are multiple parties involved.

The power of a mandate is derived from the extent to which everyone involved on your side of the deal feels that it represents their interests. That last thing you want is to work tirelessly to achieve an agreement only to find out that your mandate only represented a narrow slice of the group you were representing. Certainly, there can never be unanimous agreement when there are complex multi-party negotiations, but there are productive ways to proceed toward stakeholder sign-off on the mandate that will ensure a much more positive outcome. It is also essential to

ESTABLISHING A MANDATE

"I was one of the first guys that Gary Bettman hired when he became Commissioner of the NHL. I had only met Gary a couple times before that and I was really impressed with him. So when he offered me the role of Executive Vice President and Director of Hockey Operations, I said yes. He said, 'I need a five-year commitment from you. I do not want this job to be a parking lot for out of work GMs.' I said okay and we did all the contracts.

"And then I said to him, 'I'm a hard hockey guy. I like the game played physically. If I have one concern about where our game is going, it's that we're gonna somehow lose our roots. This game was always meant to be difficult and hard to play. That means we want the game played hard. We want guys right on the edge. And when they cross the edge, we are going to bang them, but we want them right on the edge. That's what's distinctive about the game in North America — how much hitting there is. And there is difference between a great hit that's on the news or the highlight film and a penalty.' So keep track of the interest and views of the people on your negotiating team, especially if it's large.

When representing a major entity negotiating a large contract, I bring together stakeholders from finance, human resources, procurement, technology, the President's office, and sales and marketing to discuss the mandate and the strategy. Often, I use flip charts and ask each stakeholder in the room to identify what they deem to be important for the purposes of this negotiation. Their answers may vary widely and if you have ten people in the room, you might get ten or fifteen different priorities to consider. If a consensus can easily and readily be achieved, you are in good shape, but if not, you need to be ready to facilitate one. It helps

I said, 'Are you committed to hard hockey?' He said 'Yes, I just don't want the crazy stuff.' Back then most of the stuff we had was stick related. You go back and you'll see baseball grip swings and the cross-checks to the face. We got rid of all that.

"Gary's a great boss. He'd give you enough direction that you knew what he wanted, but then he'd let you go to; he didn't micromanage or anything. I've heard rumours he's a screamer. I've never heard him scream. I really enjoyed my five years."

Watch the interview at tinyurl.com/negotiating-burke-mandate

BRIAN BURKE, President of Hockey Operations for the Calgary Flames and former General Manager of the Toronto Maple Leafs

to have the individual stakeholders rank the importance of those priorities: 1 to 3 is "very very important," 3 to 5 is "important," 5 to 7 is "if we can get it — great" and 7 to 10 is "not important at all." Having everyone in the room at the same time assessing priorities and then discussing the results of their valuations builds momentum toward a mandate you can pursue. In an exercise like this, it is extremely helpful to go through a second and third round of prioritizing the goals to build toward an agreement because the different emphases and perspectives — such as the differences between HR and IT — means seeing the issues differently. A process that allows everyone to assess options and share opinions makes consensus about the mandate more possible.

This is a process that negotiators rarely consider, who instead accept the mandate as assigned by the leadership and proceed into the negotiations. But I can assure you that whether you are involved in a multi-million-dollar insurance claim, a major environmental concern or an IT procurement, a fulsome, free-running discussion focuses your people to establish accurate, specific and shared goals that you can work with as you proceed. It is also a process that develops a richer understanding of

THE QUALITIES OF A GREAT NEGOTIATOR

"People who are not afraid to say 'I have reconsidered that' or 'I understand your perspective on that.' People who can say, 'When we started this, I did not see it that way, but now that you have been talking to me about it, I do understand your perspective. It's hard for me for various reasons, and I will have to go back to my Board, but I hear you on that issue and let's see what we can do about that.' People who do it that way create a bigger basket of solutions because everybody is now working to see where we can move the pieces, so that you get what you want and I get what I want."

your side's interests and aligns the internal politics around the various issues.

David Andrews deals with negotiations of various sizes that require very different approaches in terms of buy-in from the stakeholders: "When we are going into a collective bargaining negotiation, it requires a fair amount of face-to-face discussion with stakeholders. For example, I will meet with our full Board and then with the National Hockey League General Managers, another group of stakeholders with an interest in our collective bargaining agreement. The people we are negotiating for are their employees, and the decisions we make will affect player development in the American Hockey League, so we need to know what the NHL GMs would like to see in a new agreement. We also need to know what our owners would like to see in a new agreement. And we need to think through how a new agreement will impact various aspects of our business beyond just the relationship with the players. Whereas, there are other initiatives that I would take on, for example negotiating a new officiating agreement with the NHL, where I would probably not engage the stakeholders at all. I know what our objectives

Watch the interview at
tinyurl.com/negotiating-
hansell-qualities

CAROL HANSELL, former Director of the Bank of Canada, Founder and Senior Partner at Hansell LLP

will be and I know what the NHL position is likely to be. So the preparation is mostly me sitting down and trying to sort out what I hope to achieve on behalf of the organization and what the challenges are that I am likely to face."

Watch the interview with David Andrews at tinyurl.com/negotiating-andrews-agreement

REPUTATION

As Distinguished Counsel in Residence at the Ted Rogers School of Management at Ryerson University, Ralph Lean is aware of how reputation affects the negotiation process: "Trust comes from your body of work over time. People talk and you can develop a reputation as a person who is a fair dealer or someone who isn't. You want to be a person who people know that when you make a commitment, they can trust that you are going to live up to that."

Watch the interview with Ralph Lean at tinyurl.com/negotiating-lean-reputation

Keep reputation in mind as you establish your mandate for a particular negotiation, because it is an important component of both your career and your ability to achieve success for your client or the organization you represent. If there are conditions, tactics, goals or priorities in the mandate that could be detrimental to the way you are perceived, you are best to either alter the course of the negotiation before it begins or get yourself off the file. For example, aggressive tactics may work well sometimes, particularly if the issue is one just dealing with price. However, if you continuously strong-arm people, your approach will become known and you will not likely be well trusted. Ultimately, keeping track of your reputation is a surefire way to proceed in the negotiations with the right mindset, because you will inevitably take a long-term view knowing that your professional identity is part of your success.

Bob Rae — lawyer, negotiator and former Premier of Ontario — characterizes the role of reputation in a negotiator's approach: "One of the problems is that people see a negotiation as a way of taking short-term advantage. People will say, 'I really screwed him.' To me, that's not the way to think about negotiations. I see it in two ways. One is that your reputation follows you wherever you go. How you behave stays with you, and you are known as either somebody that can be trusted or somebody that can't be trusted. You are either known as someone whose word is good or not. People learn very quickly whether they can shake hands with you or whether it has to be down in writing. The second thing is that if you are trying to develop a relationship with a person over time, it doesn't make any sense to take advantage of them in the short term. A very good friend of mine, Jack Rabinovitch, who is a real estate expert and a superb negotiator, said to me a long time ago, 'When I negotiate, I always leave something on the table because you don't want to make the other guy feel like you fleeced him. You are going to want to do business with him again.' Jack was talking about the reputational issues associated with how you proceed."

Watch the interview with Bob Rae at tinyurl.com/negotiating-rae-reputation

One of my most memorable experiences with reputation came when I began working with the Honourable Allan Rock, Canada's Minister of Justice from 1993 to 1997 and current President of the University of Ottawa. His reputation was that of a person who was friendly and cordial but tenacious, competent, tough and, above all else, principled. He was also known to follow through whenever he gave you his word.

THE QUALITIES OF A GREAT NEGOTIATOR

"If you don't have a good relationship, you can't expect to get a deal done. If either party doesn't respect the another, it's not going to happen. You have to respect one another in terms of what you are trying to do and what the objective is. If there is emotion in the way, it's not going to happen and you have to get somebody else in to take over. I had a set of circumstances once where I was the wrong guy to be at the table and I knew that. I brought somebody else in from the team and let him negotiate it and we got the deal."

Watch the interview at tinyurl.com/negotiating-cleaner-qualities

MICHAEL CLEANER, Franchise Agreement Negotiator

When I was working to establish new tobacco control legislation for Canada, Rock more than anyone else could have easily derailed or delayed the process. He did not. In fact, he was key to the entire process going smoothly. We often met in advance of cabinet meetings to ensure that we had covered all the bases and were aligned in our thinking and in the discussions about the proposed legislation. Rock was true to his word, despite being pressured internally by some Members of Parliament and externally by business interests to slow down my efforts to move the legislation along. From the beginning, Rock had agreed with the overall objective of the legislation, especially as it related to controlling advertising of tobacco, and he worked tirelessly to deal with the various issues that came up along the way. He was committed to the goals of the legislation and proceeded to do everything he could to bring it into law. Rock's reputation as a person of integrity added another level of trust that smoothed the process.

TIME FRAME

"Timing can sometimes be price sensitive," explains Paul Zed of the role of time frames in the technology negotiations that dominate in his industry. "You might say, 'Look — I can offer this price because this product is on an assembly line and it is offered at a certain price with a certain discount associated with it, but after a certain date, we can't honour that price.' And sometimes price can help nudge a negotiation. Another timing factor in negotiation is delivery. Very often, particularly in technology, there may be a system that is being implemented and the integration of the system will require a two-year delivery lapse."

Watch the interview
with Paul Zed at
tinyurl.com/negotiating-
zed-timing

As I have said, time needs to be on your side during negotiations as much as possible, which means that a key part of establishing your mandate is to acquire from your superiors or client a clear indication of the factors affecting the timeline, especially as it pertains to the minimum and maximum allowable time. In addition, effective preparation and mandate construction includes understanding the timing on the other side, so that you know how their constraints or options might influence your decision making. Careful consideration to the timing of your negotiations allows you to be more strategic. Timing considerations include the availability of people for both sides, the clarification of various issues, the need to get additional information and the possibility of visiting the site of operations that are the focus of the negotiations. And while it is important to prudently manage expectations — those of your team, your superiors or clients and the other side — it is even more important to see clearly, in advance, how long it will actually take to complete each particular negotiation.

DEADLINES

As the saying goes, nothing would ever get done without a deadline. The astute use of intermediate and final deadlines can work in your favour as you go through the process and should be considered when you are drafting your mandate. But deadlines can also be an obstacle to reaching agreement if not carefully designed and fail to take into consideration the realities of a particular deal. Begin by ensuring that your mandate contains reasonable deadlines. If you do not have time to do your job properly, or you are forced to jam the other side, the odds of reaching a mutually agreeable and beneficial arrangement rapidly decline.

Once your own deadlines are clear, proceed to establish deadlines with the other side and then continually loop back to revise your mandate as you go along. My approach to deadline clarification contains three steps before the primary live sessions at the table. First, when discussing the agenda with the other party by telephone, I make sure that we clarify the deadlines which have typically been agreed to in advance. In many instances, the other side will deviate from the initial timing but not substantially. Second, I will confirm the deadlines when I send an email with the written agenda for the meeting. In particular, I am very careful about the wording. An email might look something like this: "I wanted to follow up regarding our agenda and the time frame for our discussions concerning *xyz*. I believe we have covered all of the agenda items, which are attached to this email, and I look forward to hearing from you within the next forty-eight hours in terms of additions and/or sub-components to what we had discussed. In addition, we agreed that we would attempt to have this matter resolved by *abc* date. Please confirm this date at your earliest convenience." Last, as I sit down at the table with the other party, I review the agenda and the time frame once again so that everyone is clear. Sometimes you will run into a negotiator who is not well prepared and will try to fudge the deadlines. Consider reminding them of what they said on the two previous occasions, especially if the client and/or other parties are in the room.

AUTHORITY

In 1994, I had the great honour of representing Canada on a visit to Israel. This was the result of efforts by Canada and other countries to arrange for approximately $300 million of financial aid for housing, water and infrastructure in the war-torn areas of the Gaza Strip. I was scheduled to meet with Prime Minister Rabin before he was called away to meetings in the United States. In his place, the Israelis arranged for me to meet with Shimon Peres, the legendary international politician who was Foreign Minister at the time. I will never forget my meeting with Peres. I learned as much about negotiation from him as from anyone else before or since. Referring to me as "young man" throughout, Peres talked at length with me about the complexities of the ongoing bargaining taking place in the Gaza Strip and he asked me detailed questions about who I would be meeting with in the subsequent days. I explained that, among others, my delegation and I were hoping to meet with members of the PLO to discuss the possibility of financial assistance with infrastructure and housing.

Peres was eloquent and clear as he articulated his thoughts on our efforts. "People in the Gaza need clean water, good housing and infrastructure," he said. "But, young man, try as best as you can to

---

CLARITY ABOUT AUTHORITY

"The biggest case where we had a problem was during the Charlottetown negotiation. Prime Minister Mulroney was away in Germany and Mr. Clark was the negotiator and the minister responsible for negotiation. We were getting down to the short strokes on a discussion about the senate, and it became very clear to me at a certain point that the dynamic of the conversation was going in a certain direction. So I pulled aside one of the senior public servants who was working for Mr. Clark and Mr. Mulroney and said, 'Is this actually the federal government position? Is this actually what Mr. Mulroney wants to happen?' He said that it was, but as the process unfolded and Mr. Mulroney came back, he was not happy with what had happened and we had to start over again, because Mr. Clark did not have the authority but he thought he did have it. I don't challenge his

---

ascertain whether or not the people you are meeting with have the actual authority to consummate an arrangement." His advice was odd to me, because I could not imagine how the negotiations could go awry given that we were offering $300 million in relief.

During meetings with several representatives of the PLO, including Yasser Arafat's brother Fathi Arafat, we talked at length about the Gaza residents' needs, and everyone at the table seemed to be in agreement. Yet when it came time for us to comply with the regulations and demands that the United Nations had set down for this sort of process, the PLO representatives were less than enthusiastic. They indicated that they would have to check with other members of the PLO before they could agree. In the end, the conversations were unproductive and no monies went to the Gaza at that time. Peres's advice had been spot on.

Some people are reluctant to raise the issue of authority for fear that the other side might become annoyed, thereby getting the negotiations off on the wrong foot. Their concerns are

integrity for a moment. I think he believed that that is what he had. But Mr. Mulroney had a different approach to it."

Watch the interview at tinyurl.com/negotiating-rae-authority

BOB RAE, former Premier of Ontario, current faculty at the University of Toronto School of Governance and Public Policy

unfounded, as it is easy to raise this issue in a comfortable manner. For instance, you could start by saying, "I wanted to share with you that I have the authority to be here today and to resolve this particular dispute in its entirety. I was hoping that you could give me some sort of assurance that you too have the authority to resolve this outstanding matter." The mere fact that you have raised this question and "gone first" will oblige the other side to provide an answer. If the other party can give you the assurances that they have the authority to proceed, all is good. But if they are vague or seem reluctant to talk about it, you should take this as a cautionary note. When creating your mandate, you have to know who is calling the shots, internally and on the other side. On your side, understand your own authority and the various conditions that will require you to seek approval from superiors, clients or the Board. In dealing with your opponent, develop a clear sense of their decision-making processes so that you can craft your approach accordingly and speak with the right people.

Early in my career, I was burned by not clarifying authority when I was running Dial-A-Student Co-Op Services Limited. The co-op was attempting to purchase three surplus trucks from the Department of National Defence, and we were in discussions with a senior official in Nova Scotia. After days and days of meetings, postponements, exchanges of information and the verification that Dial-A-Student had the money to purchase the trucks, the official finally admitted he had no authority to do the deal. As a result of this inordinate delay, we almost lost the opportunity to secure the trucks. Several members of our group had to fly to Newfoundland to meet with an official who could sign the deal, incurring additional expenses and using up more time. The lesson I learned is that it is much more advantageous to raise the issue of authority at the beginning of your negotiations than to wait. Discussing authority early on saves the money, time and tension that arises from confusion.

One way to understand issues of authority clearly is to look at an aspect of legal proceedings called an "undertaking," which is a legally binding personal promise to do what you say you will do. Section 5.1-6 of the Model Code of Professional Conduct, Federation of Law Societies of Canada, reads: "A lawyer must strictly and scrupulously fulfill any undertakings given and honour any trust conditions accepted in the course of litigation." Because an undertaking occurs within a legal framework, the lawyer is obliged to follow through exactly as committed. This is a helpful framework for all negotiators. If you view your promises as ironclad, you will learn to be very careful about what you commit to. Almost every lawyer will say that when they give an undertaking, they are certain it describes something they can actually do. For example, if requested to produce documents from a third party, you may only be able to undertake that you will ask for the documents, because that party may refuse to give them to you. A negotiator needs to be very careful to ensure that they have the authority to follow through on their promises — especially since requests, like undertakings, are quite often made in the heat of a negotiation. Long before reaching the point where the other side asks something of you, be clear about what you can and cannot deliver.

Understanding authority issues is also essential in situations where you cannot avoid talking to an intermediary. For example, consider your interactions with a headhunter if seeking a senior position in an organization. You know upfront that they are merely a representative of a particular client. Sometimes a headhunter actually assesses different candidates and makes a recommendation that is automatically accepted, but that is not generally how it goes. It's been my experience that decisions are made by various committees and executives who develop a mandate for incumbents which covers responsibilities, characteristics, skill sets and a host of other qualities and conditions. The catch is that if you fail to impress the headhunter with your ability to perform, it is unlikely you will move along in the process. While the authority to make the final decision lies with a senior vice-president or CEO, the headhunter will likely hold sway in how the process unfolds.

The same is true of a negotiator acting without authority to close a deal but on behalf of a client who has that capacity. Just as you have to work with the headhunter to be considered for the job, you have to work with the negotiator to consummate a deal. Whomever you are dealing with is your conduit to the people who have authority. You need to impress upon the representative the significance of the offer you are proposing, the positive impact it will have on the other party and the negative consequences if your recommendations are not accepted. Failure to work co-operatively and meaningfully with the representative runs the risk of your position not being accepted or being altered substantially.

RATIFICATION SYSTEM

The ratification system in place to approve deals is related to authority. Ed Clark describes the role that the Board of Directors of TD Bank played in its ongoing assessment of potential acquisition targets: "We constantly update the Board to say, 'This is what we are looking at.' We ask them, 'Do you have views that we should or we shouldn't?' and 'What's the size of the bet that we are willing to take?' All of those things are extensively discussed. And we have two rules for decision making at the Board about potential deals. One is that they have multiple occasions to discuss an opportunity, so I can't come with an acquisition and say, 'This is hot, I have to get it done now and I need your approval.' These are the kind of deals where you really do want your Board members to go home and think about it for a while and then come back and tell you if they are comfortable with it. The other rule, which is a learning from the financial crisis, is that the Board cannot take the vote on a particular acquisition until all of the management — including me — leaves the room. The Board has to meet alone without management. The reason is that you don't want a very aggressive, powerful CEO standing there and hammering the Board and saying, 'I want to do this deal now and I want to take a vote,' because, frankly, a CEO can overwhelm a Board. They need to take some time to talk with each other on their own and decide if they want to do the deal."

Watch the interview with Ed Clark at tinyurl.com/negotiating-clark-ratification

TD's careful process of ensuring good decisions is one kind of ratification system. As you establish your mandate, be clear about how a deal will be ratified at the end of the process, both on your side and the other. It's enormously frustrating to reach an agreement after many hours, days, weeks or even years of negotiations and then discover that the ratification process is an obstacle to finalizing the agreement.

When dealing with sophisticated clients concerning major issues, there is usually a complex ratification system. And, if the issues are serious enough, they will require the approval and recommendation by a CEO to a Board of Directors. If that is the case for your particular subject matter, it's best to understand that well in advance of your negotiation. Michael Cleaner explains how he would take the ratification process into account when beginning a franchising negotiation: "I had a $10 million approval. I could make an arrangement, sign all the documents myself and bind the company for up to $10 million. But if a deal was going to exceed that number, I needed to know well in advance because that had to go to the Board. I needed to make sure there was time for the approval process to take place. So I always began by being very careful about cost overruns."

Watch the interview with Michael Cleaner at tinyurl.com/negotiating-cleaner-process

In many instances, the other party may be reluctant to demonstrate the ratification system currently in play within their organization. If so, you may be limited to asking good questions about the negotiator's authority, but hopefully even that will reveal some information about how the final decisions will be made. In general, I try to separate questions about the other party's authority from questions about the ratification process in order to develop the clearest possible picture of what is happening, but it is not always possible. I don't consider an absence of information about the ratification system to be something that derails the process, but it is a warning to proceed in a prudent and strategic manner.

TAKEAWAYS

ORAL VERSUS WRITTEN MANDATES

1. Get it written — even if the mandate is delivered orally, send a written version for sign-off.
2. Be proactive — do not be shy to raise and settle all questions with your superior.
3. Press for clarity — include goals, time frame, authority and other details.

EXPECTATIONS AND STRATEGIC GOALS

4. Dream big — set high expectations and be ambitious in your goals.
5. Be realistic — you will lose credibility if your stated goals are unattainable.

RATIONALE

6. Fill in the picture — work to discover what the negotiation means to both parties.
7. Develop depth — understanding why your client wants the deal empowers you.
8. Know what success looks like — it will be partly built on the "why" of the negotiation.

GETTING AGREEMENT

9. Take the initiative — the mandate's power depends on how many interests it represents.
10. Build consensus — bring the stakeholders together to rank the priorities and align interests.

REPUTATION

11. Build your name — your ability to achieve success will be partly based on your character.

12. Don't compromise yourself — avoid tactics or drop a file that will stain your reputation.

13. Keep your word — you will become known as a trusted figure.

TIME FRAME

14. Know the limits — clarify minimum and maximum allowable time on both sides.

15. Break it down — plan in advance to acquire all resources and complete each stage.

DEADLINES

16. Be astute — design and establish deadlines that drive the process forward.

17. Confirm in writing — send an email to corroborate stages and dates with the other side.

AUTHORITY

18. Clarify your own approval level — there may be limits or conditions attached.

19. Raise the issue — share your level of authority and invite the other side to reciprocate.

20. Watch for evasion — you may not be dealing with someone empowered to resolve issues.

RATIFICATION SYSTEM

21. Pursue knowledge — ratification processes can be more or less layered and complex.

22. Start a dialogue — try to learn about the other side's approval structure.

CHAPTER 6
Communication

"It is better to keep your mouth shut and let people think you are a fool than to open it and remove all doubt."

— Mark Twain

When I took over as President and CEO of the Royal Canadian Mint in February 2003, my mandate was to increase revenues and address a variety of internal difficulties that were hampering profitability. Once I arrived, I began to see that one of the leading issues was a lack of commitment to building and sustaining relationships — with customers, government officials, the union, international contacts, suppliers and banks across the country. So one of my initial priorities was to help the entire organization alter its approach to relationships.

I began with my Leadership Council. These were highly capable members of the team in their various areas, but a handful had little or no capacity for — or interest in — building interpersonal relationships. These individuals rarely attended social events with union members, reached out to important contacts in the network or went out of their way to spend non-meeting time with people. The lack of skill in this area was hurting their performance and was having a detrimental effect on the team overall. So I met with these members several times to tutor them about why and how to approach relationships. I then used this process as a model for how everyone in the company would operate. I made it part of the Leadership Council's Terms of Reference (the official document that outlined the responsibilities of every employee) that they attend functions and have coffee or lunch with customers and other important stakeholders in our network on a regular basis.

Based on our interactions, those members of the Council were able to make a 180-degree turnaround in the way they related to people. As they improved in this area, their confidence grew, they made more effective use of social interactions and they saw the value of regular, ongoing casual communication. By making this part of their work an obligation, we begin a process that spread from a handful of people to the larger Leadership Council and then to the whole company. This was a key part of the turnaround at the Mint that saw revenues climb from $250 million to $350 million in eighteen months.

There were other initiatives that focused on relationship-building through open communication, and they too had a transformative effect. For example, I insisted — despite significant resistance from the senior management team — on having four union representatives added to the President's Leadership Team. While tough at times, having those members in the room for key conversations about the operations and strategic direction of the Mint created a shared view of where we were heading and how we would get there.

Perhaps the best example of how a strong commitment to regular, open and informal contact is helpful came with a new routine established around Friday lunch. I began a process of taking six to eight of the Mint employees out to lunch on my tab on a regular basis. We'd head out to a local restaurant and talk about whatever came up, which I made sure was a balance of personal lives and interests with the workplace and how it could be improved. My lunch mates were often blue-collar types — hard-working, straight-shooting people who pressed coins for a living. Their perspective on the revenue and expense issues and challenges the company was facing was always enlightening, and once they got over the initial hesitation about talking to the boss, there were frank discussions about what they thought, including pointed questions of me about why we were doing this or that.

As one of the lunches was wrapping up, a long-standing employee said to me, "You know, Mr. Dingwall, I'm the kind of guy who believes that you work your forty hours and take your pay and are thankful for having a job, but that isn't necessarily the way that everyone who works for you sees it." And then, after a look around, he leaned in, lowered his voice and said, "You might want to look into the overtime." Then he got up and left.

When I got back to the office, I began looking into it right away. Sure enough, the overtime was a huge mess and many employees were abusing it. And there was a widespread practice of management putting in for time off in lieu of overtime pay. As I got into it, I was able to make changes in the work ethic and the culture by addressing people's conception of the value of their work and the time they spent. By the time we issued the 2004 annual report, we were able to state that value-added sales revenue per employee was up 130 per cent and gross profit had risen by 32.1 per cent. These were changes that began with a commitment to communication and ongoing social interactions. I believe that engaging and authentic communication plus a willingness to act on what you hear can pay enormous dividends.

The importance of communication is more and more evident in normal business operations, especially with the instant interaction and "citizen reporting" that this era of social media has made possible. But it remains an area that most negotiators need to develop further. How you approach communication during your bargaining and deal making has a significant impact on your ability to accomplish your objectives, fulfill your mandate and accelerate your career. Strategic negotiators develop the skills, understanding and perspective to make considered and calculated choices about communication.

THREE FORUMS FOR COMMUNICATION

To begin thinking about how to approach communication strategically, be sure you are clear about the three forums and how they interrelate.

1. Internal communication within your own organization and team.

Depending on the size of the negotiation or the organization you are representing, it can be incredibly difficult to ensure effective, timely and collective communication about the issues at hand. The more you can get everyone on your side on the same page, and the more your approach reflects a shared view of the negotiation objectives and strategy, the more capable you will be of achieving the mandate. But when dealing with large groups, this is a challenge that requires you to be both relentless and creative about how you proceed. For example, I have dealt with complicated insurance arrangements where it was virtually impossible to get all of the relevant parties in a room at the same time. We had to use Skype, telephone-conferencing and email to create communication chains to keep everyone informed and up to date. Aside from organizational size, it can be incredibly difficult to get even your own people in the same room, and skilled use of time and written, oral and interactive communication is paramount.

2. Horizontal communication across the table with the other side.

At times, I find that negotiators pay careful attention to the *content* of their interactions with the other side but not enough to the *form* of those interactions. How you say something is as important as what you say, so take the time to be strategic about communication choices. Maurice Mazerolle specializes in negotiation and dispute resolution at the Ted Rogers School of Management and has several rules about communication. Based on his work, I consider the following to be key considerations for horizontal communication.

a) Rehearse your communication in advance. Too often, negotiators and their teams proceed to the table with a strong agreement about their position on various issues but without a clearly developed plan for how they will communicate their position. Commit to running a simulation that forces you to clarify and hone your approach to various topics. It is not enough to think, "I have to be organized in advance." Make sure you and your team do some trial runs so that anyone who speaks in the meetings is ideally positioned to succeed.

b) Choose a spokesperson in advance and support them throughout. Every negotiation team needs a spokesperson who is genuine, passionate and knowledgeable about the subject matter. Then, team members should work together to support the lead in identifying issues to communicate. Collaborative decisions such as what is asked for when, how much you will ask for and how issues will be framed are all very important, especially given the critical importance of avoiding outlandish demands or claims. Good negotiations are grounded in facts and realistic claims, and it takes a very careful team to make that happen. You also want to avoid situations where members on your side talk over each other or with crossed wires while at the table. A clear quarterback avoids much of the potential muddle, especially if there is no dispute about their authority and capability to lead.

c) Be concise. Sometimes, there is nothing more import-ant in a negotiation than cutting to the chase. Wasting time, wasting words and saying more than you ought can undermine your success. During your overall prep-arations, you will have developed clarity about your position on various issues. With that established, use your communication prep to construct the clear and precise language needed to articulate your position. All of the superb negotiators with whom I have worked are able to succinctly express the key issues during any part of a negotiation process. Ensure that any members of your team who will speak during meetings have the same capacity.

d) Always focus on the benefits to the other party. It is easy to fall into a mode of expressing your position and interests. While this is important, even if done bril-liantly, it creates distance from the other side because it is exclusively about you. I advise negotiators to focus on discussing shared areas of agreement as much as pos-sible and, in particular, the benefits to the other party of whatever you assert. Framing your position in terms of their benefit is a powerful way to move toward an agreement. Of course, the catch is that if you are off base when it comes to their interests — or if you are insincere or condescending — you will sound either ill-informed or manipulative. Part of your preparation should be a thorough understanding of their needs. And remember that if you are not completely clear about that, go ahead and ask how a particular position or outcome affects them. This is a courtesy that will build rapport.

e) Ask the other party to comment on their response to what you are saying. A powerful technique is to ask the other side point-blank how your message is being received and how it fits with their interests. If all you do is send out your message and then respond to their reply, you miss a valuable opportunity to find out what they think about what you are saying. Asking for a person's impressions of your comments and assertions is a way to show respect and build trust.

f) Be an attentive and careful listener or reader. One of Mazerolle's main rules is "listen more than you speak." I have already identified that being an active listener is a game-changing habit, but it is worth underlining here. Whenever reading or listening, be attentive to both what is and is not being said. At every stage of my career, I have found that listening attentively generates likeability, understanding and sincerity, all of which convey that you are working together toward a resolution rather than wrangling around each other. Being attentive means asking genuine questions, seeking clarification and restating what the other party has said. Another respectful and strategically advantageous way to listen is to take notes while the other party is making its case.

3. External communication with third parties such as regulatory agencies, government agencies and the media.
Communication with parties not directly involved in the negotiation but interested in the outcome can have a strong effect on the

process — in both negative and positive ways. At heart, this is an issue of trust, because what is said to the media or external regulators has to be consistent with what is said in the room. And more importantly, all of that communication has to present a fair, supportive and accurate picture of the other side. Working with the other side to develop a shared approach to communication with external parties is beneficial and gets you closer to your goal of an agreement. On the other hand, undirected and unplanned external communication opens you to unnecessary rifts and risks. And even when you are not operating with a mutual agreement about third-party communications, it is always preferable to be fair to the other side to avoid creating unnecessary conflict that adds to the complexity of the negotiation. Obviously, in highly public processes between major entities, there is the potential for a war of words in the media. But in those cases, your communication is still a planned and carefully orchestrated process.

AGENT-PRINCIPAL RELATIONSHIPS — A SPECIAL KIND OF COMMUNICATION

It is a normal practice for an agent to act on behalf of an individual or entity in negotiations, and it is often the case that the same representative will be used for a variety of negotiations over time in order to build a strong working relationship. In some instances, an agent may be a lobbyist, a lawyer or simply a subject expert. You may act as or encounter an agent when that is standard in the nature of the industry, such as residential real estate or professional sports. Regarding the world of hockey, Brian Burke once explained to me, "I think an agent acquires a place in the player's life that's almost comparable to being a family member. These guys will often ask their agent for advice before they ask their own dads because the agent has the expertise. It's a very important relationship, and teams should never try to damage that relationship. I always try to find a way for my players to think that I respect their agent, even if I might be having a difference with one of them. There are a lot of moving parts to win a championship and keep a team together, and treating the agents respectfully and not trying to get in between them and their player is one of them."

Watch the interview with Brian Burke at tinyurl.com/negotiating-burke-agents

A principal considers a variety of issues when selecting an agent to represent them in a negotiation. Each issue can only be addressed through open and ongoing communication, which is the responsibility of both the principal and the agent. If acting as an agent, the strategic negotiator wants a lot of candid conversation to take place before stepping into the role. Below are some issues to sort out together:

1.   Do you have an agenda of your own that will get mixed in with what the principal is trying to accomplish?

2.   What is your subject matter expertise and how does it help the principal's cause?

3.   What resources and relationships can the principal provide access to that are unavailable to you and would be useful?

4.   If the principal is more skilled or experienced as a negotiator than you are, how does their expertise alter your approach to decisions and conversations?

5.   How can you be used for strategic advantage to the principal — for instance, in a good cop/bad cop scenario to insulate the principal and protect their relationship with the principals on the other side?

6.   What impact will a decision to have a lawyer at the table have on the process if the principal decides to go that route?

7.   How much flexibility and freedom is the principal willing to allow you and how will the extent of your authority be decided and described?

8.   How will the other side be proceeding in terms of using an agent and how does that influence the principal's choices?

INVOLVEMENT IN MEETINGS

"You not only need to have constant dialogue, but you have the membership in the room so that they hear for themselves, form their own opinion, express their own views, ask questions of the other side and all the rest of it."

Watch the interview at tinyurl.com/negotiating-fehr-face-to-face

DONALD FEHR, Executive Director of the National Hockey League Players' Association and former Executive Director of the Major League Baseball Players Association

All of the considerations listed above illustrate how important good communication is between you as an agent and the principal. Maintaining ongoing contact means that any of the major obstacles that can muddle your approach to a negotiation can be resolved both in advance and whenever new issues and complications arise. For example, it is not abnormal for an agent's expertise and experience to create a situation where there is asymmetric information and the principal knows less than the agent, both about the subject matter and the nuances of negotiation. As a result, agents and principals need to be very careful about their approach to communication. I suggest you consider the following guidelines:

1.   Communicate as often as possible — more frequent, shorter interactions are better than long breaks and long meetings.

2.   Have a well-defined structure for communication and be clear about expectations for information flow right from the start.

3.   Candour is essential. The more that the agent and principal understand and trust each other, the better, which is why clients often work with the same lawyer for years.

4.   Ensure there is shared clarity about all of the major issues, objectives and interests. Any confusion for the principal, for the agent or between them will inevitably create problems.

5.   Develop the game plan and ensure it makes sense to both of you.

By definition, lawyer Carol Hansell always operates as an agent. This is how she approaches updating the principal — her client —

during a negotiation process: "One of the most important things, I think, is to communicate back to the client really promptly. They may be very anxious about the fact that I am now on the phone with the other side or that I had a meeting — and there is nothing that is more difficult for them than my going from that to two other meetings and updating them at the end of the day. Often what I work on is mission critical and matters a lot to the client, so getting back to them quickly is essential, if only to say 'I'm done and it went well' or 'What's your time frame; when can you be available for a call?' It is also important to be balanced in the reporting back about the tone of the conversation. In many cases, a negotiator can really enflame their principal by reporting back every sarcastic comment or every stray nuance of the discussion that was about the principal. Unless a detail is reflective of where the deal is going, it's not necessary to go through it. You really have to know how to frame the discussion."

Watch the interview with Carol Hansell at tinyurl.com/negotiating-hansell-agents

THE MESSAGE

Give serious consideration to your message so that the spokesperson and all other parties are consistent in what they communicate at all times. Discordant messages coming from various members of your team — or differences in what the agent and principal are saying — create no end of headaches and problems. This is where talking about the what and how of your approach to communication is as important as any other part of your preparation so that you can cover the impact you want your message to have, the tone and words you will use, the substance of the message in terms of the mandate, and how the message reflects the views of various team members. And as you work through those preparations and begin to communicate at the table, there are a handful of considerations irrespective of whether the issue is a matter of public policy, collective agreement, health and safety, the environment, corporate relations, commercial enterprises, family law or real estate:

1.   Is your message one of substance? You want to give the other side a comprehensive proposal in terms of what you are seeking. It is not wise to play games or waste time. When you speak, make sure it matters and is on the mark.

2.   Is your message delivered with passion? If you believe in what you are saying, you should say so eloquently, concisely and with a clear focus. Every part of a negotiation is an act of influence and people are swayed by commitment and vision.

3.   Is your body language aligned with what you want to say? If you can't look the other party in the eye, they will conclude you are not sincere or there is something else that you are angling for, which will undermine your credibility.

4.   Are you prepared to account for the demands you are making? Whatever you are seeking, you need to have a justifiable rationale that includes supporting data such as reference to a precedent, a market force, a market study or an industry-associated standard. You will no doubt expect that the other side provide a detailed justification of their demands to make them accountable, so you should do the same. Failure to be accountable can quickly impede the negotiating process.

A wonderful example of a negotiator preparing how to convey their core message and then executing the plan brilliantly comes from Bob Rae: "One of the best trial lawyers in Canada in the twentieth century was a man named John J. Robinette from McCarthy & McCarthy [now McCarthy Tetrault]. I once saw him present a case at the Supreme Court of Canada on the *Anti-Inflation Act*, which Prime Minister Trudeau brought in in 1976. I was a young law student acting on behalf of the United Steel Workers and was working on the file. On the province's side, it was all very technical about contracts and how the constitution worked. Mr. Robinette, who was arguing against the province, reached into his pocket, pulled out a dollar bill and held it up and said, 'My Lords, this is a dollar bill, and I see here that it is signed by the Governor and Deputy Governor. It's a Canadian bill. The Bank of Canada is a federal institution. This law is about protecting the value of the Canadian dollar. So it falls within federal jurisdiction.' He understood that when you are making an argument, you are really trying to focus on what the argument is about and you don't want to get it confused with a lot of other things."

Watch the interview with Bob Rae at tinyurl.com/negotiating-rae-message

Communicating the message is a skill that requires verbal clarity, tact and precision. A spokesperson who just likes to hear themselves talk is not the person who will move the mandate along.

TOOLS OF MESSAGING
Face-to-Face Meetings
For me, live meetings are by far the best form for delivering or receiving a message while also developing a relationship. There

is just no substitute for looking people in the eye and then taking in their reactions to your proposal or counterproposal. In an increasingly digital and fast-paced world, it can be difficult to justify and arrange live meetings, but do it whenever humanly possible so they can experience the tone, authenticity, passion and nuance that you want. Live interactions can be both genuine and strategic acts of influence at the same time. The give and take of live conversation is also ideal for allowing the two sides to ask questions or counter a position in immediate and accurate ways.

Many of the negotiation experts I know emphasize face-to-face meetings. Consider these comments from three of the best:

David Peterson: "I am completely a verbal guy. I don't like communicating in serious ways by email. I have seen email screw up more deals . . . and I have seen more people get mad over the written word. If you say something, it can pass in the wind sometimes. But if you write something down, people look at it and cogitate. I have seen a lot of mistakes. So I never negotiate by email on anything sensitive. I like talking face to face. I like understanding the person I am dealing with. I like to try and find their point of view. And I always try to find something in it for them because finding the mutuality of interests here is the key to these things."

Watch the interview with David Peterson at tinyurl.com/negotiating-peterson-contact

Chris Rudge: "I may be old-fashioned, but I still like a one-to-one discussion. When something is really important to me and someone says, 'I'll call you tomorrow morning at ten,' then I say, 'Where is your office, I'll come over and see you.' I'd rather sit one to one because so much is communicated in body language and eye contact like demonstrating you care and you really are listening. So I always opt for a face-to-face meeting, if I can. Barring that, I will talk to someone on the phone if I have to. And I use email and text simply for the perfunctory stuff — conveying information."

Watch the interview with Chris Rudge at tinyurl.com/negotiating-rudge-face-to-face

Brian Burke: "Face-to-face meetings are essential, I think. When I used to have a major player to sign, I would go and present the offer in person at the agent's office. I think that's critical, that level of respect. No one else does it. But I know that the agents and players all appreciate it. And I think it helps us get deals done."

Watch the interview with Brian Burke at tinyurl.com/negotiating-burke-face-to-face

Email

Of the various forms of electronic communication, email is most frequently used for negotiations because it permits a wide range of written interactions that can vary in length — in terms of the content and the time taken to respond — and allows a negotiator to be very detailed in a communication or response. It is naive to suggest that negotiators, their teams and other parties ought to avoid email, but there are particular benefits and limitations of this form. In my practice, I use emails extensively for forming agendas, scheduling meetings, communicating simple messages and seeking information about the subject matter.

There are numerous benefits of email: convenience when parties are at a distance; time to consider the next move; a clear record of proposals; ease in conveying large amounts of data to back up your proposals and counterproposals and the power to quickly mobilize large coalitions of like-minded people via group distribution lists. There are also challenges. For instance, it can increase the risk of an impasse because most emails come across as more aggressive in tone than the spoken word. There is also the potential for careless clicking when sitting in front of the computer screen if people lose track of the fact that a message can be forwarded and shared easily. In general, if careful attention is not given to the content and the style of an email, there is a risk of major misunderstandings amongst the parties.

Essentially, your task is to be strategic about your use of email. Put some thought into when it is most and least effective. Never forget that you have no control over where a message is forwarded and that tone is very easy to misinterpret. It is most useful for communicating very specific information and for quick, low-stakes communications that expedite the process and help keep parties connected. Here's how Leonard Asper and Carol Hansell explain their approach to email:

Leonard Asper: "I use email so that my points are clear. For example, if you are dealing with a person who interrupts a lot, it can be helpful to write a nice, long, clear email that outlines what you are trying to say. In general, I find email really useful when you need to make points, especially if you expect them to come up again and again in the conversation. In that case, you want to have a record. In a lot of cases, you want to build a record of what you are saying and what they are saying. Then, when it comes to getting things done, I usually reach out and get in touch for a discussion."

Watch the interview with Leonard Asper at tinyurl.com/negotiating-asper-email

Carol Hansell: "Email is so helpful because it is quick and it is contained. It doesn't seem like much to pick up the phone and call and do all the social conversation that happens before you get to the substance of the call, but it is time consuming. Email keeps things moving, keeps people up to date and creates a record of things so they can go back and look at what I said to them and I can remember what I said to them. That is helpful. Email is problematic, obviously, because it is flat, subject to misinterpretation and if you are being quick about it, people can sometimes be offended. But if you are careful, it can be very helpful in making sure you are all on the same page."

Watch the interview with Carol Hansell at tinyurl.com/negotiating-hansell-email

Telephone

Phone calls are an excellent middle ground between electronic communication and live meetings. Devise a system for keeping a record of calls made to the other side and what has been discussed. And be careful about your tone because in this format, the tone of voice is the only non-linguistic evidence of your intent. As with any other part of the process, make sure you prepare for calls, especially if you are at a complex stage in the negotiations.

Be clear about your priorities as they pertain to your mandate and your specific goals of the current stage before you engage in a phone conversation or meeting. If you enter into a call without a plan and assume you can sort out your priorities as you go along, you are likely to be ineffective and miss something. A plan is especially important because telephone negotiations are much shorter than face-to-face sessions and involve far less socializing time during which you can gather your thoughts.

Under the heading of doing the little things well, it's best to have needed materials at hand — such as documents, a calculator or online resources — and not be interrupted by staff or another phone ringing. Little things make a difference to the tenor and flow of calls. Also, make careful decisions about the use of a speakerphone. It may be necessary at times, but a speakerphone conversation is not as fluid and clear as a handheld, and that loss of call quality has an effect because tone of voice matters so much on a call. During any call, take notes about what has been said and agreed to. Often, I send an email shortly after a call to confirm the content and any commitments, including timeline agreements.

The Letter

There are numerous instances when negotiators write an offer, counteroffer or amendment and send it via a paper letter. My colleague Janice Payne, one of Canada's top labour lawyers, uses letters extensively. She begins by expressing her mandate and the key issues to her own client in a letter following an extensive interview. Then, she turns her attention to the other side. "In my practice, it is very rare that I wouldn't set out my client's position in a letter. It does not need to go on for pages and pages, but you need to let the other side know where you are coming from and what matters to you and why. And I am often talking to the client on the other side when I am writing a letter so that they understand. I might, perhaps, push buttons that I know will be meaningful to that client. Until you do that and give the client on the other side something to bite on or maybe even worry about, it can be difficult to get a good negotiation going."

Watch the interview with Janice Payne at tinyurl.com/negotiating-payne-letter

By using letters as she does, Payne pushes all sides to clarify outstanding items after the initial discussions to ensure there is a shared and solid understanding from the beginning.

The Media
Depending on the nature of the negotiation, it is possible that the press will be very interested in what is going on — maybe because you or your client are high profile or because the nature of the dispute or deal is newsworthy. In these situations, I always advise negotiators to proceed carefully and not to engage in media relations unless they are, first, very clear about what they are trying to accomplish and, second, have a strong understanding of the priorities and emphases that members of the media bring to the interactions. I have seen several situations in which public

relations firms have been engaged to help negotiators navigate the complexities of speaking with the media, but it is also interesting to hear various views from experienced negotiators.

Janice Payne: "You cannot manage the media. I do not — just about never — try to use the media. I can think of less than a handful of occasions where I have felt that the media might be helpful. Sometimes I have had a client who is high profile — perhaps even with a journalistic background of some kind — who really can use the media and knows what he or she is doing, and as long as I am talked to in that process and things don't get wildly out of hand, I cope. But it is rare that the media is helpful to advance a particular case. The media wants a story. They want the fight. And sometimes it is better not to fan the flames by saying anything and the story goes away. It varies, but if there is one thing that I have learned, it's that you can't manage them."

Watch the interview with Janice Payne at tinyurl.com/negotiating-payne-media

Buzz Hargrove: "I was the national leader of a union that, at its peak, had 265,000 members. The bulk of the auto industry employees are in Ontario, but if you look at the airline industry and the rail industry and others, they are spread right across the country. You have to recognize that probably 30 per cent of our members will read email, but if you communicate through the media, most of them will get the message. So the only way that I could communicate on a direct basis was through the national media. The national media used me to get a story and I used them to get my story out. I worked very hard at it. When I announced on July 12, 2008, that

I was leaving the union, the first thing that happened was that my phone quit ringing. What a shock for me. That cell phone or my home phone used to start at 5:30 a.m. It would start in Newfoundland and Labrador and then Halifax and then across the country and I would end up at nine, ten, eleven at night speaking to media on the West Coast. I didn't realize how much I was doing until all of a sudden it stopped. I used the media — especially in major bargaining — but there are a lot of company people who don't like the exposure of the media and would not open the door and allow the cameras in to take a shot of the bargaining before it started. You have to know that going in, because you don't want to start with a fight about what they would call a media circus and what I called communication with the members and the broader public."

Watch the interview with Buzz Hargrove at tinyurl.com/negotiating-hargrove-media

Marie Bountrogianni (Dean of the Chang School of Continuing Education at Ryerson University and former President and Executive Director of ROM Board of Governors): "First, know your stuff. Know your facts. Do your homework. In other words, if you are going to be interviewed on a topic, do your research. Particularly if it is a new topic. Second, try and personalize it . . . Have a personal story to share. For example, when we were announcing the disability measure for the Royal Ontario Museum, we had people with disabilities come and be part of the event so that the media could see in a straightforward way how our changes affected people. At the Chang School, when I speak to the media, there are always students that the media can speak to or other colleagues from the university. Third, always be accessible. People who avoid the media, particularly with a controversial topic, are making a mistake. By speaking with them, you at least have the opportunity to give your side and your opinion. A good journalist will post that. They may only include it as 1 per cent of the column, but they will post it. And that's your only opportunity. Rebuttals are secondary. You have to be there from the beginning."

Watch the interview with Marie Bountrogianni at tinyurl.com/negotiating-bountro-media

Social Media

Advancements in social media have revolutionized communication and can have an enormous impact on the negotiating process, such as during the revolution in Egypt, which gained momentum from a Facebook page with photos of an Egyptian businessman who was beaten to death by police officers. With this barbaric act visible, more examples began to pop up from all over the country, and the world paid attention in real time on computers and mobile phones. Eventually, the Egyptian government was overturned based on the momentum created through social media, which had led other governments throughout the world to condemn Egypt for its brutal methods.

During a negotiation process, anyone involved can tweet, like or post at any time, and those public pronouncements can alter private negotiations. The effect is so widespread that most publicly traded companies have taken steps to move beyond merely keeping a close eye on what analysts are saying about them to tracking what bloggers of all shapes and sizes are posting. This is an especially relevant consideration because the general public can be relatively undiscerning about the source of available information.

It is wise to manage how your side uses social media to influence the outcome of the process. Negotiators need to be sensitive about posting anything at all, as this can be high risk, particularly if information sent turns out to be inaccurate. Social media can also expose divisions within your team when various members say different things because they have not coordinated their message.

Just as professional sports teams have developed guidelines for the use of social media, negotiators must not leave anything to chance. Only use social media to your advantage. Two examples of the use of Twitter as a form of influence — one intentional and the other inadvertent — come to us from the realm of professional sports negotiations.

The first happened in 2011 when Eric Winston, President of the National Football League Players Association and a former right tackle with the Houston Texans, joined the social media frenzy during the NFL collective bargaining talks. Winston used his Twitter account to chastise the NFL owners regarding their positions on the collective bargaining. Then many of his colleagues joined in and tweeted similar views. Their attempt was to build public support for the players' position. Winston was intentional about his communication and used the form to put pressure on the owners.

The unintentional example is simpler and singular. David Andrews, the President of the American Hockey League, was sitting at home one night watching an NHL game and took to Twitter. He explains, "I was frustrated watching NBC coverage of the NHL playoffs and the commentators ignoring the fact — almost it seemed purposely ignoring the fact — that a player had come up from the American Hockey League. They would give the background of the player and where he played junior or college and where he was born and what his mum's name was, but the fact that the player had been for the past three months playing in the

AHL and was just recalled — we didn't seem to be getting our due. At that point, I was an active Twitter guy and had lots of followers. I tweeted something to the effect of 'Is it possible that NBC Sports and Pierre McGuire are almost intentionally not mentioning the AHL? It would have to be intentional for this to go on game after game.' Well, it was retweeted I don't know how many million times. It ended up being effective in a way because it did make a difference going forward, but it really irritated some very powerful people at NBC. And though it didn't irritate Gary Bettman, he was aware of it and I heard about it because that is the NHL's media partner. That situation had some positive effect, but I had not intended for that sort of exposure, so it is a lesson in the way that you have no control over what happens with social media."

Watch the interview with David Andrews at tinyurl.com/negotiating-andrews-media

Visuals

Always keep in mind what Harry Mills in his book *Artful Persuasion* says about learning (which is what the other side is doing when they listen to your case): visuals make up 75 per cent of the learning process, hearing is 13 per cent, and smelling, taste and touch combined are 12 per cent. You don't need a visual with everything you present at every meeting, but a properly prepared and accurate visual representation or image can be very powerful, especially if you begin by explaining your position and then proceed to a visual to support what you are saying. All visuals should be clear, in a font that is easy to read, in colour and, where possible, use graphics. Avoid starting with a visual because people tend not to listen to what you are saying while processing what you are showing them. The eyes trump the ears. Talk first, then illustrate, or you may mangle a golden opportunity to communicate.

MIXING IN-PERSON MEETINGS WITH ELECTRONIC COMMUNICATION

"Meeting in small groups is really important because what you learn by the interaction and conversation is much more than you could ever learn by seeing a videotape or listening to a lecture or reading a memo. You have to communicate with the players in a way that the players appreciate and will actually respond to. Twenty years ago, if you said there is going to be a device in your pocket and you should read it when it dings, people would have thought you were from Mars, but that is what this generation of players do. So we developed a strategy for email and smartphone applications and we would send out information that way. It gives you the ability to reach large numbers of your membership very quickly. One of the benefits of having your members in the bargaining meeting is that they can leave the meetings, pick up the phone and call the other guys. Players talking to players is a method of communication which in almost every situation is preferable to lawyers talking to players."

Watch the interview at tinyurl.com/negotiating-fehr-communication

DONALD FEHR, Executive Director of the National Hockey League Players' Association and former Executive Director of the Major League Baseball Players Association

BODY LANGUAGE — ACTIONS SPEAK LOUDER THAN WORDS

I have already emphasized the importance of behaviour and attitude in interactions with the other side, and non-verbal communication is an integral part of that process. In a superb little book entitled *The Charisma Factor*, Robert Richardson and S. Katharine Thayer address the importance of non-verbal communications by using the triangle pictured here to show that our words account for approximately 7 per cent of our message while our tone accounts for 38 per cent and body language is the remaining 55 per cent. This doesn't mean that words and tone are irrelevant to communication, but it underlines how much we all have to pay attention to body language. It is best to align all three forms of expression in all interactions.

We have all come across conversations where people say one thing but their gestures indicate something totally different. What they say is not what they mean. Good negotiators see the value of body language and use it. Carol Hansell describes it this way: "Even though a lot of the offices of people I work with are very close by in the downtown core, a lot of meetings are conducted by phone. I think it's important to go over to the client's office or have them come to yours. If we are on a conference call, particularly when the other side is on the line, it's critical to see the client's body language. To see whether they are engaged, to see whether they are reacting to the conversation, to see whether I need to step in. I prefer the in-person because the back and forth that is possible live is so much easier than if we are on the phone. It's a much more effective way to talk to somebody than if you are doing it on the phone."

Watch the interview with Carol Hansell at tinyurl.com/negotiating-hansell-gestures

The strategic negotiator is careful about what they do with their body when speaking or listening. Looking away, speaking without making eye contact, rolling eyes, eyes glazing over, raising an eyebrow or looking intently at a person are all taken as indications of how you feel about the exchange. And there can be various interpretations of our visible actions that we don't intend

A Communication Perspective

See: *The Charisma Factor: How to Develop Your Natural Leadership Ability*
Robert J. Richardson & S. Katharine Thayer

but that send strong signals. For example, it has been brought to my attention on several occasions that, when speaking in public, I have a tendency to talk out of one side of my mouth. It came to light that audiences were annoyed by this signal because they felt it indicated that I didn't really care about them or my subject matter. They assumed it was like the old saying — those who speak out of one side of the mouth may perhaps speak out of the other at a different time. It conveys inconstancy and even deception. So I attempted over the years to address this.

The key is to assess and understand your own mannerisms and then work at knowing which actions convey the messages you want. For example, how do you sit in a chair? Upright, sideways, lounging? Does your approach convey preparedness, a laid-back attitude, superiority? These are all real considerations — especially with people who don't know you well and can only infer from your physical expression. Even something as simple as your demeanour during a handshake can speak volumes about your intentions. Are you frowning and cool or open and receptive? If cool, it is likely that the other person will respond to that rather than your spoken message. As with visual presentations during a meeting, your body as a "picture" trumps your words. Offer a firm (but not crushing) handshake, make eye contact and smile. You will be received well.

THE MAGIC OF LIVE MEETINGS

"Mediation is actually a way of seeing the impact of a live meeting, because the parties always arrive in the same room with a gap — sometimes a very big gap — and a very different view of the facts that have brought them to the table. Looking across the table at each other, talking to each other directly or through the lawyers, really does have an almost magical effect in terms of changing ideas on both sides of the table."

Watch the interview at tinyurl.com/negotiating-payne-face-to-face

JANICE PAYNE, leading labour lawyer and partner at Nelligan O'Brien Payne LLP

As technology has come to define more and more business processes, we participate in virtual meetings such as conference calls where we can hear what is being said without seeing body language. All the research tells us that this is disorienting. I have mentioned already that conference calls run the risk of misunderstandings. If they are a necessity, limit them to less important items and arrange for a live meeting on the substantive issues. Without the flow of live interactions, extended calls can lead to muddles. With no visual cues, it is easy to lose track of people. Videoconferencing, such as Skype, can help a bit with meetings across distances but have similar limitations to conference calls.

Compare two Democratic Presidents when it comes to body language: Clinton and Obama. Obama has a reputation (accurate or not) for being closed, reserved and not engaging. Clinton has a reputation (ditto) for being open, warm, approachable and engaged. This impression comes, in large part, from the way they handle themselves physically. Clinton sits back or stands with his body open, uses his arms to communicate, smiles as he speaks and expresses his ideas in warm Southern tones. Obama tends to use short gestures, stand or sit with a tight body posture and have a serious look on his face. We know that President Obama can be quite funny and engaging and that he is an excellent public speaker. But his body expressions send particular messages to the audience that have contributed to his reputation.

OTHER COMMUNICATION CONSIDERATIONS
Emotions

I've already talked extensively about body language, which has the benefit and disadvantage of expressing your emotions. You need to know how you come across physically. But in addition, great negotiators are aware of their emotional state: they don't take things personally, they manage emotions carefully by slowing down the speed of their remarks, speaking sincerely and frankly, and they choose their words carefully. This is an idea that many negotiators emphasize.

Bob Rae: "Conflict is a normal part of life and it is a part of everything we do. Often times, as Canadians, we talk about trying to resolve conflict, but I think it is more about managing conflict. And one of the things that you have to do is to avoid taking things personally — which is very difficult to do. A lot of times in a discussion, somebody will say something horrible because they are trying to assert their position and you can make the mistake of taking it very personally. Asserting yourself is natural and good — but only up to a point."

Watch the interview with Bob Rae at tinyurl.com/negotiating-rae-emotions

Gary Corbett (President and CEO of the Professional Institute of the Public Service of Canada): "I have been in many negotiations where emotions were high and people needed to vent. And then once the emotion is out of it, we can get on with looking at the issues. Sometimes there is very colourful language behind closed doors or even with the other side. Tough exchanges can take place, but you can never take it personally. It's not personal. It's fact based. You sit across the table from somebody and you can be a tough negotiator and then afterward you can go for a beer."

Watch the interview with Gary Corbett at tinyurl.com/negotiating-corbett-emotions

Impact of Words

The specific words used in any negotiation make an impact. If you use jargon or a specialized vocabulary, that should only be because it's best for the particular situation and listener. Even being mindful of the fact that language changes over time can be helpful, such as the way that "purchasing" replaced "buying" and then became "procurement" and now "strategic sourcing" is commonly used. Complex vocabulary and phrasing should usually be avoided, even if you have a sophisticated vocabulary and it comes easily to you. In my experience, the more concise and direct your language, the better. Long, multi-part sentences and complex phrases tend to create distance. Sometimes, a person will use fancy diction and phrasing in an attempt to intimidate you. Or they will try to impress, even when they evidently don't know what they are saying. In all cases, I encourage you to focus on your most important objective: to achieve clarity of communication. And, if you are not clear about what someone is saying when outlining their position, make sure you ask in the moment rather than assume you know what they mean. It is very hard to do that later on.

One last consideration is to be careful about language that might offend members in the room. One potential area for offense today is that some people are more comfortable than others with language considered in various circles to be profanity. Make choices that suit the audience and context. If you are at all unsure, take a conservative approach. I would also suggest that you avoid the use of acronyms, which can cause offense when they are received as jargon. Don't assume that everyone in the room — including members of your own team — are familiar with various acronyms and their definitions. If you use them, you risk coming across as lazy at best and distant or elitist at worst.

Authenticity

As I have said about the entire negotiation process, authenticity and integrity are important considerations for influencing the other side and building a strong relationship. This also applies to communication, and I strongly advise a sincere, open, direct and honest approach to every interaction. The best way to demonstrate authenticity is to be very well briefed on the subject matter and to present it in a formidable, concise and passionate manner. And even if you think your presentation skills are superb and your intellect and knowledge of the subject will carry the day, you still need to practise, practise, practise. Authenticity isn't about "being yourself" or "being nice." It's about being prepared, consistent and doing what you say you will do. If no one ever doubts that your word is your bond, then you have authenticity.

Focused Listening

I discussed active listening in chapter 3 and I am mentioning it again briefly here because it is the backbone of effective communication. Sometimes, saying nothing speaks volumes, and *how* you say nothing conveys even more. Everyone wants to be heard and they want a listener who is focused and engaged. There is a big difference between "just" listening and openly illustrating how attentive you are. Active listening provides a strategic advantage from both an influence and a content perspective. People feel good about you — and you don't miss a thing. But don't offer a

189

series of gestures that are a hollow performance. Being genuinely curious lies at the heart of focusing and builds rapport, mutual understanding and respect. Use the honest techniques of active listening: eye contact, nodding your head, seeking clarification and summarizing the information that has been forthcoming. Some people argue that they can fake interest in the other side. I have not met too many successful people who use this tactic.

Visualization in Advance of Meetings
Athletes are well known for using visualizations to help them prepare for competition, and I am a believer in this approach for negotiators. Whether you rehearse the scene in your head while walking your dog or in a meeting with colleagues, work toward a clear picture. Practising and seeing a clear image of how the meeting will go sets you up to execute your plan in real time. You also create a positive affirmation loop for yourself that builds confidence as you envision what success looks like. Far from empty affirmations, seeing yourself succeed is a key way to ensure that you do. Visualize yourself delivering the message, and you will be on your way to doing it well.

Breathing
It is a simple but effective technique for preparing yourself for a negotiating session: take a moment or two beforehand to do a few deep breathing exercises. Deep breathing has been shown to lower stress and improve focus. Releasing tension sets you up for an open and engaged dialogue. A negotiator shares much with a competitive athlete or public speaker, so part of your routine as you prepare yourself for negotiations, presentations and important meetings should be deep breathing.

TAKEAWAYS

THREE FORUMS FOR COMMUNICATION

1. Internal — ensure that all parties on your side receive effective information and timely updates.
2. Horizontal — rehearse in advance, use a spokesperson, be concise and attentive, focus on benefits.
3. External — work with the other side for a consistent message for the media and other third parties.

THE AGENT-PRINCIPAL RELATIONSHIP

4. Open the channels — working as an agent requires early and ongoing dialogue with the principal.
5. Make time — frequent, shorter interactions are better than long breaks and long meetings.
6. Build a structure — devise the communication system for optimal information flow.
7. Be candid — honesty leads to mutual understanding and trust.
8. Create clarity — all issues, objectives and interests should be equally known and shared.
9. Develop a game plan — it should make sense to both of you.

THE MESSAGE

10. Be consistent — your spokesperson and other parties on your side should speak with one voice.
11. Have substance — offer real content connected to your mandate and goals.
12. Find your passion — believe in what you are saying and convey your conviction.
13. Support it physically — align your body language and look your listener in the eye.

14. Be accountable — support your demands with the necessary details and data.

TOOLS OF MESSAGING

15. Do it live — face-to-face meetings are best for communicating and building relationships.
16. Hit send — email is best when you need to write it down or manage logistics.
17. Make a call — pay attention to tone of voice and keep written records of all phone calls.
18. Write a letter — offers, counteroffers and amendments are often conveyed on paper.
19. Address the press — only deal with the media directly if you are both clear and experienced.
20. Go social — your side should be consistent and only tweet/post to your advantage.
21. Paint a picture — explain your position first then offer a high-impact visual as support.

BODY LANGUAGE

22. Embody your message — body language communicates 55 per cent of our meaning.
23. Send the right signal — avoid looking away, rolling your eyes, tapping your fingers impatiently.
24. Posture speaks — it can convey preparedness, a laid-back attitude or superiority.
25. Limit conference calls — without body language, it's easy to misunderstand.

OTHER COMMUNICATION CONSIDERATIONS

26. Develop awareness — tune in to your emotions and don't take things personally.

27. Choose your words — avoid fancy diction and showing off — your goal is clarity.
28. Be authentic — adopt a sincere and direct approach and do what you say you will do. Listen carefully — never underestimate the power of active listening.
29. Visualize and breathe deeply — borrow techniques from athletes to raise your game.

CHAPTER 7
The Set-Up

"Trust is enhanced if a negotiator can demonstrate a genuine interest in trying to help the other side reach its objectives while retaining his own objective and making the two appear compatible."

— William Zartman and Maureen Berman,
The Practical Negotiator

I had never been so glad for a snowstorm in my life. It was February 1980, and after a short period of time working as a lawyer I had won the nomination of the Liberal Party to run for election as the federal Member of Parliament for the Cape Breton–East Richmond constituency. I'd never been involved in an election campaign, let alone one that took place in the heart of an Atlantic winter. It was an invigorating exercise, but the weather made it a particular kind of challenge.

Early in February, my team and I had learned that the former (and future) Prime Minister Pierre Elliott Trudeau and his senior team, including my mentor Allan J. MacEachen, would be making a stop in my electoral district. This was a huge opportunity for my campaign. Though the peak of "Trudeaumania" was behind us, the nation was intrigued and enthusiastic when Trudeau reversed his decision to retire and committed to leading the Liberals after Prime Minister Joe Clark's Conservative minority was forced into an election by a vote of non-confidence.

The party organized an event with about one thousand people in attendance, many of whom had never seen me in the flesh. As the hosting candidate, I was responsible for giving the opening remarks and introducing Trudeau. I was twenty-seven at the time and had grown up watching Trudeau run the country and become an international personality. For me, it was a daunting task. When the harsh weather rolled in the day of the event and made campaigning impossible, I was relieved to stay home to prepare my remarks. I'll never forget standing in our family room facing the blank TV screen with my cue cards laid out on the ironing board in front of me. Over and over again, I rehearsed and revised my remarks, recording the time and working to condense them to a little over three minutes.

Sometime in the middle of the afternoon, my wife came into the room and listened to a complete run-through of my speech. When I was finished, I saw a look on her face that told me all I needed to know: boring and long-winded — juice it up! So I worked and reworked the remarks about twenty-five times, with no shortage of self-recrimination, until I had a sense of something worth listening to and the seal of approval from my biggest support and most honest critic. With cue cards in my jacket pocket, I headed off to the most important three minutes of my public life to that point.

After the various duties of hosting were out of the way, I was moved into position to deliver my remarks. The room was buzzing with energy. It was quite an event for a small community like Cape Breton to have access to a politician of Trudeau's stature. Working hard to concentrate on the passion and focus I had rehearsed with my ironing board, I spoke with enthusiasm and roused the crowd into a standing ovation to welcome Trudeau.

Arriving at the podium with the mix of poise and flair that always defined his public style, Trudeau quieted the crowd. When he thanked me for my introduction, he used the phrase "great orator" to describe me. The label was so powerful that

Mike Duffy (who has since gone on to be famous for all the wrong reasons but was just a junior journalist at the time) reported on the nightly news that "a young orator named David Dingwall moved the crowd here." At the end of the campaign, I was elected by a fairly slim margin, and I am certain that Trudeau's choice of phrase played a role in putting me over the top. I was left pleased and proud to have taken the time to prepare my remarks so carefully.

Twenty-eight years later, I learned something else about that night on the topic of planning in advance. I was attending an event in Ottawa in honour of Jean Chrétien and had occasion to sit down with former Premier of Newfoundland Brian Tobin. While we waited for the entrée to arrive, we got to telling stories and I recounted the public speaking event that had been so important in my election campaign. No sooner had the word "orator" come out of my mouth than Tobin interrupted by exclaiming "are you kidding?!" Trudeau had attended an event during Tobin's election to the House and had said exactly the same thing about him. A master politician, Trudeau had all the tricks he needed to win an election, which is essentially a long and complex negotiation.

This is not a book about politics, but the strategic negotiator can learn a few things from a former prime minister about foreseeing moments of influence in the negotiation process and doing some forward thinking. From due diligence and information gathering to planning out the smallest details, look ahead and decide how you will proceed.

UNDERSTAND THE SUBJECT MATTER AND THE NATURE OF THE DEAL

"One reality of negotiations that deal with technology is that everybody in the room understands what you are talking about, because it is technical, but when it goes up one more layer into the business organization, nobody in the business understands it."

Watch the interview with Paul Zed at tinyurl.com/negotiating-zed-understanding

That's how Paul Zed, President and CEO of Rogers Communications Canada, describes the nature of negotiations in his highly technical industry. His observation points to the importance of understanding the subject of the negotiation and how negotiations in any particular industry will unfold.

THE QUALITIES OF A GREAT NEGOTIATOR

"One of the best negotiators that I have ever met was Sheldon Levy [President of Ryerson University]. He had each and every one of us in his office when we were ministers. He would tell us not only the needs of his university but the needs of universities in general. By making it about the bigger picture and making it about society and then also about Ryerson, he was very successful in establishing a very trustworthy relationship with the Ontario government. He was also a straight shooter, a great communicator and a down-to-earth person."

Watch the interview at tinyurl.com/negotiating-bountro-qualities

MARIE BOUNTROGIANNI, Dean of the Chang School of Continuing Education at Ryerson University and former Member of Provincial Parliament

It may be obvious but it is worth saying that your preparations should include acquiring a thorough understanding of the subject matter. A negotiation can vary widely depending on whether you are dealing with, for example, a product, service, policy or commercial agreement. You can't enter into a negotiation about a particular aspect of a medical device, for example, and not understand the impact it can have on an individual or the healthcare system. Expertise in the subject matter is a strategic advantage and includes knowing the facts of a situation, the history of the file, the issues in play, the risks and the regulator's perspective, if that is relevant to the subject. It is also useful to access the various checklists readily available on the Internet in areas such as real estate purchases, mining acquisitions, shareholder disputes or the purchase and sale of products and services.

In addition to doing your homework on the subject matter, it is helpful to understand the type of deal you are working on and the way that deals are created in different contexts. In general, I think there are two ways that deals are reached: inductive and deductive. An inductive deal is put together piecemeal and built primarily through mutual compromise or exchange of concessions on specific items. A deductive deal is achieved by establishing the general principles or formula governing the issues and then working out the implementation of details. As a general rule, international negotiations tend to follow a deductive process while commercial, corporate, collective bargaining, family or other forms of domestic negotiations tend to use the inductive method much more often.

UNDERSTAND THE ENTITY THAT IS THE FOCUS OF YOUR NEGOTIATION
Ed Clark describes the process that TD Bank uses to assess an acquisition target: "Everybody that is on the other side of a deal with us would say they have never seen the kind of due diligence that we do. We would typically, even in small acquisitions, have

one hundred to two hundred people involved. So we try to make sure that we have the best person in the bank on that part of the due diligence and we go through a process at the end where there is a large meeting — often with two hundred people on the call — and every single person goes through all of their items and they opine whether what they have seen would cause them to do the deal or not do the deal. And we have our internal Head of Audit audit the due diligence and certify to the Board that we have not changed the due diligence process since previous acquisitions so that the Board is comforted that we are not somehow short-changing the challenge function as we do acquisitions."

Watch the interview with Ed Clark at tinyurl.com/negotiating-clark-understand

To effectively negotiate for or with an entity and to tailor your proposals and counteroffers appropriately, learn as much as possible about the organization. This can be challenging with privately held organizations (compared to public entities with a wide range of available data), but do what you can. Start by sorting out the nature of the company (wholesaler? manufacturing? service?) and determine who the customers and suppliers are. Then search for information about the industry and attempt to place the company relative to its peers. In some cases, such as a firm that belongs to a pharmaceutical or environmental association, there is generally free information available about the member companies and the issues of concern to the industry association.

Investigate the company in any way you can. Remember that with publicly traded companies, you can access the work of well-educated marketplace analysts who have a comprehensive perspective on the company and the industry. They are also generally happy to respond to questions you may have once you have read their reports. Spend some time looking at the organizational chart to see how the sales managers, directors or VPs relate to each other. And call people you know. "Having a personal relationship with people makes all the difference," explains Ralph Lean. "My clients know that my network of contacts can be valuable to the whole process because I have been able to gather information that other people couldn't get because I have a network of people to call."

Watch the interview with Ralph Lean at tinyurl.com/negotiating-lean-understanding

Collecting financial information about the company is also important. This can be hard for a privately held firm, but you can at least get a sense of its financial structure and health, and you can ask the other party to provide you with information, if they are representing the entity under negotiation. Even the basic financial statements can be useful. An income statement shows the relationship between revenue and expenses and illustrates if the firm translated revenues into net income or profit. A balance sheet offers a snapshot of the assets, liabilities and equity in the company so that you can understand the debt situation, shelf life of various assets and percentage of the company that is owned by the firm. And the statement of cash flow reveals the company's operating, investing and financial activities. The statement of cash flow is also useful in determining short-term viability and, in particular, the company's ability to pay its bills. You can also read the management team's discussion of these statements to develop a clearer sense of how the firm perceives itself.

FIGURING OUT WHERE YOU ARE HEADED

"When I was working on the Greater Toronto: Report of the GTA Task Force in 1996 for the provincial government on the future of the Toronto area, I had four brilliant task force members that I had invited. We had Robert Prichard, President of the University of Toronto, Jack Diamond, who is a world-class architect, Dr. Joseph Wong, a community physician, and Tom McCormack, an economist. I knew that you have to know where you are going or you won't get there. Like the Alice in Wonderland quote: 'If you don't know where you are going, any road will take you there.'

"So I asked these very busy, talented and brilliant people if they would come away for the weekend. We met in a motel in Oshawa and talked about the vision. Then at the end of the exercise, I asked each of them to go into a room for an hour and write the outline of the Report — not what the recommendations would be, but the outline — and we all came back in the room and shared our outline. We were off just by one chapter."

Watch the interview at tinyurl.com/negotiating-golden-vision

ANNE GOLDEN, former President and CEO of The Conference Board of Canada

Once you understand the financial situation, it is often worthwhile to perform a SWOT analysis on the company you are trying to buy or do business with to determine how robust the operations and possibilities are. As mentioned earlier, SWOT stands for strengths, weaknesses, opportunities and threats. This analysis helps to avoid being hoodwinked by news releases and public relations events. It is also a path toward understanding the overall negotiation strategy of the other side. For example, what are the key factors for their competitive success and their greatest industry opportunities? What are the potential obstacles and pitfalls they will face in the near- and long-term future? And how do their strengths and weaknesses compare to current and potential competitors? You may have to make some initial assumptions and then fill in gaps as you proceed by asking the other side (if that's your target company) for some data.

With a basic understanding of the organization under consideration, you could also seek other forms of information:

1.   The most recent auditor's report

2.   Compound annual growth rate (CAGR)

3.   The certificate of the CEO/CFO (if the entity is a publicly traded company)

4.   Press releases

5.   Accounts receivable and accounts payable over a three-year cycle

6.   How the company defines materiality in its financial statements

7. Any revenue manipulation or off-balance-sheet liabilities

8. Weaknesses in the effectiveness of internal controls

9. Benchmarks and industry association reports

10. In a merger or acquisition, the makeup of the special board committee, valuations, shareholder rights plans and change of control provisions

11. Background checks on some of the principals

12. Social media reports

13. Special audit reports

14. A value curve analysis of the company versus competitors

15. Key performance guidelines for CEOs and senior executives such as company results, key initiatives for the year and key responsibilities

16. Compensation for senior executives in terms of base salary, annual incentives, long-term incentives, benefits and perks

UNDERSTAND THE OTHER NEGOTIATING TEAM

"The first thing you have to realize before you enter into any negotiation is that you have to understand the people you are negotiating with," explains Michael Cleaner. "You need to get as much background information as you can on them with respect to their personality, their negotiating style and their hot buttons and things that may concern them. You need to do it well ahead of time and you can only do it with proper research."

Watch the interview with Michael Cleaner at tinyurl.com/negotiating-cleaner-understand

Begin by outlining the various stakeholders involved and attempt to understand the role they will play. This includes using your personal contacts to find out whatever you can about the personalities. You and your team can do some digging, or you may have established an advisory panel to support your efforts. As you get to know the other side, ascertain how they will be making decisions, who the key influences on the decision makers are (such as CFOs, VPs, outside legal counsel or consultants) and establish the various levels of authority. Variables such as status, self-esteem and motivation will also start to become clear.

Janice Payne describes this process: "One of the things you do before embarking on the negotiation is to try to get some sense of the opposing party and spend some time talking with your client about the other side and what they perceive to be the priorities of the opposing party. And if you have a pre-existing relationship — particularly with counsel on the other side — and if that relationship is positive, you can probably get into a meaningful negotiation faster, get to the point faster and get the matter resolved faster. Conversely, if you know you are dealing with someone difficult because you have dealt with them before, you might not waste time on relationship building because you know that they will push the process to more adversarial options. It depends."

With a sense of the players, assess the other side's stated positions and interests, keeping in mind that the interests actually driving the other side are often quite different from their publicly stated positions. And as you assess their needs, objectives and limitations, take time to estimate their BATNA (Best Alternative to a Negotiated Agreement) to gain a sense of where their bottom line is likely to be when you begin to make proposals and counteroffers. As a simple example, a person selling their home for a price below the market value may have purchased a new home already or may have been relocated to another city and thus need to close immediately. Like a prospective home buyer, you are seeking any information that provides leverage.

Watch the interview with Janice Payne at tinyurl.com/negotiating-payne-understand

With your sense of the other side and their interests in place, you can see whatever common ground may exist between you. As the negotiations proceed, you will learn much more about what you have in common, but an initial outline guides your strategy. This will lead to assessing where there are competing needs and interests, how some of those conflicts are likely to be resolved, and which issues you may have to give way on. If you give something away which is not overly valuable to you but is important to the other side's ability to fulfill their mandate, that will create opportunities for you to reach your own objectives. This kind of assessment helps you anticipate questions and prepare properly, remembering that as you make the other party accountable for their demands and positions, they will do the same to you.

When Anne Golden was leading the homelessness task force

in Toronto, she was faced with understanding and balancing the needs of multiple stakeholders. "We spent tons of time reading, listening, going to consult — trying to get educated. And when there was a disagreement, spending time with people. Sometimes we would say, 'look, can we agree to disagree on this' and if it became impossible, on that particular issue, we would say, 'let's study this further.' In other words, if we couldn't get common ground where we needed to, we would try to find another way. Keeping in mind that you have to recognize that sometimes, it's not going to work."

Watch the interview with Anne Golden at tinyurl.com/negotiating-golden-understand

PLAN YOUR INFORMATION SHARING

One of my primary rules about sharing information is that if I want to get something from the other party, I always offer something first. This creates a sense of reciprocity and builds trust. But this approach requires significant preparation in assessing the information available and predicting the information the other side has that will be of value. And, more than any other aspect of information sharing, be clear about how you will protect sensitive information that you don't want the other party to have. I always advise negotiators not to play games with the other side. If there is information you are not prepared to share, be transparent and offer a rationale as to why you cannot provide it. This can be done thoughtfully and without offence.

Prior to the first meeting with the other side, map out what you will and will not exchange. Unlike lawyers in litigation who are compelled by the rules of court to exchange a table of documents, negotiators have no obligation about what they share. This positions information exchange in a negotiation as a strategic process. Parties who establish open communications at this stage are more apt to set a friendly and personal tone, a base that can lead to helpful sharing on both sides regarding perceptions and issues. This sharing both creates leverage at times and helps to establish a rapport as you probe, listen and disclose. Of course, many messages exchanged during a negotiation take only a second to convey. Effective interpersonal communication is required for both parties.

THE QUALITIES OF A GREAT NEGOTIATOR

"What I value most is someone who is going to be candid and frank with me. Tell me what you can do. Tell me what you can't do. As Minister of Labour, if I am involved, we are at zero hour — something is going to happen. I want to know if you can do a deal, and I want to know whether or not you can get it ratified."

Watch the interview at tinyurl.com/negotiating-raitt-qualities

LISA RAITT, former Minister of Labour and Minister of Transport

Gary Corbett, CEO and President of PIPSC, outlines the role of information sharing in his work with government negotiations: "You really have to have good information. We have a research department and so do other organizations that we work with to garner information for questions such as, 'Does Canada need professional engineers in the government?' We would prepare and gather our information based on what we are trying to achieve — and the other side does the same thing — but to a certain extent, it is not an open sharing across the board — at least not in the beginning. It is a bit like a card game and you keep your cards close to your chest. At some point, they have to be revealed, but you make those decisions as you proceed. In bargaining, as you get closer to the end point, it is best to have more cards on the table."

Watch the interview with Gary Corbett at tinyurl.com/negotiating-corbett-info

One item of particular importance when it comes to the sharing of information is the price or financial value of the entity, product or service under negotiation. Enter into every negotiation with a clear idea of your pricing, but also have a plan for how you will reveal that information, or, more specifically, *when* you will reveal that information. In any deal, you will be called on to justify the financial value, price, cost, premium, compensation, reward or toll, but here is an essential rule that I always follow: *explain and offer the rationale before you give the numbers.*

If you are too quick to share your numbers, the other party will close their minds and start thinking only about that figure, eliminating any opportunity for you to engage them in conversation about your justification. It's just the way our minds work: we get a number and right away start to think about it. Do we have the money? Where is that number in relation to what we thought was coming? How does it compare to the industry standard? Can I sell that number to the principals? Et cetera. Avoid this at all costs. Delay the number so that your side's position and reasoning are already present and known when the sum arrives. That helps you to shape the thinking and reception on the other side. The other side may press you to give your numbers up front so they can "assess the discussions in light of the number you have in mind." Their request does not need to be answered, especially if doing so undercuts your strategy and advantage. Maurice Mazerolle always reminds his students that each negotiation has a qualitative as well as a quantitative aspect and that it's best to save numbers for as late in the process as possible because "once money is spoken about, all creativity leaves the room."

My approach is to go through a series of steps before sharing the price. The first is the all-important rapport and relationship building that matters in every negotiation and sets you up for success in finding a mutually beneficial agreement. The second is to ensure that all of the issues involved in the negotiation have been identified and discussed, so that any price you offer arrives in the context of the entire deal. Third, try to get some level of agreement with the other side, not only about the issues but about how to address some difference so as to arrive at a solution. Even if you can't get an agreement prior to revealing the price, try at least to talk about the nature of the deal or dispute. Fourth, make the connections for the other side about how your proposals address problems that have been identified and how your suggestions are of value to them. Deals get done if both sides get as much of what they need as possible, so it's advantageous to help them see what they're getting. Finally, after all of that set-up is done, give the price. Be sure that the numbers you suggest are well researched, industry standardized and carefully considered.

Done properly, these steps will leave the other side seeing the value of what you are proposing — like when someone who wants quality spends the money on an expert — and accepting your numbers as a fair and accurate reflection of market value. If there is resistance to your price, shift the conversation from the specific number to the broader costs involved or emphasize the relationship, the future value of your proposals or the fact that the solutions on the table are better than any of the other side's alternatives. The goal is to avoid getting into a highly positional shoving match about price. Obviously, there may come a time in the negotiations when you are back and forth on price, but I suggest not allowing any conversation to be exclusively about numbers.

No matter what, remember that price is never the first thing you talk about.

PLAN THE MEETING LOGISTICS

I was once an adviser to a charitable organization dealing with significant internal conflict. As I helped it prepare for an important set of meetings, I suggested that we find a working space that would allow for a semi-circular arrangement of the furniture with all participants facing a whiteboard. This layout limited the possibility of confrontation between the members and encouraged everyone to concentrate on the issues at hand. It was a small thing, but it relieved some of the tension in the room and was a good choice for this particular group.

In chapter 2, there was some discussion of how to manage meetings and where to locate them, so I just have a few additional considerations regarding set-up. Always consider the three factors of any gathering — human, environmental and geographical — and do what you can in advance to ensure comfort, convenience and suitability. Human factors include fatigue, alertness, travel, food, and putting time to good use. Your team should be well rested and, if you are hosting, do what you can to help the other side be at their best. Don't schedule a meeting right after a long international flight. Think about good options for food, beverages and rest breaks for both sides to optimize the energy and quality of the discussions. When it comes to the environment, you are looking for comfortable seating, the right kind of furniture arrangement, enough space for everyone (including breakout spaces), no hot or airless rooms and generally pleasant surroundings, as a run-down space has an effect on tone. And is it too obvious to say that there should be easy access to washrooms, printers, projectors and Wi-Fi? It's surprising how often these niceties are overlooked. As I keep saying, the details matter. Your reputation is partly built on them, and an excellent reputation is a strategic advantage.

I have already discussed options for the geographic location of the meeting — your turf, theirs or in a neutral place. Give it careful consideration. Most negotiators like to have the session at their own place of business, but that isn't always the best choice. Benefits of home turf include having familiar surroundings; the psychology of home field advantage; access to support personnel, files and executives who may drop in to the meeting as needed; and control over the human and environmental factors. But there are downsides, too, such as interruptions from co-workers and a sense on the other side of a competitive disadvantage, which can create an adversarial dynamic. In many cases, negotiators opt for a neutral site to avoid any negative effect on either side. There is no right answer, but think this through in advance and make a calculated decision.

PLAN THE SCHEDULE

In early 2000, American Airlines and Onex, the Canadian private equity firm known for its ability to acquire assets effectively, joined forces to create a team with Onex as a major shareholder and American Airlines as a minority shareholder. Their goal was to purchase Air Canada and the process quickly became a hostile takeover.

I was a member of the team representing American Airlines, and the rest of the group from Onex and American Airlines was made up of very capable and very busy people, including lawyers, domestic consultants, international consultants, corporate executives, financial specialists, regulatory experts, government relations experts and communication specialists. It was a high profile case that got a great deal of media attention and it dragged on for quite awhile.

It was a major challenge to get the various members of our team together in the same room to plan and discuss the issues. Several weeks into the process, it was evident that the principals, Onex and American Airlines, needed to convene a meeting of all of the players. Gerry Schwartz, Onex's renowned CEO, stepped forward with a solution: he invited everyone to his Toronto home on a Sunday evening. The meeting allowed for a wide-ranging discussion of the objective, the strategy and the tactics. It also led to a solution to the problem of communication and coordination: we would meet every day either in person or on the phone to discuss the issues from the previous day (and for the next day) to be certain we were in alignment. It was a great solution, but there were significant time costs which could have been avoided if we had started from the beginning with a clear sense of how time needed to be blocked off.

As you prepare for a negotiation, be proactive about blocking out time for meetings, considering length, frequency and who needs to attend what. For example, it could be catastrophic if, in the midst of a negotiation pertaining to a financial arrangement, your chief financial officer indicated that she had to be out of the country because of another pressing priority. The take-away here is that you can cancel meetings, but you can rarely find time to add them. Planning the schedule requires both time up front and an attention to detail.

PLAN THE AGENDA

"I find that there is not enough discipline around agendas, which is why meetings go on for four and five hours when most people aren't productive after two hours," says lawyer Carol Hansell. "For me, I think it is certainly important to know what the other side's agenda is. I know what my agenda is. It is very helpful to me to know what you are trying to get out of this. If I am faced with a party that does not want to lay out an agenda, if I run through my agenda and say, 'I need to discuss these six points' that can sometimes create a flashpoint where somebody will say, 'I'm not talking about that' or 'I'm not authorized to talk about that' or 'the clients are offline dealing with that.' If we can get to that place at the beginning, it provides a lot of shape to the discussions. Or say somebody wants to move the items on the agenda around, it helps me to understand which issues they think are linked. For example, if they move an item to the end, that's a big signal to me about where they are attaching the most value."

Watch the interview with Carol Hansell at tinyurl.com/negotiating-hansell-agenda

Hansell's comments are consistent with what Chester L. Karrass says in *The Negotiating Game*. He contends that the agenda items you or the other party put forward tell a story. The agenda is more than a mere organizational process; it's a reflection of the importance of the issues for the particular negotiation. Karrass feels that it is better to have more issues on the agenda than fewer, because it helps the sides understand each other more thoroughly.

Agenda formation and its control are critical elements in the set-up for your negotiation because they influence how the discussions will unfold, which is an opportunity not to be missed. I always prepare a substantive agenda, having thought strategically about the issues I want to address and the sequence that would best support my goals. I also know that an agenda that both sides agree to in advance minimizes conflict and confusion at the table. At heart, agenda formation is a shared process that can generate energy and build relations. Of course, there will be issues that do not make the agenda, so your planning should include anticipating what will come up between the time the agenda is formed and the meeting occurs. Always put the agenda in writing — even just via email after a conversation — so that everyone can see what has been agreed to and can sign off on it. Quite often, I will email the agenda to the other party saying, "This is what we agreed to but if there are additional items that you wish to add, I would appreciate hearing from you forty-eight hours before we commence our negotiations." If you have a relationship with the other side, this process can go forward without incident. However, there will be times when the other party will not abide by this suggestion and come to the table seeking to add items on the fly.

Once the agenda for any particular set of meetings has been established, assess the value of each item in relation to the overall negotiation so that you are clear about the relative importance of each. In particular, make sure that you and your client are really clear about the deal-breakers well in advance. Having a clear hierarchy for all of the items allows you to be creative in generating value for both sides as you develop the various proposals and packages that will form the final agreement. In my experience, the simple process of talking about the relative merit of each item leads to highly creative discussions, because teams are able to see how the negotiation will unfold.

Negotiations involve winning on some items and losing on others. Your success is based on which items you give away and get. If the other party is determined to deny you something that is a deal-breaker for your side, you will know very quickly that the negotiation is not likely to be fruitful. Effective agenda planning can help you to see what's coming and is the easiest way to build momentum toward a mutually beneficial agreement, because it generates highly productive discussions within your team. All is not lost, however, if you are in a negotiation without a team to discuss the agenda or any other aspect of the process. Simply reach out to someone you trust who can add value and engage them in assessing the agenda items.

I remember a situation in the mid-1990s when, as Canada's Minister of Health, I received an urgent telephone call from the Chief of the Federation of Saskatchewan Indian Nations (FSIN), who wanted to meet to discuss several issues. I asked why there was such urgency, and he responded that the cap on healthcare money was the issue. I was keen to be supportive, so I agreed to a date and time and he travelled to Ottawa to meet with me and my team.

I went to the meeting with my Deputy Minister and Senior Policy Adviser for Aboriginal Health. As we entered the boardroom, we were stunned to find only a few seats available. The Chief had arrived with several other people in tow and, as the meeting unfolded, it became clear that most of them had issues unrelated to healthcare that were well beyond the scope of my portfolio. It was an extremely awkward situation and emotions in the room ran high. The participants were deeply invested in their issues and had travelled a long way to get to the meeting. Many of them expected me to do something about it.

Faced with the prospect of creating a political firestorm by turning participants away with a promise that someone would be in touch, my team and I did our best to make the meeting worthwhile for all the representatives without creating any confusion about what would or would not be possible as a result of the discussion. In almost every case, even though I could not help with the issues, the participants took the opportunity to tell me in clear and frank language what they thought of the Government of Canada.

It was a lesson in agenda formation that I have not forgotten. No one benefits from confusion. Work well in advance to ensure that everyone agrees to what will be discussed.

A final word about the agenda: use it to insert deadlines into the process. A deadline can increase the competitive nature of the negotiation when that is appropriate and compel the other party to make decisions. Don't be afraid to take the initiative in setting deadlines that require the other side to concur or to suggest alternatives. So long as you are operating with your mandate in mind, use deadlines to create momentum and keep your overall timeline on track.

PLANNING FOR MULTIPARTY NEGOTIATIONS

In industrial Cape Breton, a tidal estuary known as the Sydney Tar Ponds is the site of one of the largest environmental disasters and one of the most impressive cleanup efforts in Canadian and even North American history. The main environmental damage occurred during the steel boom in Nova Scotia in the early twentieth century when the Dominion Iron and Steel Company of Boston, Massachusetts built a massive mill that was, at one point, the largest steel producer in North America, generating more than 800,000 tonnes of pig iron and 900,000 tonnes of crude steel annually, nearly half of Canada's production. But the pollution continued through to 1988, when the plant was closed. Until then, the coke ovens had been dumping hazardous chemicals into the water and spewing toxic red dust into the air. I remember my mother always deciding whether to hang laundry out to dry in the backyard based on the direction of the wind. On the wrong day, it would come back into the house stained red.

The steel plant benefitted from being located close to the coal tar refining plant operated by Domtar, which made it possible to power the steel plant quickly and efficiently. Unfortunately, the coke ovens that produced the steel created a run-off of toxins into the watershed.

For years, there were efforts to begin a proper cleanup in the area, but they were always piecemeal and doomed to fail. But in 1996, I was involved in a multiparty process that had the commitment and energy needed to succeed. Working with Environment Minister Sergio Marchi, Nova Scotia Transportation and Public Works Minister Donald Downe, Nova Scotia Health Minister Bernie Boudreau, the Nova Scotia Minister responsible for Economic Renewal, Richie Mann, and other senior officials, we began a widespread series of meetings with community leaders in Sydney.

As a result of that process, we recommended a radically different direction: the creation of the multi-stakeholder Joint Action Group (JAG) to conduct broad-based public consultations and devise an effective remediation plan. A memorandum of understanding between the various parties was signed that included a total of $62 million in funding from all three levels of government and a commitment to a $400 million cleanup effort. This successful coalition concluded in 2013 with the opening of Open Hearth Park on the site of the former steel plant.

As Carl Buchanan, JAG's chairman, described it, the tar ponds project was "the most complex environmental cleanup ever undertaken in this country, and maybe anywhere. It's never been done on this scale, and right in the middle of a city." The success of the project came from creating a complex multiparty process in which each worked with all to find a solution.

The secret of the success wasn't the number of parties involved, but a productive and positive approach combined with many small steps needed to reach the end. JAG's mandate was to "educate, involve and empower the community, through partnerships, to determine and implement acceptable solutions for Canada's worst hazardous waste site and to assess and address the impact on human health." Prior to this extensive consultation and shared process, there had been regular protests and significant hostility from citizens toward the provincial and federal governments. But through clear direction, ongoing coordination, extensive efforts at all levels and significant transparency, the mandate was achieved.

In some ways, negotiating with multiple parties is the same as dealing with one. The planning and preparation follow the same steps I have outlined, but you do it on a much bigger scale. You have to research and understand each entity and sort through how their needs relate to each other, including their relative attitude toward making a deal. As a result, multiparty preparations are far more time consuming. Once you have done your due diligence on the individual parties involved, there are two particular considerations for this kind of preparation.

The first is to be consistent in your approach to everyone so that you are not perceived as biased or as creating unequal access to information. If you treat one party differently, it will become known in a hurry and will hamper your opportunity to work positively with them all. Be transparent at all times when communicating information that all parties need, and adopt the same tone and behaviour with everyone involved. You may sometimes need to communicate with only one party, which is fine so long as exclusivity is required. When it's not required, I often copy the other parties on information I am exchanging with one, particularly if the information has some relevance to everyone, such as when one party requests a copy of a document. I also try to share information when it's not substantive because it creates a sense of trust and openness. Whenever communicating about something substantive, I often opt for phone calls to tell participants in person about what is happening.

Second, forming the agenda with many parties can be tricky and time consuming, but it is important because large groups require structure and a clear process to be productive and collaborative. Establish as much clarity as possible about who is advocating for which agenda items and try to understand their rationale. It takes time, but knowing the rationale and interests behind each agenda item can help you shape your strategy more effectively.

In preparing for the G8 summit as the personal representative of the Prime Minister, Peter Harder has some experience with multiple parties. "When dealing with a multiparty negotiation, there are several things I try to keep in mind. The first is that you need to form a personal relationship with your colleagues. The second is that you really do have to be informed about the agenda. You can't go without a point of view and you can't get into the room without knowing the position of the Prime Minister for whom you speak — and that would involve various ministers who would have input on the issues. Third, you need to make sure there is alignment on your side, in my case the Government of Canada. So in advance of any G8 summit, we would have very large multi-departmental reviews to determine what position Canada was going to advocate. It is essential that whoever the personal representative, they speak for the institution that they are representing."

Watch the interview with Peter Harder at tinyurl.com/negotiating-harder-parties

TAKEAWAYS

UNDERSTAND THE SUBJECT MATTER AND THE NATURE OF THE DEAL

1. Be a subject expert — do your homework on the subject of the negotiation.
2. Know the nature of the deal — it may have either an inductive or deductive quality.

UNDERSTAND THE ENTITY THAT IS THE FOCUS OF THE NEGOTIATION.

3. Gather general information — from marketplace analysis, the organizational chart and the people you know.
4. Study the financials — start with the income statement, balance sheet and cash flow.
5. Do a SWOT — sketch out the company's strengths, weaknesses, opportunities and threats.
6. Dig deeper — from auditors' reports to background checks on the principals to social media.

UNDERSTAND THE OTHER NEGOTIATING TEAM

7. Know the roles — who is involved, what they do and who makes decisions.
8. See the positions — uncover the interests that drive them and estimate their BATNA. Recognize common ground — separate the overlap from the competing needs.

PLAN YOUR INFORMATION SHARING

9. Be prepared — map out in advance what you will and won't exchange.
10. Go first — establish reciprocity and trust by sharing something with the other side.
11. Protect what's sensitive — be open about what you can't share and explain why.

12. Delay the price — there are four steps, including your rationale, before you offer a number.

PLAN THE LOGISTICS

13. Be human — make decisions about timing, food, drink and rest breaks to maintain energy.
14. Shape the environment — provide comfort, the best furniture arrangement and enough space.
15. Determine geography — your turf isn't always an advantage — a neutral site is often best.

PLAN THE SCHEDULE

16. Be proactive — consider length, frequency and list of attendees to establish a meeting schedule.
17. Go ahead and subtract — it's almost impossible to add meetings, but nobody minds a cancellation.

PLAN THE AGENDA

18. Pay attention to their items — an agenda tells a story about interests and priorities.
19. Share the process — shaping an agenda together generates momentum and build relationships.
20. Put it in writing — send an email to agree in advance about items and order.

PLANNING FOR MULTIPARTY NEGOTIATIONS

21. Go big — the research and planning process is the same but the scale is much greater.
22. Coordinate extensively — put in the time to form the agenda with all parties.

CHAPTER 8
Forming and Designing the Deal

"Our business is really simple. When you look at a deal and its structure looks like an octopus or a spider, just don't do it."

— Timothy Sloan, President and COO of Wells Fargo

Paul Martin was one of the most outstanding Finance Ministers Canada has ever had. From the time he was appointed to the role in 1993, he led the government and the country through a series of very difficult decisions that radically altered the financial situation in Ottawa and, ultimately, erased the deficit. As a member of the cabinet during that first mandate, I was heavily involved in the efforts to cut spending and get the fiscal house in order, but Martin and I didn't really see eye to eye on most of it. Ours was a clash between opposites, and while we have gone on to have a positive relationship since then, at the time it was strained.

Martin and I grew up in very different circumstances. His father served for thirty-three years as a Member of the House of Commons, was a Senior Cabinet Minister and was the High Commissioner in London, England. Martin attended private school and went on to graduate from the University of Toronto in history and then law. I was the son of a janitor raised in the basement of a school, attended the local college and graduated from Dalhousie University in law. But there was more to our uneasy relationship than our different backgrounds. While I supported the overall goals of the government, I often disagreed with the cuts Martin was making, especially to transfer payments for healthcare and post-secondary education. In 1996, when I took over as Minister of Health, I was not the only person in the ministry with a tense relationship with the Finance Department.

I knew that I needed to find a way for our two ministries to work together or we were never going to be able to achieve our mandate and serve the Canadian public effectively. As I assessed options for bridging the gap, one possibility was to use an agent to help with communication and decision making between the two parties. I needed someone with a strong relationship with both camps, though with no particular affiliation with either, who would be taken seriously. I found him in the person of Paul Genest.

Genest was an affable young man who was well liked by the Minister of Finance staff and the Prime Minister's office and who had a clear understanding of the impact of the healthcare cuts. He had a PhD in philosophy from Johns Hopkins and was extremely astute about political issues and processes. His insight and social acumen meant that he could do things with Martin and his staff that neither I nor anyone else on my staff could. Through Genest, we were able to secure monies for the modernization of healthcare, tobacco control and several other major items, despite the cutbacks underway. Understanding his role, Genest was very careful about representing the needs of both sides and helped the Finance staff see that our requests were both reasonable and needed.

Paul Martin and I eventually settled our differences, but at the time, we did not have what it took to create workable agreements between our two ministries. Foreseeing the need for a different approach to deal making prevented animosity from getting in the way of results and created the agreements needed in the country. In that way, Paul Genest illustrates the power of choosing the right action to create the right conditions for deal making, which is what every strategic negotiator should do.

When the initial stages of due diligence and set-up are over, a negotiator begins to shape a potential deal that will then be honed during the live session at the table. The choices made at this stage — including concessions offered, options created, degree of leverage generated and new information acquired — all have a significant impact on the final agreement. And, as always, the core principles of authenticity, integrity and openness underlie everything.

ELEVEN PRINCIPLES OF INFLUENCE FOR NEGOTIATORS

Once into the first stage of working toward a deal, your ability to influence and persuade comes into play. Over time, I have read dozens of books about the art and science of influence and tested every approach relevant to a negotiation. Below are eleven ideas that I find very helpful. The first seven are heavily indebted to Kevin Hogan's book *The Science of Influence*, which I highly recommend, and the rest are some ideas of my own that I have picked up along the way.

1. Law of Reciprocity

If you were helpful to me in a previous negotiation, it is reasonable to assume that I will be helpful in return. We are oriented toward responding in kind when someone does something for us, often giving back even more. If I am generous, it generally begets generosity. If I am trustworthy, it is likely to be reciprocated. If I am fair and reasonable in my demands, there is a high probability that the other side will be as well. This is a version of "I did you a favour, now it's time for you to do a favour for me." This normal business practice can play a significant role in a negotiation.

It explains why business leaders seeking concessions from their opponents will quite often entertain them in a kind, thoughtful and friendly manner. I know from thirty years of negotiation work that just taking someone out for a meal can provide a better understanding of the real interests in play.

Reciprocity is a prime driver behind most customs related to hospitality and gift giving, and the practice has become so widespread that many governments, large corporations and international organizations have developed strict policies against hospitality and gifts to remove this element from the negotiation process. Be careful about the expectations you set around gifts and, in particular, about the gifts you accept. The countermeasure to this power is to not accept gifts or favours from individuals with whom you do not want a reciprocal obligation. In some instances, you may have to say no to the hospitality and kind gestures of the other side. This is an important judgement call, especially depending on the gift. A cup of coffee is one thing; a Montblanc watch is quite another.

As one example, gift giving is a particular issue when dealing with officials and executives in China — a subject with which Sarah Kutulakos, Executive Director of the Canada China Business Council, is very familiar. "You have to be careful with gifts these days in China, but showing appreciation is important. One of the pieces of advice that we give to foreigners visiting China is to try and bring something that is unique to your culture or country that your Chinese counterpart wouldn't be able to get from an average contact. Something that is not of excessive value, so it is not uncomfortable for the other party to reciprocate. Also, it's usually better to have one of your staff talk to the staff of the other side and let them know you are bringing a gift and ask them if they want to prepare something. They don't like to be surprised."

Watch the interview with Sarah Kutulakos at tinyurl.com/negotiating-kutulakos-gifts

2. Law of Contrast

When two items that are similar but have evident differences are displayed side by side, the differences become magnified and one of the options will be seen as more desirable than if presented alone. When negotiating for a particular service or product, the data indicates that if you show an expensive product or service first and then reveal a considerably cheaper version, the other party is most likely to focus on the second option. There are exceptions to this rule, but I think you will find that when you shop, for instance, for a hotel room and the price comes back at $259 and then you are offered a second hotel room similar in style, comfort and location at a price of $199, you are much more apt to proceed to the second. The same can be said in any type of negotiation. If you first assert what the other side deems to be a somewhat unreasonable demand and then follow up with a second submission, your second proposal is more likely to be viewed as reasonable, well thought out and accountable, and you are more likely to make headway.

3. Law of Consistency

When a commitment is made in writing or out loud in front of others, it is more likely to be kept in the future because it has become part of a person's identity. If you can get your counterpart to agree with certain principles before, during and after a negotiation, you will increase the likelihood of them following through on their commitment. The key is to get them to commit to the option, principle, idea or course of action by saying it in a group setting or writing it in a letter, email or text, and don't be reluctant to thank them for their commitment. It is always a good idea to constantly reinforce your foundational principles so that the other side has multiple opportunities to concur with them — out loud or in writing.

4. Law of Scarcity

A basic rule of economics — and influence — is that we value something we believe to be scarce more than something that is widely available. For example, a university negotiating with the only nuclear physicist in the world with the relevant international experience, research history and publication background is eager for the hire because there is no one else available to fill that role. Equally, governments seeking individuals who can assist in fighting ISIS highly prize knowledge of the language, the culture and the background of the terrorist organization — a rare set of qualifications. So as you map out your proposals and options, do what you can to illustrate the distinctive and singular nature of your offerings.

5. Fear of Loss

People are far more motivated by the possibility of losing something they already have than of gaining something they do not have. Most of us, myself included, tend to think that the key in a negotiation is to emphasize what the other side will gain from the deal. It is true that a negotiator should explain the benefits along the way. But as Hogan's data indicates, you will make an even greater impact if you emphasize what the other side risks losing if they pursue a certain form of agreement. The best strategy is both to clarify the gains and play on the very real fear of loss.

6. Limit Choice

When faced with too many choices, people become over-whelmed and give up, because the energy required to sift through the multitude of options is perceived to not be worthwhile. They become paralyzed and reluctant to do anything. It is a good idea to limit the number of proposals or options you present and to make the choices succinct and clear.

7. The Power of Testimonials

We are highly influenced by a recommendation from people we know, admire or have heard of. The more often you can offer strongly supportive commentary about your proposals from individuals or organizations familiar to the other side, the more likely you are to convince them that your offer is of value and should be accepted. Be aware of your best timing to pull out some testimonials — perhaps when making or responding to a first offer. Hold onto your key references for times of greatest impact.

8. Focus on Problem Solving

My experience is that negotiators who adopt a problem-solving approach are more likely to sway their counterparts than those who are adversarial and contrarian. This means presenting your options or scenarios as possible solutions that meet the needs of both sides. As always, your demeanour is key to conveying your desire to work together to find a solution, but the surface behaviours will follow naturally if you really do pursue a shared approach toward a mutually beneficial out-come. This is not about attempting to grab whatever you can get. If you take a problem-solving approach to your work, you will develop a reputation as an asset in any negotiation, even to the other side.

9. Mix Up the Environment

It can be very effective to change the setting of your negotiation in order to alleviate a rut or log jam in the deliberations, especially if you can do it before a conflict or controversy develops. New settings breathe fresh air into the process and allow you and your counterpart a new way to interact that can be quite lucrative. For example, you might call for a health break or a chance to go for coffee. Or you might, as I have done often, ask your counterpart to go for a walk outside. There is something magical about walking in step as you talk through the issues in a softer, more indirect fashion than tends to dominate in a meeting. I am not saying that a mere change of environment will automatically result in agreement, but it can be a useful boost along the way.

10. Appearance and Demeanour

As I have underlined throughout, how you act and appear are of critical importance in a negotiation. When first working with the other party to shape and form the deal, you create all kinds of first impressions that have a bearing on the outcome. Looking tired, frustrated or dishevelled sends a message. It is better to be well-groomed, fresh and eager to begin the discussions. And make a particular point of using humour at the outset, because almost everyone appreciates some levity and it helps to build rapport. Don't dominate the room with long stories or outlandish jokes, but simple humour such as a few self-deprecating remarks can set the tone for a productive negotiation.

11. Likeability

While maintaining an authentic and honest approach, keep in mind a basic reality in life: we work more openly with people we like. We all know people with highly likeable personalities who benefit from the energy they generate. The same is true for deal making. There are many ways to generate likeability, but I have found it best to just be yourself and be as open as possible. We all respond well to people who come across to us as approachable and accessible.

KEY CONSIDERATIONS FOR DEAL FORMATION

As you enter into the deal formation process, these priorities will positively affect the early stages of your work and ensure that you are being strategic right from the start.

Keep Mandate and BATNA Top of Mind

When Sarah Kutulakos advises Canadian businesses working in China, she helps them understand how the priorities of the government influence the priorities of the executives they are negotiating with. "The long-term planning cycle is an integral part of how the government works in China and they do it extremely well. They have a five-year plan. They roll it over every five years and it is so comprehensive that you can go from the highest level targets to the individual city or sector level. It's something that very few countries do and do well. As difficult to understand as China can be in many ways, it is an open book in terms of what its goals are, and if you can understand what its goals are and you can understand how your product or service can help China meet its goals, doors can be opened to you extremely readily."

Watch the interview with Sarah Kutulakos at tinyurl.com/negotiating-kutulakos-mandate

NON-NEGOTIABLES

"When I was a young lawyer, I was drafting something and the client told me that they did not assume any environmental liability at all. He said, 'We will not take on anybody's environmental liability.' I tried it on a few different ways and he said to me, 'Look, we just aren't going to do it. We've never done it and we are never going to do it so let's get that out on the table right now.' Over time, I did a lot of work with them and it was really helpful to be able to say to the lawyer on the other side — look, this isn't ever going to change."

Watch the interview at tinyurl.com/negotiating-hansell-hard-line

CAROL HANSELL, former Director of the Bank of Canada, Founder and Senior Partner at Hansell LLP

The Chinese government and its businesses keep mandate top of mind in every transaction and negotiation. As you form the deal, constantly refer back to your specific goals, the impact of achieving those goals and the interests of the other side — all of which are easy to lose sight of when other considerations arise. In addition, be cognizant of the BATNA on both sides because you have to be willing to walk away or, at a minimum, make clear to the other side that you are willing to walk away if your mandate cannot be achieved.

Follow through on your communication strategy regarding your mandate and goals and make deliberate choices about how you will describe your offers and counteroffers. In addition, be careful about the degree to which you affirm or reject the other side's proposals, because the implications of your early reactions will be magnified as the deliberations proceed. If you are able to clearly dismiss a proposal or offer, do so in order to send a clear message about the limits of your authority and possible alternatives. My recommendation is that you and your team explicitly discuss how each stage of the deal forming process relates to your mandate by taking five or seven minutes to review each proposal and counteroffer so that you don't lose track of your priorities. I have seen many negotiations where what seemed like a productive day ended up being viewed as a setback when the parties compared their "progress" to the mandate and goals.

On top of revisiting your goals, consult your carefully crafted assessment of the other side's BATNA to measure the significance of their proposals and concessions. The quality of your research into their BATNA will show, as will how well you have anticipated their *actual* interests rather than their stated positions. While some situations involve BATNAs that are strictly monetary, most include a wide range of goals and considerations beyond price.

Leverage

I think of leverage as the power to control the outcome of the negotiation through a perceived situational advantage. Leverage is fluid, not static, shifting back and forth between parties. Assess and try to predict where the leverage in a particular negotiation will be created. Leverage is typically based on three elements: first, the needs and wants of each party; second, the BATNA of each party and, third, the current perceptions of each party of the relative strength of each side's position. The greater a party's need, the weaker the leverage. The more you have something that the other side wants, the stronger your position.

Avoid misrepresenting your situation or being untruthful about your leverage. Any lies, whether big or small, will come back to bite you. Better to work hard to establish actual leverage and then be frank about it at the appropriate stages of the process. And keep in mind that in a tough negotiation, it is not enough to show the other party that you can deliver what they want. Show them that they have something to *lose* by pursuing other avenues. Remember, leverage is not just about the facts — it is about the party's perceptions of those facts.

One of the best recent examples of leverage came in the last lockout in the NHL. At the time, Donald Fehr led the players through a process that was exceptional in many ways but in particular in creating a united front amongst the players, whom Fehr credited with being the source of all decisions despite his reputation as a tough and savvy negotiator. In the lead-up to the negotiations which took place in New York City, Fehr met with all members of the thirty-two NHL teams, mostly in small groups and sometimes individually. When I asked him why this onerous process was critical, he outlined the role that leverage plays in a negotiation.

"You need to learn everything about the subject or the likelihood that you will make mistakes skyrockets. Then, you have to educate the membership. The members, in my case the players, need to understand what the facts are, what the issues are, what can be done, what's difficult to do, how management is likely to respond to one proposal or another and what the risks are. The reason for that is the final thing you need to do. Standing alone, no one — no lawyer, no executive director — has any particular authority, clout or leverage. If the players support your position, and the owners believe that the players support your position and they are willing to fight for it, then the owners will pay attention to you, not because they care about the negotiator — smart lawyers who can make articulate speeches are a dime a dozen — but because they think the players will support a given position. Far and away, the most important thing you need to do is educate the membership and develop a very widespread consensus — on the order of 100 per cent. So you spend an enormous amount of time meeting with the players, talking to the players, making sure they understand, finding out from them what they think is important, what they are prepared to fight for."

Watch the interview with Donald Fehr at tinyurl.com/negotiating-fehr-understanding

Fehr's approach is one kind of leverage — particular to a situation where the negotiator represents a group — but in any industry or type of negotiation, you can sometimes look ahead and determine how to be in the driver's seat. Other times, it's a matter of patience and timing. As Fehr said after he described what leverage means in the NHLPA, "Verbiage has very little to do with reaching an agreement — it's simply a question of leverage. And who has the most leverage is not often apparent at an early stage in the negotiation. So you wait. Negotiations are not often about logic and persuasion. And leverage can change over time because it consists of two things: what you are prepared to do and, just as importantly, what the other side believes you are prepared to do."

Watch the interview with Donald Fehr at tinyurl.com/negotiating-fehr-leverage

Fair and Objective Criteria

In *Bargaining for Advantage*, Richard Shell highlights the importance of ensuring that supporting your negotiating position with some standard benchmark or precedent. As you enter the deal formation stage, think about the kind of standard or criteria that will be beneficial to you. Parties will often refer to objective criteria as the basis of their demands and/or counterproposals, and it is important to understand what is at stake with the choices you make here. In some instances, fair criteria may be a subjective matter. In others, criteria can be industry standard measures that are legitimately objective. If the other side uses precedents, as most lawyers do, it will be incumbent upon you to find precedents that work in your favour.

You will often work with the other side to select which benchmarks or criteria will be used, so be prepared to defend your proposals and counteract theirs. For example, a common objective criterion used is "market value," especially in the commercial world. Typically, this involves pointing at the standard that the competition is presently using: "Well, so and so is offering x amount for their particular business, so that is why we are asking for this amount." If this sort of standard is helpful to your case, you will choose it and defend it. On the other hand, if the other side uses this criterion and you do not want it, you can rebut it by questioning the definition of market rate. This approach is particularly helpful if you can genuinely distinguish your service or product from those being sold at so-called market rate. You can also argue that the circumstances of this deal are different or have changed since the ones being referred to as a standard.

In his book *Gain the Edge! Negotiating to Get What You Want*, Martin Latz refers to objective criteria as a "power" and points out three types of criteria that tend to be used in negotiations:

1.   Expert and scientific/judgement power derives from the expertise and knowledge of an industry insider who has substantial experience with the subject matter and can credibly attest to the value of proposals being made. If you intend to use this kind of criteria, it is essential that you and your team know a great deal about the expert including qualifications, accomplishments, reputation and everything they have said on the public record, which is the easiest target for the other side to undermine your expert. The only countermeasure for this kind of power is another expert of your own who can provide an alternate interpretation and position. So doing the background work to find the best expert possible is essential. In particular, I find it is really helpful to access experts who can speak to both sides of an issue with candour and insight, which builds credibility and helps to support your proposals. And you should definitely avoid anyone who is dogmatic and inward-thinking about the issue in dispute.

2.   Policy power comes from your ability to refer to established guidelines and practices in the organization you represent as a standard by which you will assess proposals and counteroffers in a particular situation. To begin with, it gives you a consistent basis for explaining how you have developed your proposals. It then allows you to say, "Well it's not me who believes this to be the situation, it's the policy of the organization and it can't be changed." When faced with an opposing side using this kind of standard, focus on a principled response to work around the policy. For instance, mount a thoughtful and substantive argument that the policy does not apply to this particular timing, environment or circumstance and will either negatively affect the outcomes for the organization it supposedly helps or simply ought to be ignored. You can also argue that when the policy was originally conceived, it did not address the issues in play in this negotiation.

3.   Industry standard agreements are existing frameworks for deals that have been used in a particular sector for an extended period of time and should, therefore, apply to all individuals, including you and your organization. They tend occur in industries such as real estate, mining or retail, where industry associations support the existing types of contracts and other arrangements. The best way to counter such a measure is to assume that such standards are in fact negotiable and that you are free to develop your own kind of agreement and put it on the table for the purposes of discussion. If you do, you will definitely raise a few eyebrows, especially if you provide a new standard in writing, but it can be an effective way to structure the deal in your favour if the existing practices are not beneficial to you. Obviously, you need to do your homework and research whether or not the standard agreement in fact represents the industry or whether you have some leeway to amend it. In my experience, changes to standard agreements are resisted because of the heavy work involved rather than because there is a prohibition against it.

Irrespective of the criteria you choose or your methods of rebuttal, be sure to understand the implications of each choice and do not rush through the phase of deciding which standards to use.

Determining and Assessing Your Price

Your goal is to provide price proposals that are credible and accurate while also anticipating how the other side will evaluate your proposals. Three standard methods can be used for both determining and assessing price:

1.   Worth analysis occurs when both sides look at your suggested price and compare it to the price the other side will

charge their customers. In essence, this is the use of margins to determine prices. If you sell coin sets to Walmart, for example, you need to know its markup on that particular item. If you know that they want to have a 75 per cent to 100 per cent markup, then a $100 coin set has to sell for somewhere between $175 and $200. Understanding the markup and final selling price allows you to assess your suggested price from their perspective. If you can offer a price that gets them the margin they want while you receive good value, you have found a mutually beneficial solution.

2.   Market value analysis is the perceived value of your product or service on the open market — even when there is not actually an open market for this particular item. When you make a decision based on the market, be ready to explain any divergence from market standards and illustrate how the circumstances of this situation are different from those used for the market price. For example, legal rates at the top law firms in downtown Toronto are quite different from legal rates charged in rural Saskatchewan. Examine the domestic and international markets for your product or service through a comprehensive study. In many instances, there will be sector analysis or trade associations that can provide this kind of valuable insight. Also, if you are operating internationally, you can review websites of different organizations for any pricing information there.

3.   Cost analysis occurs when the pricing you offer is measured based on the inputs required to create the product. If you sell lobsters from Main-à-Dieu, Nova Scotia to Beijing, you assess all costs domestically and internationally, such as labour, fuel, fishing gear, insurance and transactional governmental fees. You would also look at the costs of transporting lobster, such as the actual containers, tariffs and taxes, and fees associated with the

quality assurance programs demanded by various countries. This method requires you to look carefully at the final price you suggest and know all the costs involved to determine whether it is reasonable.

One final note about your process in setting the price: remember the fear of loss mentioned earlier in this chapter. The data suggests that decision-makers weigh information about potential losses more heavily than they do information about potential gains. Over the years, both in my practice of law as well as in international commerce, I was more interested in identifying the benefits to the other party as I worked to get them to acquiesce, but the data suggests that what they really want to know is what they stand to lose if they reject your proposal. This is where being accurate and open is critical. If you make grandiose statements about the negative effect of not accepting your proposal, your offer will not be seen as credible. But if you can state it with precision and outline some reasonable losses at stake — perhaps in quality, cost or delivery times — you will have the decision-maker's attention.

Concessions or Options

Leonard Asper has a particular approach to concessions that connects what he wants to what he is willing to give up. "I don't go in already planning to give something up. The list is more what I must have and what I would like to have. And I go for the whole thing. It's only when I get pushed that I go back and look at my list to see if I have to have this or that. And sometimes a must have can fall off the list if you get something else that you didn't anticipate getting. It's not a linear process that way. Negotiations take twists and turns, and suddenly you got something you didn't expect to get, and suddenly you're okay about giving up this or that. I learned from combat sports, and fighters will tell you, there's the game plan and then there's what happens after the first punch."

Watch the interview with Leonard Asper at tinyurl.com/negotiating-asper-concessions

In forming and designing a deal, rest assured that both parties will want concessions as part of their various proposals. Some individuals claim they never make concessions, but if you dig, you will find that it is a normal part of the process. Perhaps the most vocal example of that is labour leaders, whose position on concessions I fully understand. Politicians in the true sense, these leaders have a constituency to which they owe their position and never want to appear weak in the eyes of their members. As a result, they rarely use the word "concession." Nevertheless, when agreements are reached, you can read between the lines and see that several concessions were made throughout the process. Sometimes I refer to suggested changes as options rather than concessions, since that word takes away the stigma of seeming weak.

As you begin to form the deal, know your non-negotiables and always get something in return for anything you give. Also, when making a concession, be sure to articulate the costs associated with it so you get full value for what you give up. Even if you don't really value the option you have accepted, it is still critical to emphasize its impact. And only make concessions that the other side deems to be important.

THE QUALITIES OF A GREAT NEGOTIATOR

"You have to know what you want and what you can give. Never give something without getting something back in return. So anytime someone says to you, 'I want this,' you say, 'That reminds me, I wanted that.' Because that will give them pause. If they know that every time they try to grind you that it is going to cost them — you are going to come back with something — it is less likely to happen. Because what typically happens is that you agree on the six points and then they start grinding you for things.

"Also, always say to the person across the table, 'Don't give me things piecemeal. I want to see the whole package.' Because what a lot of people do is they get you to agree to one thing and then they come back and ask for something else."

Watch the interview at tinyurl.com/negotiating-asper-qualities

LEONARD ASPER, former CEO of Canwest Global Communications Corporation and current President and CEO of Anthem Sports & Entertainment

I am also careful not to be too quick in responding to a proposal with a "yes." If the other party counters with a good offer which you believe to be in full compliance with your mandate, take some time to think it through. At a minimum, you will want to think about whether there are contingencies associated with this offer not immediately evident, but your main priority is to not show your hand by responding so quickly that you reveal information about your position and interests. If you are too quick to agree, the other party might conclude that they have given away something terribly important and want to slow down the process. This is a time to act strategically and not from your gut, especially when it comes to assessing the timing and size of a concession. It is fine to readily accept a counteroffer on a smaller item if really clear about the value or if entering the later stages of the deal formation process when the time passing between offers and concessions shrinks. But in the early stages of the process, be very careful and move slowly because early concessions usually include large moves by the parties.

As you work with the other side to form and design a deal, plan in advance to take several caucuses to consider the offers and counteroffers. For example, when I notify the other party that we will negotiate for an hour and a half and then I would like to have a health break, I find they are usually agreeable. I can then use the break for a caucus. In this way, I set up institutionalized caucus meetings that assure my team members they will have an opportunity to talk in private about the proceedings. Negotiators sometimes feel that they need to keep pressing on with the negotiations. Resist this in favour of the effective use of stopgaps.

One book with valuable ideas about concessions is James C. Freund's *Smart Negotiating*. Here are nine of Freund's ideas to inform your perspective:

1. All concessions send a signal.

2. Your first concession needs to be strategic and aligned with your overall objectives.

3. Reciprocity of concessions is essential in the negotiating process.

4.   Initially, concessions ought to be small and infrequent.

5.   Most concessions come at the end of the negotiating process.

6.   Most negotiators think in dollar terms rather than percentages.

7.   A firm deadline can help to drive the concession process.

8.   Assume that it will take movement on your part to generate movement from the other party.

9.   Never say, "Let's split the difference." Say, "I wonder if there is any value in splitting the difference?" So that if the other side says, "No, I don't think so," you can reply, "I agree, that isn't useful for either of us."

Contingency Contracts
An item related to concessions and options but that involves a slightly different approach is the use of the contingency contract, which is an arrangement that outlines a new set of prices, timelines, provisions or agreements if the delivery of the service or the terms of the deal don't play out as they have been described and agreed to. A common practice in many sectors, it involves offering the other party a certain price provided they are able to deliver something, but not being completely sure that they will actually be able to deliver. You might even have some misgivings about their undertakings. If that is the situation, a good approach is to create a contingency contract to protect your interests in the event that the other side is not able to deliver. Yes, there is risk with contingency contracts because they suggest you are not completely confident in the main agreement, but they are also a creative and beneficial

option to ensure that you get some value of out of a particular arrangement.

YOUR APPROACH

Throughout the negotiation, think about how you manage yourself and your team. At the formation stage, there are a few particular considerations that I want to emphasize.

Candour and Responding to Attacks

Donald Fehr told me a story about Marvin Miller, the famous negotiator from Major League Baseball Players Association, who was committed to bluntness as an obligation to his clients. "When there was no free agency in baseball, which is basically the right to go apply for a job elsewhere, there was a famous lawsuit filed against Major League Baseball by Curt Flood in the early 1970s. He was asserting that what the owners were doing, in terms of closing down the player market, was a violation of the United States anti-trust laws. The union funded that lawsuit. Curt, in a very brave and sacrificial way, went forward with it. A lot of people think that he won that case. He did not. He lost it. Free agency came a couple of years later in an arbitration case. But what Marvin Miller did, along with Richard Moss, who was his general counsel at the time, is they went to Curt ahead of time, and I don't know how you get more blunt than this: 'Curt — it's the right thing to do, it's the right thing for the players and we applaud you for it. But the odds are against you in this case, the Supreme Court is stacked against you in this case and if you file this lawsuit, the great likelihood is that your career is over and you will never play again. You are done. So you have to decide what you want to do.' Marvin did that because even though sacrificing the career of one player might be good for the benefit of all players, you have to be as blunt and direct as possible with the player in that situation or you are in derogation of duty."

Watch the interview with Donald Fehr at tinyurl.com/negotiating-fehr-candour

When attempting to design a deal attractive to the other side, be aware of how you present options. Your proposal will not be taken seriously if you oversell or exaggerate its benefits. In fact, it is actually beneficial to point out mistakes you have made or the limitations of your proposals. This sort of candour is emphasized by Robert B. Cialdini, Regents' Professor Emeritus of Psychology and Marketing at Arizona State University, in his book *Yes! 50 Scientifically Proven Ways to Be Persuasive*. Cialdini notes that arguing against your own self-interest creates the perception that you are an honest and trustworthy person, especially if you follow a comment on your failing with something very positive that neutralizes the particular drawback. My interpretation of Cialdini's idea is that it is best to be upfront with the other side. If you have certain limitations, drawbacks or have blundered along the way, especially with public comments or proposals, it is very wise to openly acknowledge it rather than wait for the other side to point it out for you. Raising it yourself demonstrates sincerity and trustworthiness.

Candour is a technique to be used strategically and infrequently, but it can be very effective if, first, you have a relationship with the other side, second, you are able to read their response to what you are saying, third, you have a decent understanding of whether or not they are likely to accept your comments as legitimate and, finally, you are careful about timing, because context has a significant effect on how candid comments are received. Cialdini is also very clear that you should be as candid as possible about the rationale behind your proposals and take time to outline your reasons very clearly, even when you think they are obvious. Don't make assumptions about what the other party is thinking or believes to be correct.

THE QUALITIES OF A GREAT NEGOTIATOR

"Marvin Miller is generally regarded as the person without whom baseball would be the most different in the second half of the twentieth century. Jackie Robinson in the first half. Marvin had that kind of influence. He came from a union background. He had worked for a number of them, and for a decade and a half before he came to the MLB players' union he had worked for the Steelworkers and was assistant to the president, chief negotiator and economist in major continental-wide negotiations. Marvin believed that you always tell the truth and that means that you don't shade either. Secondly, you are direct with your member-ship — even blunt — especially when it's things that they don't want to hear. You never promise what you can't deliver. And you make sure that you have buy-in from the players."

Watch the interview at
tinyurl.com/negotiating-fehr-qualities

DONALD FEHR, Executive Director of the National Hockey League Players' Association and former Executive Director of the Major League Baseball Players Association

Another aspect of designing a deal is how you respond to an attack, especially if it is unjustified or has limited basis in reality. I never advise being nasty or personal in a response, but you cannot allow false accusations or information to go on the record without an immediate clarifying response. Maintaining silence in the face of an accusation can jeopardize the entire process and keep you from achieving your mandate. More typical than an attack on you is a situation where the other side makes inaccurate or untrue claims about your client. If that happens, offer a thoughtful response into the record that you, first, don't agree with the assertion, second, view the assertion as false and, finally, see the facts differently as they pertain to this case.

Accountability

In the formation and design of the deal, be prepared to be accountable for anything you ask for or commit to providing. Just as a lawyer is clear about whether they can follow through before they give an undertaking, you need to know the cost, impact and rationale of any decision you make, which requires being fully informed about the features and the benefits of every proposal on either side. Otherwise, you end up looking like one of those shady salespeople who outlines the features and benefits of a product, makes a series of claims about how the product delivers value and then cannot follow through on the promise. Know your stuff, take your time and only make commitments you can follow through on.

Equally important is for you to demand from the other side that they also be accountable. Why would you accept an offer if you didn't fully understand its impact? Even if you think you understand the impact of a proposal, it is best to assume that you do not. Take your time, ask good questions and consult with you team. I have seen numerous negotiations where the parties were not held accountable for the commitments they made to each other. This is a waste of time, damages reputations and limits the potential for agreement.

ADDRESSING THE ISSUES DIRECTLY

"I remember the first meeting between business representatives and people with disabilities about an accessibility act. We rented a huge room in a hotel near the airport, and when I walked in one of the activists said to me, 'You should issue a press release — we have never had a meeting like this before.' I thought, how can you negotiate anything if you don't have the parties that disagree in the same room?

"Business was afraid of what an accessibility law would cost. People with disabilities felt shut out of businesses. So we sat at the table and I listened to their concerns. By the end of the morning, it was obvious that there was 98 per cent agreement — as there usually is, but everyone tends to focus on the 2 per cent of disagreement — but in this case, business was simply in the dark about what an accessibility act would mean and how much it would cost. One business man who was an executive from Hamilton summarized it best. He said, 'As a businessman, you are scaring me, but as a father of a disabled girl, you are not moving fast enough.' That was the beginning — laying out the fears and the challenges and then working on them."

Watch the interview at
tinyurl.com/negotiating-
bountro-understand

MARIE BOUNTROGIANNI, Dean of the Chang School of Continuing Education at Ryerson University and former Member of Provincial Parliament

Be accountable for the offers and counteroffers you make and demand that the other side be accountable for theirs. This is where anticipating what they will offer and having a sense of what they are actually able to provide is critical so that you can respond appropriately.

Quality of Proposals

Your proposals should have substance and be delivered with passion and clarity. Remember Harry Mills's assertion that people learn 75 per cent through visuals and 13 per cent from what they hear. If Mills is correct, you should accompany your key proposals when required with some form of visual presentation. Most negotiations do not involve or require visuals, but some subjects (such as real estate) naturally lend themselves to a visual emphasis. There are many excellent resources to help you with this part of the process, so all I will say in general is know your audience, know the issues and create clear visuals that are easy to read and interesting to the eye. It can also be useful to develop videos for your purposes, if you have the time or the funds to do so.

The quality of your delivery matters. To be at your best and represent your interests effectively, use mock presentations in advance of the meeting, even if you have to prepare three different versions for three different possible scenarios. Practising with your team and gathering their feedback improves the quality of your proposals. You should also consider practising your opening statement (more on this in the next chapter), responses to questions, counteroffers and concluding statements. In a sense, I am suggesting a form of simulation similar to those undertaken by pilots to practise their skills.

TAKEAWAYS

ELEVEN PRINCIPLES OF INFLUENCE

1. Law of reciprocity — people will generally respond in kind to your tone and attitude.
2. Law of contrast — magnify differences between two similar items by placing side by side.
3. Law of consistency — commitments made out loud or in writing are more often kept.
4. Law of scarcity — things felt to be scarce have more value than things widely available.
5. Fear of loss — the fear of losing something is greater than the desire to gain something.
6. Limit choice — too much choice leads to paralysis — limit the options you present.
7. Power of testimonials — recommendations from people known and admired go far.
8. Focus on problem solving — problem-solvers are effective and appreciated.
9. Mix up the environment — change settings to breathe new energy into a meeting.
10. Appearance and demeanour — be well-groomed, positive and use self-deprecating humour.
11. Likeability — likeable personalities create a productive and co-operative dynamic.

KEY CONSIDERATIONS FOR DEAL FORMATION

12. Remember mandate and BATNA — weigh every offer and option against your explicit goals.
13. Gain leverage — it is based on the perception the other side has of the strength of your case.
14. Find the right criteria — use the benchmarks and precedents that support your position.

15. Determine your price — use worth analysis, market value and/or cost analysis.
16. Prepare for concessions — know your non-negotiables and always get something in return.
17. Understand contingency contracts — you can fall back on it if the other side doesn't deliver.

YOUR APPROACH

18. Be candid — point to your own failings and be frank about the rationale behind your proposals.
19. Respond to an attack — never maintain silence in the face of an unfair accusation.
20. Be accountable — support your claims and rationale with data and keep your promises.
21. Offer quality proposals — practise in advance and support with high-impact visuals.

CHAPTER 9
Live at the Table

"A sense of humor is part of the art of leadership, of getting along with people, of getting things done."

— Dwight D. Eisenhower

The G8 is a group consisting of the leaders of the Western world's most advanced economies. It was formed in 1975 and meets once a year in a member country. In June 1995, Canada was scheduled to host the G8 summit, and as a senior member of the government and a representative from Atlantic Canada, I believed it was my duty to work with my colleagues from the east to accomplish a single goal: secure Atlantic Canada's economic centre, Halifax, as the site for the summit. To do so, I would need to plan strategically to convince my friends and colleagues in the prime minister's office that Halifax would meet their needs and be a superb ambassador for the country. The question: how do we make it happen?

Among the papers and mementos of my time as an MP and cabinet minister, there is a memorandum sent from Mary Gusella, the President of the Atlantic Canada Opportunities Agency (ACOA), to me at my office on Parliament Hill. The memo is date stamped March 28, 1994, and requests that I sign and deliver the attached letter to the Right Honourable Jean

Chrétien, Prime Minister of Canada. The letter had been carefully crafted by seasoned bureaucrat Wynne Potter, then Vice President of ACOA, after extensive conversations and input from me. So why was I signing a letter from an agency located in Moncton, New Brunswick, and delivering it to a man I had known for fourteen years whose office I could walk into any day of the week to talk about any issue that needed our attention? The answer has to do with what I was trying to accomplish.

My team began by trying to understand how the decision would be made and who would be making it. Unlike in a typical negotiation where what happens on the other side is obscured from view, both sides were entirely known to us because I worked closely with Chrétien and his staff every day. Leading ministers would offer input and the decision would be made by the PMO and, ultimately, the PM himself. I knew that when the time came, Chrétien would hear me out about why Halifax was perfect. But I wanted to do all I could in advance to make it easy for him to decide.

The first step was to deal with the two other cities competing for the right to host, each supported by another minister in the Chrétien cabinet. Ottawa, the nation's capital, was being pushed by Industry Minister John Manley, an MP from Ottawa South, and Quebec City was supported by Foreign Affairs Minister André Ouellet, an MP from Papineau in Montreal. After considerable consultation with my team, I went to visit each of those ministers to talk about the summit. I had one goal: enlist their support for Halifax as the backup option in the event that their city did not win the summit. It wasn't hard to do. There was enough rivalry between the two cities and provinces that each minister was glad to agree to Halifax as a second choice.

The next step was the letter. I spent a significant amount of time on the phone with Wynne Potter and we created a document that illustrated that Halifax did, indeed, have all of the required qualities. From security to scenery to telecommunications infrastructure, we outlined it all and then made the decision to have the letter come from me instead of Mary Gusella.

Then came the key step — meeting with the Prime Minister. He and I both knew what I was up to and he respected that fact. Politics is politics, and no good politician holds a grudge against another for advocating his position. In the meeting, I emphasized the internal considerations more so than the public reasons for the choice, because Chrétien knew there were dozens of incredible locations perfectly capable of doing a superb job of hosting. I focused on angles that I thought would meet his interests: that this was a rare opportunity to have the summit out east, having been held previously in Ontario and Quebec, and that no one was advocating for a western city. I explained that both Manley and Ouellet were supportive of Halifax as a second-best option and that I suspected they would be put out if it went to their rival's city. I outlined the significant security benefits of a city the size of Halifax: large enough to have excellent infrastructure but small enough to be well controlled. I pointed out that we could promote it as a cost effective summit, which would be a public relations coup given the enormous pressure we were under to get our fiscal house in order. Then I gave him the idea that I thought would sway him the most: the citizens of Halifax would come out in droves to get a glimpse of the world leaders, which would definitely not happen in Ottawa or Quebec City.

When the PMO announced that Halifax would be the site, my Atlantic Canada colleagues and I celebrated a great moment for our region — one that was born of fortuitous circumstances, careful planning and strategic execution. And as a side note, Chrétien referred to it as a "Chevrolet summit" because it was a powerful but cost effective option!

All the strategic planning and preparation before arriving at the table sets you up for success in the live portion of the negotiation.

Remember that your objective is to achieve a deal that meets your needs, not a deal at all costs. Being true to your mandate is critical so that you are genuinely prepared to walk away at any point in the deliberations. Proceed optimistically but carefully, keeping in mind all of the basic and advanced techniques we have been discussing.

Before discussing the complexities of life at the table, here's a reminder of several approaches that can guide you at this stage of the negotiations:

1. Be physically and mentally well-rested.

2. Demonstrate at all times unity amongst team.

3. Only one person should speak at a time.

4. Don't contradict team members in front of the other party.

5. Listen, listen, listen.

6. Ask good questions.

7. If a deal does not meet your mandate or BATNA, walk away.

BUILDING RAPPORT

I have talked a lot about the value of rapport at every negotiation stage. When you arrive at the table, your general commitment to relationships becomes a more focused exercise to build the connection, harmony and trust that underpin a successful process. The quality of the relationship is the most important factor in making mutually beneficial agreements possible.

Building rapport requires time and attention from both parties, but you should not wait for other side to initiate. Start sending good vibes right away. Ideally, you've had some one-on-

one time with key players on the other side prior to arriving at the table, but if email and phone calls have dominated the early stages, make an effort to connect right before the meeting. The best case scenario, of course, is that you already have a relationship with the other side, but that isn't always going to be possible.

USING HUMOUR

"One case where I was recently in a negotiation and there were about a dozen people on the other side and one of the parties in the room was a lawyer and it didn't matter what we were talking about — even everything that his entire team talked about — he said 'no' to it. And continued to say 'no.' So I looked at it and I thought about it carefully and then there was a little break and I went to get a coffee and there were some muffins and some croissants and I took a croissant and I put it at his desk and I said, 'You look like you need a little bit of something in your stomach because you seem a little bit grumpy today.' His whole team laughed.

"I was able to change the pattern of the negotiation just with a little humour. Some of his points were really valid, but that little move helped to lower the volume in the room and move the negotiations along."

Watch the interview at tinyurl.com/negotiating-zed-humour

PAUL ZED, Chairman of the President's Advisory Board for Rogers Communications Canada and former Member of Parliament

In her March 2007 contribution to the Program on Negotiation at Harvard Law School, Janice Nadler, a law professor at Northwestern University, pointed out three things that negotiators ought to do to increase rapport:

1. Go the extra mile and meet live.
Nadler notes that the impersonal nature of email in particular makes it difficult to establish feelings of trust and connection, so she suggests you should make the effort to create a time to meet face to face.

2. Chat first, negotiate later.
Nadler offers research findings that "small talk" sets the stage for an atmosphere of positivity, trust and openness that will ultimately create value. Develop rapport by finding opportunities to socialize with the other side and exchange information not necessarily pertaining to the negotiation. Again, this will take time and planning on your part, but it is a worthwhile investment, especially if your initial interactions with the other side are somewhat distant and cool.

3. Let the other party know you.
Nadler suggests that it is beneficial to reveal things about yourself that might seem unrelated or too personal. This doesn't mean being an egocentric showboat or social butterfly. It means being open to talking about your life, work and outside interests so that people can connect to you and then share some of themselves.

These approaches can make a significant difference, as I learned during a real estate deal in which I was selling a large piece of property to a buyer who I knew reasonably well and felt comfortable with. But as we got into the negotiations and began discussing price, fees, legal structure and timing, it was evident that we did not have a good enough rapport to sustain us through the process. The deal fell apart.

OPENING STATEMENTS

"In the opening statement, you want to ensure or validate that both sides want to do whatever it is that you want to do," explains Michael Cleaner. "And you want to show that you have a high level of proprietary interest in getting it done. And you want to verify that from the other side. Once you verify that, you are really moving forward in an amicable fashion."

Watch the interview with Michael Cleaner at tinyurl.com/negotiating-cleaner-open

Whether you speak first or second once the formal meetings begin, arrive with a deliberate plan, as you will only have one chance to make an opening statement. The tone you set has a significant effect on the early stages of the deliberations. If the other party is the first to speak and your feathers get ruffled, just stick to your plan and maintain a warm, welcoming and open approach. And if you have a negative first impression of the other side because they seem dismissive, cocky or arrogant, step back and remind yourself to be strategic and thoughtful in forming your opinions. You could be wrong about an individual and/or about the substance of their pitch because you reached a hasty conclusion. Impulse judgements are always risky.

Having engaged the other party with preliminary social niceties and your opening remarks, frame the negotiation by offering your definition of the task at hand. Are you pursuing a partnership? Trying to resolve a conflict? Or negotiating over an exclusively monetary issue? Use the plural pronoun "we" to emphasize what the whole room will be working together to solve. This approach can have quite an effect because most people view a negotiation as an adversarial process like litigation and assume they are here simply to get what they want. The more you can emphasize the goal of finding a mutually beneficial arrangement, the better. If any significant conflict exists between the parties, then recognize that for the sake of accuracy. But the main pitch is to resolve the issue together.

There is enormous power in how a conversation begins. Any social gathering launched on a negative subject tends to spiral in that direction. Positive openings generate an optimistic and gracious atmosphere. As you frame the issues for everyone in the room, create a positive outlook for the negotiation and give particular consideration to how you outline the potential losses and gains that could follow from certain directions.

Along with effective presentation skills, I always find that it is best to keep an opening statement relatively short. You may be obligated to take more time if the issue is complicated, but focus on being succinct and not offering too much detail. In addition, find a balance between being incredibly well prepared and coming across as scripted and rote. Passion and a conversational tone are most effective, along with relaxed and open body language.

There is usually a power imbalance at the beginning of a negotiation because one of the parties has leverage over the other. If the other side has some kind of initial advantage, my suggestion is that you acknowledge it up front. Why? Accurately talking about what is going on demonstrates that you have done your homework, understand the nature of the situation and have credibility, impressions that will benefit you later on. And if the other party objects to some element of your opening statement, use it as an opportunity to engage in thoughtful conversation by asking them to elaborate on what the negotiation is about. Also, don't feel that you need to make a comprehensive argument. Concentrate on making your opening statement compelling.

As for the overall tone of your opening remarks, if you have good information, a solid understanding of the situation and clearly outlined BATNAs, go ahead and express optimism at the outset. This creates a collaborative atmosphere while also giving you some power later when rejecting certain offers and counter-offers. Being positive as a baseline mode heightens the impact of those outlier moments when you need to strongly disagree, rebut, correct or be "negative." The departure from your standard tone will get people's attention.

FIRST OFFERS

"I believe that you have to put a fair offer on the table at some point," explains Michael Cleaner. "I don't think you should lowball the offer to the point that you could potentially offend the other side. So my position was always to put a fair offer on the table but have some bullets of things in it that you are quite prepared to give up. So you put those things in knowing full well that you are prepared to give them up because everybody has to win."

Watch the interview with Michael Cleaner at tinyurl.com/negotiating-cleaner-offers

Depending on the strength of your position, there can be significant advantages to making the first offer because you can set the expectations and anchor the deliberations favourably. If your information and understanding of the other side's ability to meet your demands are solid, you should feel confident making the first offer. And if the opening offers are going to be about non-price issues, you can feel more comfortable going first than if forced to make pricing suggestions right up front.

A first offer always needs to be aggressive and accompanied by a rationale that refers to the standard you have agreed to and outlines why this particular offer is being made. I always recommend to my clients that their first offer be reasonable but with room to manoeuvre. An unreasonable or exaggerated opening offer will make you look ill-prepared or disingenuous and does not create momentum for the conversations. Ideally, your first offer should be your highest realistic expectation based on the chosen standard. And select your language carefully. Most often, too-common phrases such as "frankly," "to be honest with you," and "I wouldn't lie to you" raise the hackles of the other side and indicate that you are exactly what you claim not to be. Avoid sounding patronizing or manipulative.

Think ahead about the effect your first offer will have on future concessions and proposals. You may want to ask for something upfront that you know you will give away later. When you eventually do give it away, the other side will feel an obligation to reciprocate. You can also use contrast to your advantage later on when your future offers are compared to your opening bid. Those future offers may look quite appealing to the other side in light of where you began. Overall, your first offer is a strategic move that sets you up to make further moves throughout the negotiation.

THE QUALITIES OF A GREAT NEGOTIATOR

"The well-prepared person. The person who knows the file. Knows the facts. Has taken the trouble to speak to key witnesses. And is just well prepared to deal with the demands I'm making."

Watch the interview at tinyurl.com/negotiating-payne-qualities

JANICE PAYNE, leading labour lawyer and partner at Nelligan O'Brien Payne LLP

If in a position to make the first offer, keep in mind that negotiations in almost every sector run the risk of falling into the use of bracketing, the practice where two sides express a desire for numbers that are at a distance from each other and end up settling for a number in the middle. Ideally, you will avoid the see-saw process of position negotiations by focusing the conversation on the worth of your proposals. If you think you might enter into a bracketed discussion, carefully consider the impact of your starting point. And keep in mind that if there are gaps in your information or your understanding of the other side or the issues, you are probably better off responding rather than initiating.

With much to consider about how to frame and strategically situate a first offer, hold this one thought in mind: no matter what happens, never say "yes" to the first offer or the first counteroffer.

FIRST COUNTEROFFER

Prior to making your first counteroffer, caucus with your team if time permits in order to determine the exact contents of the proposal along with precisely what will be said or written to describe it. Spend time carefully assessing the original offer and probing the assumptions that were used to generate it. The more you can understand the impact of the offer on each side's interests and mandate, the more effectively you will be able to create an effective counter. A substantive first counteroffer supported by a fulsome justification and a good number (if required) will have a significant impact on the other party.

If your response to the offer is oral, I suggest you begin with some positive but accurate statements about the good qualities of the offer, such as its comprehensiveness. Then proceed to outline your counter in detail and your rationale with regular reference to the interests of both sides and the facts of the case. Typically, I am very reluctant to provide a financial value of any kind until I have outlined my rationale completely along with the specifics of my request and the impact it will have on both sides. As I have said before, numbers should never precede rationale.

One interesting example of an impressive counteroffer comes from Anne Golden during a meeting with a particularly hostile CEO. "I was at United Way and the Chairman of the campaign was a wonderful man named Bob Martin. He was very principled. Very caring. Top integrity. We go to call on a CEO and present the case. We think we do a good job. When we are finished, the CEO tells us he isn't going to give us any money because he doesn't believe in helping people. He says he is very tough-minded and tells us that he had, that day, fired a guy who is sick and has financial difficulties and has a mother with cancer. So he proceeds to tell us, with some pride, about how cruel he is with this person. My volunteer Chair got up and said, 'I cannot take this anymore. I am out of here. I cannot listen to this. You are a mean son of a bitch.' So Bob leaves the room and I was there with the CEO. I asked him, 'You studied history, didn't you?' He said he had. I told him that I am a historian by training. So I said,

'From one historian to another, would you give me $10,000?' Right there, he took out his chequebook and gave me the money and I walked out."

Watch the interview with Anne Golden at tinyurl.com/negotiating-golden-offers

THE NUANCES OF OFFERS AND COUNTEROFFERS

In any offer, counteroffer or concession, be specific and detailed and always refer back to your rationale and standard, such as a precedent or market rate. Choose phrases that emphasize the time you and your team have put into creating the proposal, the value of this offer for your side and the benefit it has for them. You might say, "We have given this a great deal of thought and this is the best we can do under the circumstances to meet both of our needs." Never say, "this is my final offer." Also, keep in mind that an offer or counteroffer in writing will be experienced as more legitimate and definite than a conversation, so choose carefully when and on what topics you make proposals or respond in writing.

At the table, it is generally easier to start with simple issues to which the parties can quickly agree and move to the more difficult topics. Also, if something is important to you, make sure you raise it early and often. If you wait until the end of the process, the issue will not get the attention it deserves and you will lose value. When you reach the phase where you are both offering incremental moves to your proposals, insist on reciprocity of movement — if you give a little, you can expect to get a little in return. If you are not getting anything, don't give anything back.

When a proposal involves numbers, I advise clients to avoid suggesting a range, such as "we can offer $8,000 to $12,000 for this service." It is more advantageous to be very specific about your numbers and provide a clear rationale for how they were selected. And when going back and forth on shifts in pricing, how you refer to the shift will be different depending on whether you are buying or selling. For example, if a buyer offers $1,000 and increases it by $100, they have increased the offer by 10 per cent. If a seller starts at $2,000 and decreases it by $100, they have only decreased it by 5 per cent. Given this, buyers should emphasize the percentage increase of a move and sellers should emphasize the dollar figure.

THE ISSUE OF PRICE

Price is one of the most intense and complicated parts of a negotiation. I have mentioned a few times to delay the price until you have offered a substantive explanation of your rationale. No matter the context — from the private sector to government, non-profit or even personal deals — and no matter the size of the deal, price is generally the final frontier of any negotiation.

Once at the stage of hammering out the financial value of the service or product, prepare for how you will respond when the other side does the inevitable: asks you to raise or lower your price. Anticipate the request and be strategic about your response so that you can continue to build rapport and momentum. And more than anything, never take it personally. A request to change the financial value you agree upon is not an affront to you or the process. It is a normal part of the interaction. That said, there are times when you can reasonably expect that the haggling is over. If someone comes at you yet again, you have the right to be miffed, whether or not you choose to show it. And you may be a lot more than just miffed if the other side hits you with the classic line, "Reduce your price or I am walking."

In their article "Extreme Negotiations with Suppliers," authors Jonathan Hughes, Jessica Wadd and Jeff Weiss of Vantage Partners, a spinoff of the Harvard Negotiation Project, make some interesting suggestions about how to deal with price bargaining. They offer five strategies to connect price discussions to principles and interests and to avoid positional back and forth that is just about money. First, inquire about how this request fits into the overall negotiation with a phrase such as, "Help me understand how you see this particular situation." Second, uncover and collaborate by engaging the other party in a discussion about why the price request is coming at this point. Third, focus on seeking buy-in from the other party by emphasizing the value of the service and the principle of fairness so they will not react solely to your response to their price request. Fourth, don't use price as a means of building relationships — you cannot buy trust or integrity. Fifth, focus on the process and do not allow the moment of the request to become the entire negotiation.

There are three phrases the authors suggest using in a price deadlock:

1.   "We seem to be at an impasse; perhaps we should spend some more time exploring our respective objectives and our constraints."

2.   "I am not ready to agree and I prefer not to walk away either. I think the issues warrant further explanation."

3.   "Unless you are willing to work with me to search out a mutually acceptable outcome, I cannot afford to spend more time negotiating."

I prefer the first two phrases over the third because I don't like giving the other side wiggle room to get out of the negotiation when so much time has already been invested in the process and, presumably, I want to reach a deal. And I'm not keen to use an ultimatum like this when my emphasis is always on making the deal work.

In summarizing their advice about coping with price negotiations, Hughes, Wadd and Weiss offer this: "Control and power can most effectively be asserted by slowing down the pace of the negotiations, actively leading counterparts into a constructive process, and demonstrating a genuine openness to learning about and even being persuaded by the views of the others." Obviously, this is consistent with the strategic approach I am advocating, but it is especially important to apply this technique to avoid price bargaining that can cause you to drift from your strategy, mandate and goals. Armed with good questions and an emphasis on the big picture, you will be more effective not only at the overall negotiation but in price bargaining specifically.

SEVENTEEN TWISTS AND TURNS AT THE NEGOTIATING TABLE

With the major areas of live negotiation addressed, I want to take you through a series of behaviours and approaches that you might use and/or see during this stage. Some will upset you, others will empower you and still others will frustrate you to no end. Regardless, they are frequent "guests" at the table and it's best to act strategically based on your mandate and with a focus on the issues, not on your ego or the personalities in the room. Is this an easy task? No! However, being well prepared and working with your team will move you away from troubling behaviours toward resolving issues and addressing interests.

1. Anger

Peter Harder says of emotion in meetings, "The people that you want to avoid are the ones who actually lose it as a result of their emotions. Emotions are a tool of negotiation, not a result of losing the negotiation momentum."

Watch the interview with
Peter Harder at
tinyurl.com/negotiating-
harder-emotions

We've all been angry in a meeting: people go off-topic, aren't making sense, become obstructive or issue insults. You will have your own list of hot-button behaviours. In his book *The Likeability Factor*, Tim Sanders offers advice with more depth than "bite your tongue." It's "delay your anger gratification." When we lash out in anger, there is a sense of relief, power and pleasure from emptying our tank, but it almost never helps the process. Hostility is not helpful when attempting to reach an agreement. You don't have to love the other party, but your primary objective is to find common ground upon which to seek a resolution. Not giving in to your anger puts you in a better position, especially if the opposite party is deliberately provoking you into revealling something they view as important. Be very careful about how you respond if they come at you in anger. We are wired for reciprocity, but when it comes to anger, nothing is gained by responding in kind. In fact, when faced with someone who is angry or very upset, follow this principle: the next ten minutes of the discussion is theirs, not yours. Not responding is responding well.

One of my early experiences with anger directed toward me came when I met with fishermen from my constituency in Cape Breton. They would arrive at my office, often without an appointment, livid with the Government of Canada regarding fishing quotas. I can still hear them addressing my assistant in the waiting room: "Where is the little prick?" They were all good people who worked hard every day and were passionate about their communities and livelihoods. But when they got riled, they got riled. So I learned what it was to sit calmly and patiently and be receptive without making any commitments that might make the situation worse.

It's appropriate at times to display anger or be more forceful than normal, but only if it's a strategic choice. You might get a bit heated — not over the top, upsetting the table and throwing chairs around the room, but letting everyone know that you are not happy with how a proposal, position or person is being characterized. If you do tee off on the other side, make direct eye contact, avoid raising your voice too much and be very precise about the nature of your concerns. Don't do this very often, but rarely and in the right moment, it can be very effective.

2. Exaggeration

When I asked Donald Fehr about his view of inflated proposals or misrepresenting your interests, he was very pointed in his response: "There are some people who believe that the way you negotiate is, for example, if you are making fifty cents an hour and you want to make a dollar an hour, you start by asking for a dollar fifty and then at some point you announce that you are going to make a major concession and accept a dollar when everybody knows that that is what you wanted in the first place. I think that if you have professional negotiators in the room, everybody knows that game and it's really just a silly way to proceed and I think it's a waste of time. I learned that the way to negotiate is to make proposals you believe in because you think they are appropriate and because you want them — and then you try and persuade people to go with them."

Watch the interview with Donald Fehr at tinyurl.com/negotiating-fehr-exaggeration

Fehr's response is in line with my impression of how people react to exaggeration. To a novice, an exaggerated position might seem compelling, even captivating, but to anyone relatively experienced, the loud voice, over-emphasized gestures and questionable content seem amateurish and are a put-off. But it's amazing how readily any of us can plunge into exaggeration. In my career, I have come across colleagues from all political parties and organizations with the best of intent — often people I knew to have integrity — who fell into the trap of expressing their position in inflated terms.

I admit that at times, I have used exaggeration on a variety of different public policy issues with predictably poor results with the media, my political opponents or my colleagues. It never pays to overstate a situation. Precision and accuracy support your ongoing work and build your reputation for integrity. There is nothing wrong with being aggressive or direct at times, but there is never a circumstance when it is best to misrepresent things. If faced with an exaggerator on the other side, address it directly and do not allow the false claims to be written into the record.

3. Embarrassing the Other Party

Buzz Hargrove was a master at building long-term relationships with his counterparts, as illustrated in this situation when he and his team could easily have taken a high-handed approach. "I remember once that we were negotiating about pension improvements and the company made a proposal and said that there was $100 million that they could not cover. 'This is a fixed limit and we can't go above that number.' It was General Motors, of course, with those kinds of numbers. So one of our young guys, a young researcher named Jeff Wareham, spent all night crunching the numbers that they gave us on what we called penny sheets with all the data. He was up all night and the next morning when I came down to get my coffee and he came in and he was all excited. He said 'I found an error in their calculations — their costs are off by

$200 million. They could give us what we want and still be $100 million better off than what they are saying.' So I talked about it with our guys and then I went and met the company. I didn't want to embarrass them. I didn't want to bring it up in front of both committees, because a key to negotiation is never trying that one-upmanship. The company representative took the numbers away and talked to his guys and got back to me in a couple of hours. He said, 'Buzz, your guy is right — we appreciate it. That makes a big difference in the numbers, but we still need $100 million dollars.' That's bargaining. That's the way it works."

Watch the interview with Buzz Hargrove at tinyurl.com/negotiating-hargrove-embarrass

Some negotiators take great delight in attempting to embarrass the other party by producing new information or facts while at the table. This approach does not add value or build relationships and I strongly discourage it in favour of open dialogue, trust and a genuine effort to consummate a contract. I see an effort to embarrass the other side as strictly an act of ego that ultimately limits your ability to reach an agreement. It also has a negative effect on your reputation. If you have access to information that the other side does not or appears not to have, find a low-key and offline way to share it, like Buzz Hargrove's request for a private meeting.

4. Difficult Conversations

In negotiations and in life, there are situations where the conversation is very difficult, emotional and stressful, and especially in moments of confrontation. It can be particularly difficult to address an issue with an authority figure, such as our children's teacher, an unco-operative boss or a police officer. In those cases, we are sometimes looking for someone to blame, but if we take the time to listen and understand before we react, we can find a way forward that decreases the tension. That said, there are always difficult moments in a negotiation — such as letting a team member go or delivering upsetting news or information.

In their much-acclaimed book *Difficult Conversations*, Douglas Stone, Bruce Patton and Sheila Heen emphasize that "listening well is one of the most powerful skills you can bring to a difficult conversation." Listening can be a potent antidote to anger, high emotion and tension. But it must be genuine and active. The authors also point out that, when in a conflict, falling into blaming "inhibits our ability to learn what is really causing the problem and to do anything meaningful to correct it."

Based on their work and on my own experience, there are several helpful considerations for difficult conversations:

1.   Do not react emotionally to the other party's emotional outburst.

2.   Listen attentively and where possible try to make a few notes.

3.   Keep good eye contact.

4.   Be careful of the words that you choose as you respond.

5.   If the heated conversation comes in the midst of a negotiation, think about taking a break.

6.   Make certain that your body language is aligned with what you are saying. The flick of an eyebrow or rolling of the eyes will aggravate things.

7.   Be patient, respectful and civil, no matter what the other side says.

5. Deadlocks or Impasses

Deadlocks or impasses are common — whether either side intends them or not — and different negotiators have different views of how you should proceed. Here are three to consider:

Peter Harder: "There's no such thing as a deadlock or an impasse. An impasse is a tactic in the negotiations, it is not the result of the negotiations. It might be a failure of the negotiators — either a lack of will or a lack of trust or a lack of being able to deliver your side — but don't view it as an end point."

Watch the interview with Peter Harder at tinyurl.com/negotiating-harder-deadlocks

Michael Cleaner: "I have faced several impasses and I think how to look at the problem and how you can solve it as a win-win for both sides. You have to understand why there is an impasse. What created it? Was there something that was misunderstood along the way when you were negotiating? Is it something you can overcome? And if so, what do both sides have to do to get there? You really have to discuss that and continue to monitor the situation and get back to the person in terms of responding with an appropriate resolution to the matter. And as long as you have some communication going, you are probably going to resolve it. The secret to negotiations is to keep on talking."

Watch the interview
with Michael Cleaner at
tinyurl.com/negotiating-
cleaner-deadlocks

Buzz Hargrove: "I never thought that because I am the chief negotiator and the president that I am the only guy that can go and meet with the top guy in the company. If I felt that Jim O'Neil was better to go in and sit down now because I had lectured the hell out of them about their position, I would send him in and he would say, 'Pay no attention to Hargrove, he goes a little nuts once in a while. Now, what the hell does it take to settle this?'"

Watch the interview
with Buzz Hargrove at
tinyurl.com/negotiating-
hargrove-deadlocks

My advice for dealing with deadlocks is to proceed strategically and avoid acting on your gut. Here are some suggestions for getting out of a blockage:

1. Set aside that particular issue and come back to it later.

2. Take a break.

3. Brainstorm options that have not been discussed yet.

4.   Agree on a deadline for resolving the dispute.

5.   Revisit the priorities for both sides and look for any room to manoeuvre so that you can maintain whatever momentum has been built up in the process.

6.   Consider changing the objective criteria being used.

7.   Move that part of the conversation up the chain of command so that players with more authority can resolve it.

8.   Change the meeting site.

9.   Change a team member.

10.   Choose an alternative process, such as mediation.

11.   Finally, you may have to concede that particular point and/or walk away.

6. Extreme Demands

In the July/August 2013 issue of *Supply Chain Management Review*, authors Jonathan Hughes, Jessica Wadd and Jeff Weiss talk about stressful circumstances in the midst of a serious negotiation. The authors explain that extreme demands create a feeling of danger that puts the pressure on to act fast to reduce a perceived threat. They explain that negotiators often act based on gut feeling and initial perceptions before they fully assess the situation. The authors advise to be wary of an extreme demand and begin by questioning the assumptions at the foundation of the other party's claims. I am in favour of this because it emphasizes good questions and a shared process of understanding. By investigating the nature of a claim, you can address the situation in a comprehensive manner.

An extreme demand can be made at any point in a negotiation and requires a thoughtful response. You can respond
by asking for more information — essentially, by launching an
investigation into the nature and rationale of the demand. Some
negotiators react to an extreme demand with pressure tactics,
which then triggers a response in kind from the counterpart.
This is a slippery slope that benefits no one. Follow the advice
from Hughes, Wadd and Weiss: "Extreme negotiations are best
approached by slowing down the pace of the negotiations, dili-
gently seeking an unbiased understanding of one's counterparts
and actively trying to lead them into a more collaborative negotiation process."

7. Silence

There can be value in sitting in silence at the table. Don't be
afraid of or surprised by this approach, and consider ways to put
it to use. Silence will happen naturally at some times and be a
deliberate tactic from one of the negotiators at others. Consider
talking about how you and your team will use silence, but also be
flexible enough that if the lead negotiator makes a decision in the
moment to wait and let the issues float through people's minds,
you will all support that effort.

Janice Payne explains one benefit to keeping quiet: "It is so
important to know when to stop talking. In a difficult discussion, just stopping and not offering anything and letting the
pause build will be enough to prompt the other side to begin to
talk and perhaps give you what you need in order to advance
the discussion. It is one of the most important skills in any
negotiation."

Should the occasion arise when the other party wishes to
break the silence, I suggest you let them have the floor and take
careful notes. And make sure that you never talk just for the sake
of talking.

Watch the interview with Janice Payne at tinyurl.com/negotiating-payne-silence

When I asked Buzz Hargrove about silence, he explained it can be effective, though hard to sustain. "I was an expert at silence. I used to love blasting the hell out of the company and then sitting back and not saying anything. It always fascinated me how people on both sides couldn't do that. I used to sit back and just let the tension build. For me that was an important part of the process. But somebody would always break it. There would always be somebody on either side of the table — not me or the chief negotiator on the other side — but somebody in the room would feel they have to come in and say something."

Watch the interview with Buzz Hargrove at tinyurl.com/negotiating-hargrove-silence

8. Remember Names

Senator Bob Muir taught me as much about how to build relationships and respect as any other political mentor I had. He was appointed to the Senate after close to twenty-five years representing the constituency next to mine, and though he was a member of another political party, he took an interest in me in the early days. Warm, thoughtful, engaging and sincere, Muir was a pro at building relationships and positive impressions.

One Saturday afternoon early in my first term as an MP, I arrived in the Sydney, Nova Scotia, airport after a few weeks in Ottawa and was greeted by my family. As we stood at the baggage carousel, the Senator approached me and asked if we could have a quick word. We stepped aside, he enquired how I was doing, and then asked, "Can I give you two pieces of advice?" I told him I would appreciate anything he could offer. "Number one, your constituents want to see you well dressed, so stop wearing blue jeans even though it's the weekend. When you are in the public eye, you need to dress well." I looked down at my clothes and then at the Senator, who was dressed in a blue suit with a white shirt and matching tie and handkerchief. "Number two, last week, when you met with the executive of the United Mine Workers, you couldn't remember a single name in the room." I went red in the face and have never forgotten that moment. He was right, and ever since then I have tried to be well dressed in public and make a deliberate point of learning and using people's names. As Tim Sanders says, "A person's name is the friendliest word in the world."

Watch the interview with Paul Zed at tinyurl.com/negotiating-zed-relationships

In your opening statements, proposals, ongoing discussions and informal interactions with your own people as well as the other side, always use people's names and make sure you know who they are, what they care about and how they fit into the situation. If the names are difficult to pronounce, plan ahead and practise. Names matter, as Paul Zed emphasizes: "It sounds pretty pedestrian, but you'd be amazed at how often people don't know the name of the person they are negotiating with. You use that name and you develop that relationship just like it was one of your friends."

9. Bluffing

On the subject of bluffing, I couldn't say it better than James Freund in *Smart Negotiating*, so I'll offer his tips for your consideration:

1.   You can only bluff a few times, so don't waste them on something insignificant.

2.   Never bluff at the beginning of the process — save it until the end.

3.   Make sure your behaviour when bluffing is consistent with how you act normally.

4.   Mix a bluff in with other items on which you are offering flexibility.

5.   If you are forced to back down from your bluff, be ready to make an argument that circumstances have changed.

10. Bad Faith

At times, you may detect that the other party is negotiating in bad faith. This might include using documents with conclusions you know to be inaccurate, offering hearsay as fact or being very loose with key data. If you find yourself in that situation, stop the process and call them on it right away. You don't need to be angry or aggressive, but it's important to set the record straight. Name it and blame it: put what they're doing into precise language and then hold them accountable. Otherwise, you indicate that the behaviour is acceptable and effective, which undermines the process.

NEGOTIATING SO EVERYONE WINS

In addition, you may find yourself working with a counterpart who intentionally attempts to sabotage the negotiations and your proposals. This is a whole other issue and requires a deliberate and strategic approach. Slow the process down and probe into the nature of every proposition and the evidence that supports it. Misinformation and lying destroy trust, and if you cannot trust what they offer, you will need to proceed accordingly. And, of course, you should never go down the road of lying, even in a small way. It is simply not productive or worthwhile.

11. Caucusing

A caucus is a group of people retreating to a private setting in order to discuss issues that have come up during the negotiation. These private sessions are invaluable and can be used strategically. Plan breaks to meet with your team. And devise a system of signals for when you want to call an unexpected meeting while at the table. If I have only a few members on my side, we use the kick under the table method to indicate it is time for a caucus. In a larger group, any member of the team touching their hair in a deliberate fashion tells me, as the lead, that it is time to take a "health break." You can devise your own approach, but create a system that encourages people to call for a caucus when they are concerned. You never want your team to be reluctant to seek clarification any time things seem to be heading down the wrong road. As teams get to know each other better, the level of understanding between members makes this process more fluid, but begin by setting ground rules for caucusing no matter how long you have known your team.

One of the great benefits of a caucus meeting is that you can share perspectives on what is happening at the table, especially when dealing with large groups. I always encourage teams to assign each other different roles during the meetings and for each member to pay attention to specific individuals on the other side so that when we caucus, we have a perspective on the whole scene. Of course, caucusing is also essential for being strategic about each move you will make at the table. Discussion deepens insight and allows you to revisit your mandate and strategy.

It is important to be careful and strategic with a caucus, however. You don't want the other side to view a caucus as a signal that a concession is going to take place. They may assume this without having received any indication from you and then feel slighted when your team returns without a concession. Any time you come out of a caucus, be prepared to frame its purpose to the other side without providing any information you don't want them to have.

12. The Flinch

The flinch is an emotional outburst designed to neutralize the power of a proposal or suggestion. It normally occurs in the midst of a negotiation when the other side responds to what you are saying by blurting out something like, "Oh my God, that's way too much!" In most instances, this kind of intervention is planned, and so expect it to happen at some point, especially once the deliberations have moved to a discussion of discrete items. My advice with a flinch is to ignore it and act as if nothing was said. The point of the flinch is to scare you off from certain proposals. If you don't react, the effect is neutralized.

13. Time Pressure

At times, you will be under pressure from the other side to make an immediate decision about an item. They may become aggressive, even if polite on the surface. As always, check your emotions, consult with your team and resist the pressure to speed up. Quick decisions are generally bad decisions. If you are able to respond because you made a decision about that particular item some time ago and it is just coming up now, that's fine. That's being strategic. But actually making a decision in the moment is invariably a bad idea.

14. Good Cop/Bad Cop

This friend-and-foe approach is typical to negotiations: one individual is pleasant and cordial while the other cool and less co-operative. A well-known technique, it is still effective in certain circumstances because it allows you to have one party who is aggressively defending or asserting your position and another who is emphasizing reconciliation or compromise. You can use the contrast between the two styles as police do during an interrogation: to increase the level of openness toward your good cop. This approach is probably most effective in small groups but can also be used well in the numerous smaller meetings that take place away from the table during multiparty negotiations.

15. The Nibbler

At the point when the agreement seems to be in order, sometimes the other side suddenly announces that there is another item they would like to discuss. Typically, the new item is not significant and is then followed by two or three other small items — all framed under the heading of "these are just some little things that we did not get to yet." I call this kind of approach a nibbler, because it feels like a small rodent nibbling away at the edges of my patience, trust and time. Be ready for the nibblers — they are everywhere! My way of coping is to address it well in advance, particularly during the agenda formation, by pressing for all issues to be on the table from the outset. Then, if small issues come up late in the process, you can suggest that the agreement be finalized first before addressing the additions. This approach decreases the likelihood of a negotiator nibbling away at your time and sanity.

16. Threats

A basic rule about threats is that if you are not actually prepared to follow through, you should not make one. But fundamentally, even subtle threats can have a detrimental effect on relationships and stall the negotiations. Obviously, if faced with a threat from the other side, you should avoid responding in kind. For example, if the other side says, "If you don't give me a higher margin, I am going with your competitor," it is not wise to respond with your own threat to leave the bargaining table.

Just as a price discussion should be framed within the overall context of the negotiation, respond to a threat by probing into the nature of the assertion and engaging the other party in a discussion about what they are trying to achieve. In the example above where the threat is about margins, you could start by asking questions to get at the nature of the request, like "why it is so important to have a higher margin?" or "what is the market rate in this case?" You can then emphasize the value of the relationship and the benefits and cost savings of working together over a long period of time. Then you can point out that while it may appear that there are greater margins available at another supplier, there are various hidden costs that will inevitably apply. And you can emphasize the advantages of working with your firm. Anything to get at the nature of the threat and diffuse the power of the forceful assertion.

17. Ethical Conduct

It is important for your success in a particular negotiation and for your reputation long term that you never compromise on your morals. The impact of being unethical, particularly in highly connected communities can be extremely serious. It is always best to be as transparent, trustworthy and candid as possible.

Equally important is how you should respond when you sense or see unethical behaviour from the other side. Wherever possible, even though it is extremely difficult to know exactly how to proceed, I think it is best to call this kind of behaviour out. Allowing the other side to misrepresent, skimp on the facts or be silent about the causes of their activities creates a rift in the proceedings that will inevitably come back to bite you and infect the discussions. It is better to address it right away and make it clear that you know what they are doing and will not tolerate it. When I have called someone out, most parties have made a point of looping back to me to clarify that they did not intend to be deceptive — an act that usually means we can carry on with the negotiations successfully. But I have also faced situations where the lack of character on the other side made it impossible to proceed and I had to walk away from the table.

TAKEAWAYS

BUILDING RAPPORT

1. Go first — initiate a positive connection if you've not met before heading to the table.
2. Do the extras — get together in person, take time to socialize, share some personal details.

OPENING STATEMENTS

3. Set the tone — be positive and frame the negotiation as a problem to solve together.
4. Keep it short — offer the key elements and issues and stay away from tedious detail.
5. Be lively — prepare well in advance but come across as passionate and conversational.
6. Generate optimism — indicate that you have faith in the proceedings and the outcomes.

FIRST OFFERS

7. Create an advantage — if you go first, set expectations and anchor the process favourably.
8. Be assertive — support your offer with the agreed standard and a careful rationale.
9. Be reasonable — don't make ridiculous lowball offers but leave yourself room to manoeuvre.
10. Think ahead — all your future offers will be measured against this one.
11. Say no — no matter what, never say "yes" to their first offer or counteroffer.

FIRST COUNTEROFFER

12. Plan it — caucus with your team to determine the proposal and the language you will use.

13. Offer a justification — always accompany a counter-offer with a full rationale and standard.
14. Frame it — explain how the counteroffer meets the interests of both sides.

THE ISSUE OF PRICE

15. Delay it — don't offer numbers until you have provided a substantive rationale.
16. Don't take it personally — expect the other side to request that you raise/lower your price.
17. Connect to principles and interests — always put a price in a larger context.
18. Slow the pace — maintain control by never rushing and always being open to dialogue.

SEVENTEEN TWISTS AND TURNS AT THE NEGOTIATING TABLE

1. Use anger as a strategic tool on rare occasions — never act from pure anger.
2. Exaggerated proposals and misrepresented interests are a waste of time.
3. Don't embarrass the other party — meet privately if you have new or sensitive information.
4. In difficult conversations, avoid acting from emotion, take breaks and listen attentively.
5. An impasse is a problem to be solved, not a result — know how to get out of a blockage.
6. Extreme demands create a sense of danger — respond with slow, calm conversation.
7. Use silence effectively and don't rush to talk if the other side falls silent.
8. Know everyone's name — it's their favourite word.
9. You can only bluff infrequently — save it for the end and mix it with flexible items.

10. If the other side shows bad faith, probe every claim and call them out on inaccuracies.
11. Make a plan to caucus regularly and use signals in the room to call unexpected breaks.
12. Ignore the flinch — planned emotional outbursts are intended to scare you off.
13. Resist pressure from the other side to make an immediate decision.
14. Try good cop/bad cop if it will be effective — and watch for it on the other side.
15. Manage the nibblers by finalizing the agreement before addressing small additions.
16. Don't respond to threats — ask questions and engage the other side in more conversation.
17. Act with integrity — ensure that all claims on both sides are comprehensive and honest.

CHAPTER 10
The Close

"He that can have patience can have what he will."

— Benjamin Franklin

Sometimes a negotiation can be so complicated — in terms of the number of steps and stages as well as the number of parties involved — that it is actually a complex network of interconnected negotiations. These cases are particularly helpful in illustrating that closing a deal is neither a simple process nor something that only happens at the end. A negotiator sometimes has to close agreement after agreement on the way toward achieving the primary goals of their mandate.

That's exactly what happened to me less than one week after the November 4, 1993, general election. No sooner had Prime Minister Chrétien appointed me to the Cabinet on behalf of the Province of Nova Scotia and into several portfolios, including Public Works and Government Services and the Atlantic Canada Opportunities Agency, when a substantial economic crisis began to unfold in Port Hawkesbury, Nova Scotia.

I first got wind of the situation when I received a call from then Premier of Nova Scotia John Savage asking me to attend a meeting with Per Knuts, the President of the Dusseldorf Stora Feldmuhle, a subsidiary of the massive Swedish multinational corporation Stora Enso, which is the oldest known corporation in the world, founded seventy-three years after the signing of the Magna Carta. Stora Feldmuhle had run a pulp and paper mill in Port Hawkesbury for thirty years that created 1,200 direct jobs and three times that number in multiplied employment. The plant was also a substantial part of the overall forestry industry in the province.

A visit from the president of the company was a major economic event, so Savage called in reinforcements, which in this case was me. I immediately made arrangements to fly east, but was delayed due to weather and was not present when Savage and his team greeted Knuts at the airport hotel. When I finally arrived, the meeting was just ending and I had missed whatever it was that Knuts had come across the ocean to tell us. I immediately pulled the Stora executives back into the room for a full briefing and heard their position, which was that Stora was going to give notice for the closure of its operation in Port Hawkesbury. I knew that I could not let that happen.

As an MP who had fought for years to protect jobs and support the economic welfare of the region, I was shocked. I knew right away how devastating this closure would be. As the town's mayor Billy Joe MacLean was fond of saying, "In Port Hawkesbury, there's God and then there's Stora." Obviously, I opposed the closure at the meeting and suggested that the governments at all three levels could contribute to ensuring the sustainability of the operation. Afterward, I stayed well into the night talking with all concerned about the implications and possibilities for what we could do.

The next day, after delivering an address to several hundred members of the Nova Scotia Liberal Association, I began to follow through on a promise I had made to myself that morning: I would do everything I could to ensure that the plant remained open. I knew full well that it would be a difficult and complex task — and a negotiation where there really wasn't a BATNA of any kind — but I also knew that my responsibility was to use the powers of my office to try and make a deal. Before returning to Ottawa, I communicated with the local MP, Francis LeBlanc, and the primary representatives of the Atlantic Canada Opportunities Agency, President Mary Gusella and Provincial Vice-President Wynne Potter. We all agreed that our mission was simple: find a way to secure funds from the government that would assist Stora in getting through the current downturn so that when the economy recovered, the firm could once again have a thriving business here. Having formed the initial team to work on the project, I returned to Ottawa to inform the Prime Minister and plan a strategic approach.

Early in 1994, as we embarked on the wide range of activities required to marshal support for the Port Hawkesbury facility, I began negotiating and closing a series of small agreements that were vital in achieving the final goal. In the process, I had to work with government officials of Nova Scotia, several federal government departments and several municipal units, including the Counties of Inverness, Richmond, Cape Breton and Victoria. I also needed to influence and engage the unions, the business community, and the local, provincial and national media.

One of my earliest tasks was to reach an agreement with the major municipal player, Mayor MacLean of Port Hawkesbury. MacLean and I knew each other, but he was a former Tory Cabinet Minister (I was a Liberal) and I had been warned off of dealing with him directly by many of my colleagues who were suspicious of his motives. My impression of MacLean was that he was a passionate advocate for his community, and so despite the advice I had received to steer clear of him, I picked up the phone and called him myself. He immediately offered to do anything he could to help. I suggested that I would be in touch with him on a regular basis and that we would definitely need his support, especially with the media and the provincial government. That was my first close in this multiparty negotiation.

I then had to secure a commitment from the office of Premier John Savage, but I didn't know Ross Bragg, his minister responsible for Economic Renewal. As you know, I am a big fan of building relationships, so I contacted Bragg myself. He was a delight to deal with — smart, congenial and clear about his limitations. He committed to helping with the project to whatever extent he could, and I said I would keep him informed. Close number two. So far, so easy.

The core team and I then set about trying to understand Stora's needs. We travelled to Sweden to meet with the upper echelon of the multinational parent corporation. Our mission was to learn all that we could, but also to demonstrate that we were willing to do everything possible to keep the mill open. We also wanted to build some rapport with the group that would be deciding the fate of so many Nova Scotians.

Arriving in what could only be called a "war room," we met with several Stora executives, hospitable folks who were very clear with us about their objectives: cut costs and maintain the viability of all operations. And there on the wall was a graph illustrating thirty years of profit and loss for the Stora plant in Port Hawkesbury, showing each year that it had not made money. It was clear that the earnings were cyclical, which we had been hoping to see. If the company had some help in the lulls, the plant could once again run on its own. When we left Sweden, we had learned about the economics of the plant and had secured an agreement from the Stora executives to give us time to develop and recommend a course of action. That was close number three.

On our way back to Canada, we talked extensively about what could be done, and especially how the federal government could help. We all knew that given various international trade agreements, the Canadian government could not provide a direct subsidy to a company based in another country. So we focused on being imaginative and innovative about ways that the Province of Nova Scotia could provide the funding with support at the municipal, provincial, federal, business and union levels. Given the enormous negative impact of a closure, there was a widespread desire on the part of all parties in Nova Scotia to resolve the issue. I was able to get a commitment from the Savage government to provide funds for a subsidy on two conditions: first, there needed to be support from the federal government and, second, Stora would have to guarantee that, if funds were provided, the operation of the plant would be maintained. That was close number four.

With the provincial commitment in hand, I then had to get the blessing of my colleagues in Cabinet, particularly the Prime Minister, the Minister of Finance, the Minister of Natural Resources, the Minister of Fisheries and the Minister of Industry. At first, none of them were keen to support the initiative. It was a time of enormous cost cutting for the government. They were also worried about any deal that would lead to a breach of the international trade agreements. After many meetings and much creative problem-solving, I was able to get my peers to support my plan so long as the money came from existing budgets and the agreement was consistent with all international treaties. If I could make that happen, they were prepared for the decision to be my call. Having already worked with my team to map out a plan to make the funds available at both the federal and provincial levels, I accepted their commitment and carried on. Close number five.

It was then up to my team and I to secure a commitment from the senior executives at Stora. A believer in live meetings and personal hospitality, I picked up the phone and invited several of Stora's international representatives to a dinner in Ottawa, including leaders from the Stora group and executives from the Wallenberg group of companies, an entity with interests in so many companies around Sweden that by the early 1990s it controlled a third of the country's GDP. The Swedish leaders agreed to come to Ottawa, and I had close number six.

Once the commitment was made, I contacted as many of the key government, business, community and union representatives as I could to invite them to the dinner. My hope was to impress upon the Swedish executives the passion and commitment of all the players. No surprise, there was widespread support for the dinner initiative, including Mayor MacLean arriving in a snowstorm with no luggage and visiting a local tailor to get some clothes for the dinner. The guest list was close number seven.

At dinner, my staff and various leaders in the room did all they could to be welcoming and engage with the Swedish leadership teams, including local MP Francis LeBlanc making a special presentation of paintings from Nova Scotian artists to our guests and an appearance by the Minister of Finance who I had asked to drop by on behalf of the Prime Minister who was not in Ottawa at the time. The lively event built relationships all around and laid the foundation for the possibility of a deal. That was close number eight.

In the months that followed, I pursued all the formal negotiations and was able to secure a commitment from Stora to keep the plant in Port Hawkesbury open in exchange for the funds from the provincial government. Working with officials at all levels, we were able to sort through the nuances of the deal that worked for all parties and provided $15.4 million to the company over a three year period, money that was repaid in record time when the economy took off again. That was the ninth and final close of the deal.

Keeping the Stora mill up and running required a highly complicated arrangement, but it was also a process of securing one commitment at a time on the way to reaching the goal: a sustainable solution that would protect the local and provincial economy while meeting the interests of the Swedish multinational corporation. It took nine mini-closes to avoid an economic disaster.

BASIC CONSIDERATIONS FOR THE CLOSING PROCESS

The first question is, are you in fact in the final stage when you attempt to ink the agreement and secure the value you have worked so hard to create? To determine if you have arrived at closing, ask five basic questions about the agreement. If the answer to any of them is "no," assume that you need to remain at the table and proceed accordingly.

1.   Does this agreement meet the goals established in your mandate?

2.   Is the proposed agreement better than your BATNA?

3.   Will your side be able to fulfill the terms as they are currently laid out?

4.   Will your organization commit the resources necessary to implement the agreement?

5.   Do you believe that the other side intends to and is capable of fulfilling its commitments?

ON TRUST

"I'll never forget it. Years ago with Conrad Black and my father. Conrad was selling something called Crown Trust and he and my father shook hands outside their office on 10 Toronto Street on a price. Then something happened later that made the business more valuable. But Conrad had agreed to a price and unlike what happens normally where a person comes back and wants to alter the deal, and he just said, 'I shook hands on it and that's the price.' Fast forward twenty-five years later to when we acquired his newspapers and the deal got done because they had that relationship. There were parts in the deal where they could have taken advantage of each other but they didn't. They helped make sure the other person was getting a good deal."

Watch the interview at tinyurl.com/negotiating-asper-trust

LEONARD ASPER, former CEO of Canwest Global Communications Corporation and current President and CEO of Anthem Sports & Entertainment

Knowing that you are in the final phase alters your approach, as it did in one bargaining session for Buzz Hargrove when an internal disagreement threatened to derail the ratification he was trying to achieve. "Early in my presidency of the union, we had a strike deadline at de Havilland, which had been bought by Bombardier a few years earlier. We had previously agreed to a settlement that gave us no wage increases but improved pensions a little bit for the retirees for a two-year period to give

Bombardier an opportunity to start doing some things. And they did — they went and put a new operating system in, what they called the Bombardier Manufacturing System — which they used around the world. For example, the wings for the new planes were made in Japan, the fuselage was made in Ireland, and other parts were made in other places in the world. They were all shipped to Toronto and assembled in the plant.

"Our guys could handle that change because they knew the world was changing. But what they couldn't handle was that the Japanese had some real quality problems with the wings and at one point there were about a hundred Japanese workers in the plant doing the work that should have been done in Japan. Mitsubishi flew them in and put them up in hotels. Our guys could not stand the idea of having foreign workers in their plant who weren't members of the union who were doing work that our guys felt was their work. So we were heading into bargaining and had a strike deadline and the guys fought with the company for a few months on the issue. So the company provided what they called a Supplier Letter which said that when they paid for a part in Japan or Ireland or wherever, they were going to bring those workers to finish the job because they had already paid for it and were not going to pay twice.

"It was a pretty good argument. But our committee wasn't having any part of it. So we ended up with a hell of a fight. I went to a membership meeting and the chairman was saying, 'we are going to strike' and I said, 'guys, this doesn't make any sense' and of course they booed the hell out of me, including one big guy standing up and saying, 'hang him, hang him!' Finally I said to the chairperson of the committee, 'Get on a plane, go to Montreal and talk to Bob Brown yourself.' He was the one telling us that they are going to walk away — that they don't have much invested in this plant yet. The Rae government had put in most of the money, so Bombardier could shut it down and move off and make it a tax write-off and our members would be without work. So he did. He got on a plane and flew to Montreal and Brown told him, 'if we can't produce the planes the way we decide, if we have to pay twice to do the same work, we're not doing it here and we'll get out. We don't need de Havilland. We are doing very well on our own.' So we went back to the bargaining committee and they still booed the hell out of me but they ratified the agreement by about the same numbers as they had rejected it when it was just me recommending it."

Watch the interview with Buzz Hargrove at tinyurl.com/negotiating-hargrove-ending

Hargrove's unusual closing situation may never resemble one of yours, but it worked because the whole deal was close enough to the end to hinge on one final action. If your answers to the five pertinent questions are affirmative, you are also close to the end and can focus on the particular aspects of this unique stage in bargaining. To reach a successful conclusion, here are nine considerations to inform your strategy:

1.   Assume that last minute demands will come up — from both sides. And if you have an objection to raise with the other side at the last minute, ensure you are constructive and thoughtful in your approach.

2.   Apply your understanding of the other side to the closing process. You have learned a great deal during the negotiation and need to use this knowledge to predict how they will act and react.

3. Be patient and firm. It can be very difficult to stay calm in the final phase when everyone is tired and keen to conclude the arrangement. Whether you need to listen carefully, extend the time frame or revisit your goals, do so with care and attention. You can then proceed with a fair and open mindset toward the end, balancing the push to consummate with accepting additions and modifications.

4. Remember that the primary action of the final phase is for both sides to resolve their remaining issues so that everyone can arrive at the moment of signing feeling positive and comfortable about the deal. You do not need to acquiesce to every request from the other side, but take your time and be supportive.

5. If one of the issues being addressed in the final stage seems unresolvable, try factorizing it: break it into its component parts. It is often easier to get an agreement when faced with the individual pieces instead of the whole.

6. When you make your final offer, communicate clearly that this is the end of the line and deliver your proposal with passion and clarity.

7. Throughout the closing process, emphasize the gains that result from the deal. This is not the time to be drawing attention to the drawbacks of the agreement. That should have happened earlier and been left behind.

8. Be wary of the sunken cost principle. When a negotiation has been long and involved, there is significant motivation on both sides not to waste the effort and time by walking away. Hence, the longer you are at the table, the more likely you are to accept the agreement as it is. But if the agreement does not

meet your mandate and your BATNA is better, you should not consummate it.

9.   At this stage, be very careful about the language used in the final agreement. Whenever possible, hold the pen yourself. This ensures that your understanding of the agreement prevails. The other party will have a chance to review, amend or delete some of the words or clauses that you have chosen. But holding the pen increases the chances that the deal meets your needs.

ISSUES ON THE OTHER SIDE THAT CAN LIMIT YOUR ABILITY TO CLOSE

My experience over the years, and the information I have gained from Brian Tracy's excellent work on the nuances of selling, have shown me five kinds of reactions from the other side that can block the progress toward closing. A seasoned negotiator can address each objection head on in the interests of saving the deal.

1. Indifference

When the other side conveys a relative lack of interest in the deal — or certain parts of it — probe carefully to uncover what is behind their indifference. Resist the impulse to hammer them with a long list of reasons why the deal is beneficial to both sides or to modify the conditions of the deal in an attempt to appease them. Often, something has changed on their side that makes them reluctant to sign the existing agreement. Discover what that change is and you can reenergize their appetite for the deal. In addition, be careful not to come across as frustrated by their indifference — even if at your wit's end. Negative signals through body language and tone of voice betray your position to the other negotiator and diminish your capacity for a strong finish.

2. Skepticism

I have found that after an extended period of working together, some negotiators begin to doubt the sincerity of the offers and counteroffers I present in the late stages of deal formation. They may also be concerned that your side will not be able to follow through on the deliverables contained in the agreement. Listen to and respond to their concerns, with an emphasis on understanding, and don't be anxious to defend the commitments you have made. I suggest revisiting proof points you have already provided, or judiciously providing additional evidence that you will be able to deliver, but not mounting a widespread and extensive defence. Believe in what you have offered and convey to the other side that you are very confident in your ability to follow through. I also find that this is a good time to use two high-quality sources of support — factual stories and written testimonials — especially if you have not used this evidence prior to this point. Personal experiences are highly compelling and can be just the extra push you need to reassure the other side.

If the other party does not accept your proof, ask "what kind of substantiation would be acceptable for you?" and then sit quietly while they prepare an answer. Don't break the silence. Both the question and the waiting time pressures them to find a solution to the problem and helps move the agreement along. Remember, it is their job to express what they need to be satisfied, not yours. Your role is to provide the proof as best as you can in response to their enquiries. Don't let your desire to appease them lead to offering an unsubstantial proof source. This can derail the proceedings and work against you as you try to settle their concerns. You are better off suggesting that there is no additional proof available. In addition, never use phrases like "just trust me," "I have done this many times before," or "I know it's hard to believe, but it is the truth." They will have the opposite effect to what you intend.

3. Misunderstandings

Explicitly acknowledge any confusion. Once out in the open, you can focus on talking it through to settle the concern. Allowing misunderstandings to fester will undermine the process from that point forward. Use supportive language that focuses on the other side's needs, such as "I thought your need was . . ." or "since your need is x, this is how I think we might be able to proceed . . ." If you validate the issue, demonstrate that you have their interests in mind and work together to resolve the misunderstanding, this kind of blockage can generally be resolved.

4. Drawbacks

Sometimes the other side starts to highlight elements of the arrangement they perceive to be deficient relative to their interests. The problem is often that they are looking at a particular part of the deal out of the context of the entire arrangement and the circumstances under which it was settled. The best approach is to accurately replay the history of the negotiation for the everyone in the room. "We agreed to a because we had done b after you had suggested we consider doing c and I responded by . . ." This is where careful notes and the memories of your team are important. But if you don't know exactly what happened to lead to a certain decision, don't pretend. The other side will perceive this as playing fast and loose with the truth and it will work against you. Once you have revisited the conditions under which the concerning item was settled, refocus on the big picture and frame the item in the context of the entire agreement. Keep the other side from plucking an item out and looking at it in isolation from the whole story. And then, if you have to, consider ways to make non-substantive changes to a particular item to appease the other side.

5. Ratification Problems

In many negotiations, the closing stage requires that parties go back to their respective superiors for sign-off on the deal. This is where your earlier work on ratification systems and your understanding of the decision-making process pays off. If you did your homework, you should not be met with any surprises at this stage. But if the other party has not done their due diligence with the decision-makers or has misrepresented their situation to you, there can be surprises at this stage which put the deal at risk. If you meet with resistance or delays as a result of the other side trying to get sign-off, do not accept radio silence as a positive development. Keep communicating and get updates. Dealing with their superiors is not their issue alone; it is yours as well because the entire deal is at stake.

THE QUALITIES OF A GREAT NEGOTIATOR

"People who listen well. People who make the other party feel important and feel that they are part of the process. Ones that are well prepared going into a deal and know where there is a deal to be made and what the other partner wants out of it."

Watch the interview at tinyurl.com/negotiating-rudge-trust

CHRIS RUDGE, Executive Chair and CEO for the Toronto Argonauts and former CEO of the Canadian Olympic Committee

COMMUNICATION AROUND THE CLOSING OF A DEAL

"I was in constant contact with the membership and the bargaining committee so that when it came time and the company tabled their final proposal, I knew it was going to fly. But then I said to them, 'you have to come and present it to the bargaining committee. And you have to have a hard copy for people because they are only comfortable when they have that document in their hands.' They want to be able to take it, analyze it, read it. It was called a memorandum of settlement and it was usually a five or six page document that had to be ratified by the union and by the company. When it was ready, we would all sign it — on both sides of the table. Sometimes the signing page was longer than the actual document because there were so many people involved.

"Once the agreement was there, we would start our ratification process. The communications people had to be in the room the entire time because I couldn't teach it to them in a few hours. So they would put together the brochure outlining the terms of the deal. And there had to be no mistakes. Since 1979, I reviewed every brochure myself as National President to make sure there was not a single mistake."

Watch the interview at tinyurl.com/negotiating-hargrove-accuracy

BUZZ HARGROVE, former National President of the Canadian Auto Workers union and current Distinguished Visiting Professor at Ryerson University's Ted Rogers School of Management

TYPES OF CLOSES

When Michael Cleaner arrives at the final stage of a negotiation, he makes sure that the momentum continues. "I like to get things done and I express that throughout the process by creating a sense of urgency and always getting back to the other side very, very quickly — more often than not, within a twenty-four-hour period. When it comes time to finalizing the deal and getting the documents there, I believe that has to be done quickly, efficiently and you bird-dog it. In some cases, we have sat down with a legal team on both sides in a boardroom, we have hammered out what the issues might be with the documentation, I've had several caucus meetings with our legal counsel, all to get it done on that day. To show good faith. If you don't move with great dispatch, the other side might feel you are not sincere."

Watch the interview with Michael Cleaner at tinyurl.com/negotiating-cleaner-closing

Closing a deal often requires figuring out how to keep it moving along. Some approaches are better suited to certain situations, and you can mix and match them as appropriate.

Assumption Close

This close works when the majority of the major issues on the agenda have been covered and there are either a handful of smaller issues to resolve or neither side has firmly expressed that this is a deal that they can support and sign. To prompt both sides to move toward agreement, a strategic negotiator says, "It seems as though we can assume we have a deal." This statement pushes the other side to assess their attitude toward the existing arrangement and either table substantive concerns or agree with you. Either way, you're moving things along, either by addressing the remaining issues or proceeding with a mutual agreement that the deal is all but done. Ultimately, this approach is a prompt to push the discussion toward a conclusion. Sometimes, a negotiator will attempt to lower the price by acting as if both sides have agreed to that reduced price. This is not an assumption close. It's a form of manipulation and trickery that should be resisted or ignored depending on the circumstances. Be mindful of this tactic.

Surprise Close

I have been involved in several negotiations where the other party has made an out-of-the-blue suggestion intended to speed up the final process. For example, another party once said to me, "Look, since we have reached an agreement on almost everything, let's celebrate our success by having dinner and then going to a basketball game. I have the tickets right here." In that particular case, my team and I did agree to dinner and the game, but we did not agree that we had a consummated agreement. During the evening out, we were able to finalize the elements of the deal and reach an agreement. The suggestion moved the process along and my side, though on the receiving end of the surprise close, was able to fulfill its mandate.

This interesting technique can work if there is a good rapport and trust between the sides. In essence, it involves arriving at the table with something positive to offer that energizes the process. Obviously, it can be a risky proposition if you make the offer and the other side has more remaining items than you thought. They may perceive it as a distraction tactic. But if you choose the right moment, this kind of close can be well received. It requires your good judgement of the other party and of the substance of all outstanding issues. It doesn't work if there are still a lot of issues to resolve.

Off-the-Record Close

An off-the-record close is most often used between parties with a strong relationship and a high level of trust, either between the lead negotiators or between trusted advisers from each side working together on behalf of the entire group. It occurs when you find yourself on a health or coffee break during the final phase and the other side approaches you suggesting that they have a way to settle the two or three outstanding items, often in the form of "I am prepared to offer x if you are prepared to accept y." It can be a useful way to finalize the deal if the circumstances are ripe for a quick resolution, because you then return to the table with a mutual agreement. I have sometimes suggested an extension of the break time so that I could go for a walk with the other lead to see if we could settle the remaining issues.

It's important to advise your team early in the process that there may come a time in the negotiations when you will go for a walk (or a coffee or something similar) with a certain member on the other side. You don't want to antagonize members of your own team by surprising them with this approach. They may conclude that the formal negotiation has been a staged event and the real discussions are taking place off the record. Share with your team that you may need some flexibility to engage away from the table and that there is no fake versus real dynamic in place. They don't want to feel that their work has been a sham — and you need to have this option available if it becomes useful. Speaking up in advance also keeps your reputation as a trustworthy negotiator intact.

Natural Close

For me, the best close occurs in a natural and non-threatening way. This involves accepting that there will be as many back-

and-forth exchanges as necessary to complete the deal. It is a time-consuming approach that can test your patience but is highly effective for ensuring that the final arrangement is strong and mutual. The challenge, of course, is to stay focused on your mandate and calmly persevere despite the inevitable mental, emotional and physical fatigue. Do what you can to prevent the same fatigue on the other side from undermining your ability to fulfill your mandate. Respond to their requests quickly or offer to help with logistics that might put a strain on their resources. In essence, the key to a natural close is to manage expectations about how quickly the deal will be done. Stick to the habits of a strategic negotiator: be attentive, careful and let the process unfold.

The relatively time-consuming nature of a natural close requires that both sides continue to work together rather than be positioned as adversaries. If both sides are open about remaining concerns and support an exploration of the issues in order to optimize the value of the deal, this approach works very well. Then, when the moment finally arrives for someone to ask, "do we have a deal?" there is very little tension in the room and everyone nods in unison.

Invitational Close

A useful technique related to the natural close is to think of the final phase as a complete negotiation in and of itself and invite the other party to table all remaining issues. I would use phrasing like this: "Our side has three items remaining to resolve before we can sign a deal. Would it work for you if we shared those while you share with us whatever is left on your list?" You will find that the other party is often content to collect up their remaining issues, usually after a caucus meeting, and table them with you. At that point, the discussions have a newfound energy because everyone can see a single list of all that remains to be done to arrive at the end. This can be a welcome relief after a lengthy process.

Authorization Close

There comes a moment in many negotiations, especially those smaller in scope and scale, when I can move the agreement to a conclusion by asking for a signature and a cheque. Like most closes, this works very well when there is trust between the sides, but it can also be effective with negotiators who don't know each other well because it is such a simple way of focusing the discussion: are they ready to sign? The extent to which the concerns of both sides have been addressed prior to using this technique is, ultimately, a judgement call. I look for a situation where the outstanding issues are non-substantive even if they have some emotional value for the participants. People want to get a deal completed — especially if the process has been drawn out — and they can move fairly quickly through the final items if there is an appropriate sense of urgency. If my request to sign and exchange funds doesn't work, I can always use the other side's reluctance as an opportunity to pull out whatever issues remain for them. This is a good time to directly ask what remains to be addressed. A great way to speed up the process, the authorization close can be used in combination with most of the other methods.

COMPONENTS OF THE CLOSING STAGE

Describing his approach to the final tense hours before an agreement is reached, Buzz Hargrove explained, "The only rule I had about closing was that when you are going down to a deadline and you only have a few hours, there is always somebody who sees a nightmarish situation and will start bringing things up — what about this, what about that? And then someone will say, 'We're tired, let's go have a sleep and then get back at this in a few hours' time.' I would say, 'No, no guys, we are going to conclude this thing.' Because what I found in the early part of my career was that if you let people go to sleep, when they wake up in the morning, they can't see the things that we have already agreed on. And they start to change the way they see the language and forget about the intent behind the language, which is a very important part of bargaining. So during the last few hours of bargaining when you have to make the final decisions, my policy was we are going to keep at it until we get it done."

Watch the interview with Buzz Hargrove at tinyurl.com/negotiating-hargrove-closing

LETTING THE OTHER SIDE WALK AWAY

"Sometimes you have to let them know that their approach is no good so you need to express the emotion of it — but always in control. One time, after I did that, the other side walked out of the room and my client asked, 'What did you do?' But I knew what I was doing because during the preparation, I learned that they had to do the deal. The deal on the table was a very fair deal. So I knew that I could grandstand a little. Eventually, they came back and we got the deal done."

Watch the interview at tinyurl.com/negotiating-lean-closing

RALPH LEAN, Distinguished Counsel in Residence at Ryerson University's Ted Rogers School of Management

Hargrove often had a strike deadline looming, but all of us face deadlines and pressures at the end that influence the rate at which we work through the components of the final stage. Each part of the close has distinct features to consider.

Memorandum of Understanding

When dealing with complex issues, such as when nations negotiate over international subjects like fisheries, justice issues or foreign aid, it is common to use a Memorandum of Understanding (MOU) as an intermediate step on the way to a final agreement. In general, an MOU is a broadly written document that highlights areas of agreement and outlines how and when further investigation or negotiation will take place. Agreeing on a document that solidifies some parts of the deal and outlines others creates a sense of accomplishment on both sides while securing the momentum that might be lost if you continued to push toward a final agreement. An MOU is a living document that can be updated later or set aside in favour of a new MOU or a completed agreement. Topics outlined in an MOU include the term of the agreement, the monies in play, a payment schedule, services to be provided or the nature of those services.

When working out an MOU, do not attempt to push to get a complete agreement on the various issues because it undermines what you are trying to accomplish. An MOU is simply an attempt to articulate, as precisely as possible, what has been accomplished and what remains to be done on the way to an agreement. Focus on helping both sides be as specific as possible about what has and has not been settled and then outline a time frame that allows for clarifying deliverables or getting permission from superiors.

Getting Sign-Off

One of the most difficult and potentially frustrating moments in deal making occurs when negotiators on both sides reach a tentative agreement and then seek approval from their principal or superior. This process goes smoothly when the negotiators have kept in close contact with the decision-makers all the way along and operate with a clear mandate that eliminates surprises about authority. But this stage can also lead to silence, confusion, frustration and misinformation when the deal is assessed away from the context of the process by parties who were not at the table.

As I have said all along, be proactive about the ratification system on both sides because you have as much invested in how your counterpart gets the deal approved as you do in your own process. Include discussions about the decision-makers throughout the deliberations so that there are no surprises about what the principals or superiors think or want. Ultimately, you want the decision-makers to arrive at the final sign-off without any questions, issues or concerns. Keep them informed and engaged at each stage. Be sure to plan ahead, as everyone is busy and you don't want to discover that a superior is out of the country when you need them. And always offer to speak directly with the decision-makers on the other side if it is helpful. Typically, the other negotiator will not want you communicating with their client or superior, but offering to do so can help move the process along.

Legal Issues

If consummating a contract or collective agreement with parties such as a supplier or regulator, you will require the approval of counsel for both sides. Like being proactive about the role of the signatories, think about the legal issues from the beginning and consult regularly with your counsel. Your lawyers will want to address issues such as jurisdiction, confidentiality, waiver, estoppel, renewal options, term, insurance and indemnity. In so doing, make sure they do not alter the material provisions of the agreement.

At the earliest stage possible, acquire a template from your counsel that frames the legal issues particular to the current negotiation. This allows you to begin with the various headings and provisions for how the contract will be structured and then fill in the blanks. The bulk of the legal work occurs once the major provisions of the contract have been settled, but be sure to consult with your legal team in advance of your offers, counteroffers and concessions so that you understand the legal implications of your decisions at all times. Avoid a situation where the lawyers rewrite the contract. That will create tension with the other side and jeopardize your agreement.

One way to address all the legal issues in advance is to make sure that you are very clear about, and explicitly define, the key terminology in the contract. For example, if you use the word "performance," spell out what this means and how it will be measured in terms acceptable to both sides. Is there a formula? Is there a schedule? Is there a third party? If you don't outline these details in the contract, your legal team will tell you it's too vague to be binding or allows too much latitude for interpretation in the event of a dispute.

Alternative Dispute Resolution Provisions

As you near the completion of a contract, identify the mechanism to be used in the event of a dispute between the parties, which most often happens in complex contractual relationships. Making provisions for Alternative Dispute Resolution (ADR) methods is rarely included as an agenda item, but it is a good idea to do so. ADR provisions help to avoid expensive and time-consuming lawsuits and can maintain or even improve a good working relationship. In the provisions, I suggest a structure that begins with negotiation and then moves to mediation and then arbitration if each preceding method is unsuccessful. Also, identify how the costs will be shared and how decisions will be made, such as selecting a mediator. You should also allocate a time limit for mediation or arbitration processes so that they don't drag on and create unnecessary costs and delays for both sides.

Management of the Agreement

At the final stage, work together to decide how the agreement will be managed in the coming years. Some negotiators don't like to address this until the agreement has been consummated, but I would suggest doing it before you get there. In particular, I advise outlining the provisions for managing three aspects: the contract, the project and the relationships. First, especially in major deals, the parties agree to the key people assigned to monitor various aspects of the agreement including time frames, rights, payment of money, quality of product and other obligations. Second, the parties outline the scope of the project and identify both the people and the process used to monitor progress and ensure completion. Third, the parties decide how the relationship between the two entities will be managed, which is an area that gets far too little attention in final agreements. Identifying the liaison between the organizations and outlining the mechanism for reporting and managing the various issues and information that come up is extremely helpful, especially when it comes to internal and external communication.

This was my approach to the agreement reached during the mid-1990s when I represented the Government of Canada in a negotiation with the People's Republic of China. The project was a proposed twenty-six-acre site in Beijing that would allow representatives of the Canadian housing industry to showcase their materials to demonstrate the durability and quality of our product to interested parties in the Chinese residential market. In the agreement, there were specific details about all three of the management areas: first, who would monitor the fulfilment of the agreement on behalf of each nation, second, who would oversee the actual building project and, third, who would be responsible for liaising between the countries.

NEGOTIATOR'S FINAL RESPONSIBILITIES

Once the deal is complete, I believe the strategic negotiator has two final obligations. The first is to facilitate the transition from deal-making to deal-executing. I suggest you write a comprehensive memo to your superiors and anyone else who will be directly involved in the execution of the contract while the details of the deal are still fresh in your mind. The memo outlines the key issues and nuances of the discussions so they are preserved to guide future decisions. Without a summary memo, whoever leads the way during future conversations will follow their own interpretation of the contract and risk taking action that challenges what the deal intended. Include details about who was at the table, the time it took to complete the agreement, the major issues addressed throughout the negotiations and the importance that each party attached to those issues. For example, outlining the details of the pricing or pay schedule helps to avoid confusion and inefficiency later with invoicing.

Second, you have an obligation to yourself and to your principal or organization to perform a post-mortem on the process. This can be a simple memo to file or you can use a negotiation journal in which you record impressions, lessons and insights. This kind of reflective process is incredibly helpful for a person intending to build a career as a negotiator. You can look back when you encounter a similar negotiation in the future and benefit from your own learning. When I diarize my learning from a negotiation, I focus on relationships, the subject matter, positive and negative aspects of the process, difficulties that came up, and any specific successes or failures on my part. Michael Wheeler calls this WWW and WWYD: what worked well and what would you do differently? When you have had time to reflect on your own learning, think about what you can offer the organization or your principal about the process that might be of use to them in the future. Your communication needn't be long or complex. One or two solid suggestions for ways to improve their operations will add value.

TAKEAWAYS

NINE BASIC CONSIDERATIONS FOR CLOSING

1. Assume there will be last minute demands on both sides.
2. Use your extensive understanding of the other side to predict their moves and reactions.
3. Be patient, firm and fair when it's tempting to rush to the end.
4. This is a time for both sides to resolve some remaining issues — be supportive.
5. Try factoring an unresolvable issue into its component parts to settle it.
6. Your final offer really should be final and delivered with passion and clarity.
7. Emphasize the gains on both sides — drawbacks need to be left behind now.
8. Be wary of the sunken cost principle — you still need to meet your mandate.
9. Choose your words carefully and offer to write out the final agreement yourself.

LIMITING ISSUES ON THE OTHER SIDE

10. Indifference — find out what has changed and work to resolve it.
11. Skepticism — listen and respond to concerns, exude confidence, and revisit proof points.
12. Misunderstandings — address confusion right away with their interests in mind.
13. Drawbacks — put each part of the deal in context to emphasize its complete value.
14. Ratification problems — maintain contact with the other side as they deal with their decision-makers.

TYPES OF CLOSES

15. Assumption — once the major issues have been addressed, say you assume you have a deal.
16. Surprise — offer something positive such as a social event to energize the process.
17. Off-the-record — talk to the other lead during a break and come back with a plan to close.
18. Natural — continue with all the back-and-forths needed in a positive and supportive way.
19. Invitational — share what items you have left to settle and ask them for their list.
20. Authorization — ask for a signature and cheque when the outstanding issues are non-substantive.

COMPONENTS OF THE CLOSING STAGE

21. Memorandum of Understanding — draw up a list of agreements and what remains to be done.
22. Sign-off — include discussions about decision-makers throughout to avoid signing difficulties.
23. Legal issues — use a legal template to frame the issues and consult regularly with counsel.
24. ADR provisions — include provisions for negotiation, mediation and arbitration for disputes.
25. Management of the agreement — decide together how it will be managed in the coming years.

NEGOTIATOR'S FINAL RESPONSIBILITIES

26. Memo to your superiors — summarize key issues and details to guide future decisions.
27. Memo to yourself — what worked well and what would you do differently?

Final Thoughts

When I starting teaching at the Ted Rogers School of Management at Ryerson University, it was an exciting detour from my work as a politician, lawyer and negotiator. It was also incredibly educative for me. One thing I learned right away was how much my students love stories. They sat patiently if I answered a question with a long-winded explanation about a fundamental principle of negotiation, but with a noticeable glaze over their eyes. But if I told them a story from my experience — whether in public life, the private sector or even my personal life — they leaned in and listened hard. And though I didn't realize it at first, those early moments as a teacher shaped my thinking about how I would proceed with this book. To be of value, it had to be a blend of ideas and experiences with healthy doses of narrative along the way.

That emphasis on story merged with my desire to be thorough in my preparations for the Ryerson Negotiation Project. Those conversations with leading negotiators working in Canada helped me consolidate my ideas and see more clearly the differences and similarities in various approaches to deal-making more clearly. Between those interviews and my reflections on my own experiences, I was able to sort out the key ideas I wanted to convey and refine the list of techniques that this book contains. In so doing, I discovered I was exploring what is so compelling and valuable about a Canadian perspective on negotiation.

Canadians have a rich history of effective negotiations. Our skill in this area flows from the unique nature of our economic and political context. We play a particular role as a small, developed and connected Western power. We also have a complex cultural and linguistic framework for our society. A nation of immigrants and a genuinely multicultural society, we have succeeded by doing far more than saying "sorry" and going for a beer or a doughnut! We are thoughtful, positive, and collaborative. We are also resolute, because sidestepping our values or shying away when a firm commitment is needed is not productive. And our ongoing success has always required careful homework, clear communication and a complete understanding of the nuances of deal making. Canadians always have to be on their negotiation game.

Negotiation skill is evident in the rich experience of the leaders who sat for the Ryerson Negotiation Project interviews that inform this book. They are also evident in the highest corridors of power in our government. Consider the long line of Canadian ambassadors who have made a mark in the world, including David Mulroney in China, Allan Gotlieb in the United States, Ken Taylor in Iran, Jocelyne Bourgon at the OECD in Paris, and Roy McMurtry in Great Britain. Or Prime Ministers who have succeeded on the international stage, such as Nobel Prize winner Lester B. Pearson in the Suez Canal affair, Brian Mulroney addressing Apartheid in South Africa or Jean Chrétien saying "no" to the war in Iraq. There are also Prime Ministers who navigated incredibly contentious domestic issues, such as Pierre Elliott Trudeau managing the October Crisis and the repatriation of the Constitution. We are even seeing sophisticated negotiations in the early days of the new Justin Trudeau government on issues such as immigration, taxation and climate change.

Negotiating is a fine art because every negotiation is different — from the subject matter to the relative importance of the arrangement to the interests of the participants. This complexity requires a considered and careful approach and makes these skills useful to every leader and, in reality, every person. If you can improve your negotiation skills, you can improve your capacity. You can learn how to decide if walking away makes more sense than making a deal, no matter how much time you have put in. And you can accomplish what I have always sought and what drives the leaders profiled in this book: reaching agreements that work for everyone.

David's Recommendations for Further Reading

I have read literally hundreds of books on various topics closely or distantly related to the art of negotiating. Below are ten that I especially appreciate and would recommend to anyone in — or getting into — negotiation situations.

A Sense of Urgency
John P. Kotter (2008)
The Harvard professor best known for his works *Leading Change* and *Our Iceberg Is Melting* simplifies an action plan to get you and your organization to act with a sense of urgency. Kotter asserts that true urgency should focus on critical issues, not just important items. Furthermore, he notes that a sense of urgency often collapses after a few successes are obtained by the organization.

Kotter discusses the need for behaving with urgency each and every day. He believes that you ought to respond fast, clear the decks and don't have a crowded appointment diary. Clutter undermines true urgency, as does fatigue. It's important to be visibly urgent and to engage with your people on a daily basis.

If you're not sure why or how a sense of urgency can be critical, read this book.

Difficult Conversations: How to Discuss What Matters Most
Douglas Stone, Bruce Patton and Sheila Heen (1999)
This book was based on fifteen years of research at the Harvard Negotiation Project. These Harvard professors discuss a number

of aspects about difficult conversations. In particular, they focus on the importance of disentangling the concept of intent from impact.

Pay particular attention to their section on blame. It may be hard to avoid finger-pointing when something does not go as planned, but any focus on blame will hinder problem-solving. In addition, their chapters on emotion are helpful. They assert that feelings are too powerful to remain peacefully bottled and will be heard one way or another. It has always been helpful to me to focus on the emotion in the room.

This book helps anyone who has to have a difficult conversation, whether with an employee, a client, a spouse or a child. In other words, all of us.

Gain the Edge! Negotiating to Get What You Want
Martin E. Latz (2004)
For a negotiator, Latz's book is a must read. He outlines five golden rules:

1.   Information is power.

2.   Maximize your leverage.

3.   Employ fair objective criteria.

4.   Design an offer concession strategy.

5.   Control the agenda.

Within these rules are a lot of constructive suggestions — take-aways — that are worth the time and effort to uncover. Furthermore, Latz talks about protecting your reputation, establishing clear identifiable goals, designing a strategy for offers and concessions, and evaluating the power of the relationship in the negotiation.

Getting Together: Building Relationships as We Negotiate
Roger Fisher and Scott Brown (1988)
This book is the sequel to *Getting to Yes. Getting Together* takes the reader through a step-by-step process that works in business, government, between friends and among family members.

I particularly like the book because it addresses the substance of the following five issues: 1) separate the people from the problem, 2) be unconditionally constructive, 3) don't make relationships contingent on agreement, 4) always consult before deciding and 5) we can't resolve differences without understanding them.

If you want to enhance your leadership skills and become a more effective negotiator, this book is a must.

In Business as In Life — You Don't Get What You Deserve, You Get What You Negotiate
Chester L. Karrass (1996)
I have read Karrass' two bestselling books, *The Negotiating Game* and *Give and Take*. This book provides additional insights into the negotiating process. Some takeaways for me are the fourteen rules for the competitive negotiator and the idea that in win-win negotiations, you need to go well beyond just the purchase price. I was also influenced by his discussion of the power of time and the power of persistence in a negotiation.

There are a lot of practical tips contained in this book, particularly in developing a team of negotiators, understanding various approaches to winning concessions and knowing how best to defend your selling price. Karrass also gives his perspective on international negotiations.

Influence: The Psychology of Persuasion
Robert B. Cialdini (1984)

Cialdini is the leading expert on persuasion. He examines the six principles of persuasion: consistency, social proof, authority, liking, scarcity and reciprocity. His illustration of the contrast principle and his discussion of reciprocity are particularly good. Cialdini provides example after example that are beneficial for a negotiator as well as a leader. Pay particular attention to his chapter on liking and the impact it can have for a negotiator.

The Art of Negotiation: How to Improvise Agreement in a Chaotic World
Michael Wheeler (2013)
Professor Wheeler knows his subject matter extremely well. He notes the importance of the negotiator being adaptable and improvising along the way. He understands and demonstrates the impact of small moves or gestures on the negotiation. He notes that BATNA is an excellent concept in theory but, in his words, messy in practice. His whole discussion of BATNA is extremely useful to anyone looking to enhance their negotiating skills.

Other highlights from Wheeler: occasions when you might need to dump all of your chips on the table in order to be seen as a serious player, the importance of being optimistic and the shortcomings of being unrealistic in the negotiating process. This is a helpful book for developing both negotiation and leadership skills.

The Trusted Advisor
David H. Maister, Charles H. Green, Robert M. Galford (2000)
Whether you are in business, government or a non-profit organization, *The Trusted Advisor* offers an invaluable road map to developing truly special relationships with clients. This is a highly readable text aimed at professionals, and for negotiators, I think it's a must.

The authors offer eleven key principles of relationship building that apply in both personal and professional life:

1. Go first.

2. Illustrate, do not tell.

3. Listen for what is different, not what is familiar.

4. Be sure your advice is being sought.

5. Earn the right to offer advice.

6. Keep asking.

7. Say what you mean.

8. When you need help, ask for it.

9. Show an interest in the person.

10. Use compliments, not flattery.

11. Show appreciation.

This is a comprehensive, thoughtful and practical book. Read it if you value the importance of relationships.

True Professionalism: The Courage to Care About Your People, Your Clients, and Your Career
David H. Maister (1997)
Maister writes in a clear and compelling manner. For him, professionalism is believing passionately in what you do, never compromising your standards and values and caring about your clients, your people and your own career. The importance of values, teamwork and excellence in client satisfaction

and relationship building are all examined by this consummate professional. Maister also talks about the need to have fun. This is a book for would-be negotiators and anyone who wishes to enhance their leadership skills.

Winning with People: Discover the People Principles that Work for You Every Time
John C. Maxwell (2007)
Winning with People helps everyone to interact better with employees, board members, associates, or colleagues. A few highlights:

1. Don't take relationships for granted, whether with friends, colleagues or associates.

2. Attitude is one thing you have ultimate control over. Learn why a positive attitude really works.

3. Whatever your stage in life — young, middle age or old — never blame others for your failures.

4. Resist reaching conclusions before the entire problem has been laid out. For example, don't condemn an employee without a full and complete hearing from them.

5. It is wise to give out genuine compliments.

APPENDIX A
Litigation Quagmire

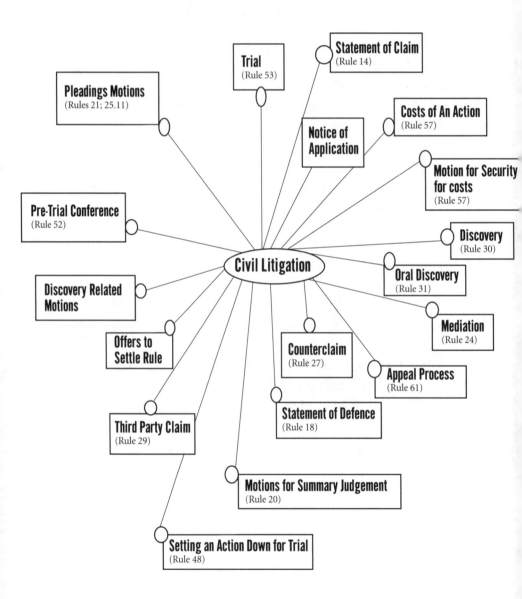

Trial
(Rule 53)

Statement of Claim
(Rule 14)

Pleadings Motions
(Rules 21; 25.11)

Costs of An Action
(Rule 57)

Notice of
Application

Motion for Security
for costs
(Rule 57)

Pre-Trial Conference
(Rule 52)

Discovery
(Rule 30)

Civil Litigation

Oral Discovery
(Rule 31)

Discovery Related
Motions

Mediation
(Rule 24)

Offers to
Settle Rule

Counterclaim
(Rule 27)

Appeal Process
(Rule 61)

Third Party Claim
(Rule 29)

Statement of Defence
(Rule 18)

Motions for Summary Judgement
(Rule 20)

Setting an Action Down for Trial
(Rule 48)

APPENDIX B
Decision Tree

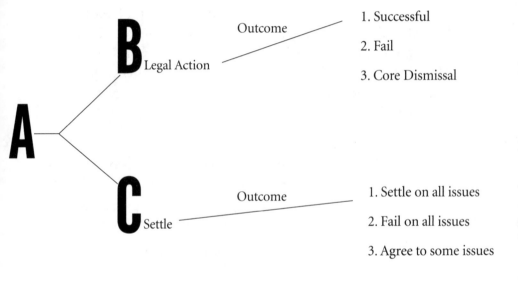

A

B Legal Action — Outcome —
1. Successful
2. Fail
3. Core Dismissal

C Settle — Outcome —
1. Settle on all issues
2. Fail on all issues
3. Agree to some issues

Ryerson Negotiation Project Video Interviews

All the quotations in the book attributed to the individuals listed below have been excerpted from the Ryerson Negotiation Project interviews conducted by the author and produced by the School of Radio and Television Arts at Ryerson University. The videos are available on YouTube at the URLs indicated below. The content of each interview is the property of David C. Dingwall.

Andrews, David   Part 1: www.youtube.com/watch?v=z06wD8MvjJ8
                        Part 2: www.youtube.com/watch?v=en9ELeGkjYk

Asper, Leonard   Part 1: www.youtube.com/watch?v=sKPUS-sBWAA
                        Part 2: www.youtube.com/watch?v=q0xy7bmrR2Q

Bountrogianni, Marie   Part 1: www.youtube.com/watch?v=2KeU_OjM-sI
                        Part 2: www.youtube.com/watch?v=c6Z2owbh27I

Burke, Brian   Part 1: www.youtube.com/watch?v=cixH8a7lHDc
                        Part 2: www.youtube.com/watch?v=ZmjJlUx6Gr0

Clark, Ed   www.youtube.com/watch?v=94FH8mY-hso

Cleaner, Michael   Part 1: www.youtube.com/watch?v=SSWnOazVK7c
                        Part 2: www.youtube.com/watch?v=PyjbWakjO2I

Corbett, Gary   Part 1: www.youtube.com/watch?v=8HHOSzmBx1I
                        Part 2: www.youtube.com/watch?v=sQ1_wdU34zo

Fehr, Donald   Part 1: www.youtube.com/watch?v=2UVP7M2Z1l8
                        Part 2: www.youtube.com/watch?v=uBNCclZsInE

Godfrey, Paul

Part 1: www.youtube.com/watch?v=QsUqh5HjmUk
Part 2: www.youtube.com/watch?v=_3xPQNsYbns

Golden, Anne

Part 1: www.youtube.com/watch?v=ReUTtci5ZVA
Part 2: www.youtube.com/watch?v=iCmzrb57Z9c

Hansell, Carol

Part 1: www.youtube.com/watch?v=eCMmmXubq_E
Part 2: www.youtube.com/watch?v=e3jUkMmQ_Jo

Harder, Peter

Part 1: www.youtube.com/watch?v=5yXFjfR93xA
Part 2: www.youtube.com/watch?v=UmwPM1loYbE

Hargrove, Buzz

Part 1: www.youtube.com/watch?v=WYF-Spx_Wrg
Part 2: www.youtube.com/watch?v=WP3xH5kUlcs
Part 3: www.youtube.com/watch?v=B-NUhuETSU4

Kutulakos, Sarah

Part 1: www.youtube.com/watch?v=UtbDNU9ycdE
Part 2: www.youtube.com/watch?v=wfy3fynBkck

Lean, Ralph

Part 1: www.youtube.com/watch?v=OyiHD9_hi-w
Part 2: www.youtube.com/watch?v=vgFcdh7rNFk

Payne, Janice

Part 1: www.youtube.com/watch?v=fxA1MmzUa7Y
Part 2: www.youtube.com/watch?v=y5xXGr_HDEo

Peterson, David

www.youtube.com/watch?v=gQ_J1RVMC3c

Rae, Bob

Part 1: www.youtube.com/watch?v=qUW3BRCVK7g
Part 2: www.youtube.com/watch?v=sMJPy8BTGL4

Raitt, Lisa

Part 1: www.youtube.com/watch?v=cdTfrBWmUvg
Part 2: www.youtube.com/watch?v=h4L9vtGRvKs

Rudge, Chris

Part 1: www.youtube.com/watch?v=b4XBAGNxy18
Part 2: www.youtube.com/watch?v=VBcWYlWEnZY

Singh, Martin

Part 1: www.youtube.com/watch?v=fXIJHNiaw7c
Part 2: www.youtube.com/watch?v=sD1hDdiblgs

Zed, Paul

Part 1: www.youtube.com/watch?v=I01QBVsgGO0
Part 2: www.youtube.com/watch?v=pw1PC-wbtBc

Acknowledgements

This book has arisen out of thirty years in law, politics, business, education and sport. Those experiences, both domestic and international, shaped my view of the best practices in negotiation. Needless to say, many people have contributed to this undertaking.

From the Ted Rogers School of Management at Ryerson University, many thanks to former Dean Ken Jones, current Dean Steven Murphy, Dr. Neil Rothenberg and, most importantly, Dr. Maurice Mazerolle, for their backing and astute counsel.

To the twenty-two seasoned professionals who agreed to be interviewed for the Ryerson Negotiation Project and whose insights are in included in this book, I am grateful for the time you took to share your experiences and for the insider knowledge you imparted.

At my law firm, Affleck Greene McMurtry LLP., David Vaillancourt, Chris Somerville, Michael Binetti and Managing Partner Peter Greene were supportive and patient and offered thoughtful suggestions. Particular thanks must be given to my assistant Linda Alexiou, who typed the manuscript with dedication and professionalism and helped keep me positive even during the most difficult times.

To my editors, Karen Sumner and Warren Lang, thank you for making this a better book. Your work ethic, professionalism and engaging personalities made this journey so much more enjoyable.

To my publisher James Lorimer and his superb team members Nicole Habib and Emma Renda, I thank you for your dedication and professionalism even when we didn't agree.

To my friends across the country who read passages, made suggestions, corrected facts or questioned the sequence, I am grateful for your many insights.

To my daughters Jennifer Rae and Leigh Anne and my son Jay, you were supporters and strong advocates for me to complete the book.

To my grandsons, Lucas and Shamus, perhaps when you are older you can look back at what Pops has written.

Finally, to my best friend and wife Nancy, I am grateful for your unconditional support. You read and meticulously commented upon the entire manuscript. Your wise suggestions, kindness and encouragement enriched my writing immeasurably. A million thanks for being one in million.

Index